Every design begins with a process of analysis. Of the place? Of the time? Of the history of the place? Of the relationship of landscape architecture to space, and to time? Of the relationship between design and history? Space cannot be considered independently of time. In designs for places and spaces that are especially representative of history because they are memorial spaces or spaces of remembrance, the actual challenge is to communicate the course of time in space.

In the creation of spaces and places of remembrance, landscape architects have a responsibility to history. More than anything, however, they are faced with the task of making remembrance possible in the here and now. After all, history is not the past of a place but the perception of this past from the present day.

The use of landscape architecture as a means by which to strengthen this perception, in turn supporting the work of historians and of memorial institutions, can be remarkably effective. In an introductory essay, Peter Reichel, a political scientist and historian whose work focuses on political cultural history, examines these challenges as seen in the work of sinai landscape architects. It becomes clear that design is much more than the adaptation of spaces to a predefined brief, and more than the bundling of information and their expression in images. The engagement with places of remembrance, with their memory, is always an individual process and yet strives to ensure that more than one own opinion or perception is expressed. It is an attempt – through its expression in space – to give history intersubjective validity, to allow it to be accepted, not least and precisely because an objective historiography is not possible.

In their designs for places of remembrance, sinai landscape architects with A. W. Faust, Klaus Schroll, Bernhard Schwarz and their team have demonstrated how history can be considered and communicated from the present. This book presents the most important of these design projects and contributes in turn to advancing and intensifying the discussion of our history and how we relate to it. However, what is more important than this discussion and the design of the places of remembrance is to visit these places themselves. Without the direct impact that space has, history, and the time concerned, can never be experienced in its full potency.

Jeder Entwurf beginnt mit der Analyse. Des Ortes? Der Zeit? Der Geschichte des Ortes? In welchem Verhältnis steht Landschaftsarchitektur zu Raum, zu Zeit? In welchem Verhältnis stehen Gestaltung und Geschichte?

Raum ist ohne Zeit nicht zu denken. In Entwürfen für diejenigen Orte und Räume, die insbesondere für Geschichte stehen, weil sie Räume des Gedenkens und des Erinnerns sind, ist die räumliche Vermittlung der Zeitläufte die eigentliche Herausforderung.

Die Landschaftsarchitekten stehen angesichts der Aufgabe, Räume und Orte des Gedenkens zu schaffen, in einer Verpflichtung vor der Geschichte. Sie stehen vor allem aber vor der Aufgabe, das Erinnern im Hier und Jetzt zu ermöglichen. Denn Geschichte ist nicht die Vergangenheit eines Ortes, sondern die heutige Wahrnehmung dieser Vergangenheit.

Diese Wahrnehmung mit den Mitteln der Landschaftsarchitektur zu stärken, und so die Arbeit der Historiker, die Arbeit der Gedenkstätten zu stützen, kann überzeugend gelingen. Peter Reichel, Politikwissenschaftler und Historiker, dessen Schwerpunkt die politische Kulturgeschichte ist, geht in einem Essay dieser Herausforderung am Beispiel des Werks von sinai Landschaftsarchitekten nach. Deutlich wird, dass Entwerfen weitaus mehr ist als das Anpassen von Räumen an vorformulierte Anforderungen, mehr als das Bündeln von Informationen und deren Umsetzung in Bilder. Die Auseinandersetzung mit den Orten des Gedenkens, der Erinnerung, ist immer individuell, und folgt dennoch dem Anspruch, mehr als eine eigene Meinung und Wahrnehmung zum Ausdruck zu bringen. Es geht um den Versuch, der Geschichte in ihrem räumlichen Ausdruck eine intersubjektive Gültigkeit, eine Akzeptanz zu geben, auch und gerade weil es eine objektive Geschichtsschreibung nicht geben kann. sinai Landschaftsarchitekten mit A. W. Faust, Klaus Schroll, Bernhard Schwarz und ihrem Team haben in ihren Entwürfen zu Orten des Gedenkens bewiesen, wie Geschichte aus der Gegenwart heraus gedacht und vermittelt werden kann. Daher stellt dieses Buch die wichtigsten dieser Entwürfe vor und leistet so einen Beitrag, die Diskussion um unsere Geschichte und ihr Erkennen weiter zu intensivieren. Noch wichtiger allerdings als diese Diskussion um die Gestaltung der Gedenkorte ist der Besuch dieser Orte selbst. Ohne die unmittelbare Wirkung des Raumes hat Geschichte, hat die betrachtete Zeit niemals ihre volle Kraft.

Thies Schröder
Peter Reichel, Essay

Birkhäuser
Basel

Difficult Places

Landscapes
of Remembrance
by sinai

Schwierige Orte

Erinnerungs-
landschaften
von sinai

Content   Inhalt

"Remembering, like politics, therapy and aesthetics, has become a social project, a form of work. It is seemingly the only remaining countermovement to the emptying out of the present."

„Das Erinnern ist heute, als Politik, Therapie und Ästhetik, ein gesellschaftliches Projekt geworden, Arbeit. Es ist offenbar die letzte uns verbliebene Gegenbewegung gegen die Entleerung der Gegenwart."

Dieter Hoffmann-Axthelm, 1994

Peter Reichel

**The Past
– an Inaccessible Place**

Die Vergangenheit
– der unerreichbare Ort

Hoffmann-Axthelm, Dieter:
Der Stadtplan als Erinnerung,
in: Kunstforum International
(1994), Vol. 128, pp. 149–153

Hoffmann-Axthelm, Dieter:
Der Stadtplan als Erinnerung.
in: Kunstforum International
(1994), Bd. 128, S. 149–153

1
Kulka, Otto Dov: Landscapes
of the Metropolis of Death:
Reflections on Memory and
Imagination, trans. Ralph
Mandel, London 2013
2
ibid., p. 75

1
Kulka, Otto Dov: Landschaf-
ten der Metropole des Todes,
München 2013
2
Ebda., S. 111f.

I

Those who journey there no longer find the place. It doesn't matter where they look. The limits of their present separate them from it. Hermetically. All the same, we harmlessly call it the past. As if it were a place we can visit whenever we please. Forgetting as we do that it belongs only to the dead, the overpowered and the few survivors. People who were murdered in these places in the hundreds of thousands. People from all over Europe. They had committed no crime, incurred no guilt, lost no battle. They had to die because a self-proclaimed "master race" had deemed it so, had stigmatised them as "social parasites", as being "unworthy of life", because they were Jews, a mere religious minority. Thus it is written in the history books. Regardless of where they look, they will not find out much more.

Nevertheless, the stream of visitors continues unabated. Relatives and descendants wish to commemorate their dead at their place of suffering and death. History-seeking tourists, nowadays constantly mobile, restlessly in search of the next special experience, are attracted by the negative aura of the place, and wish to come that bit closer to that distant event, the epitome of human malice and barbaric inhumanity. As if once in the "metropolis of death"[1] one might understand what happened in Auschwitz-Birkenau between 1942 and 1945. Even there, in the centre of the organised mass extermination of millions, the search for a lost past is in vain. As in all other places of death, there too it is an illusion, a self-delusion, to believe the past can be made present. Every metaphor of remembrance is inadequate, every gesture of remembrance illusionary. Our path back to that time in the past, our access to it, can only be abstract, symbolic and fictional.

Not even the survivors seem able to trust their memories, a phenomenon that evidently applies all the more to those who experienced Auschwitz as children. The almost 80-year-old Holocaust historian and Auschwitz survivor Otto Dov Kulka writes that all he can remember today is "the quiet and tranquillity", the "blue skies and silver aeroplanes, those toys" high up over Birkenau, when he asks himself what "the most beautiful experience in his childhood landscape"[2] was.

Those who come to Auschwitz will find no graves. The mortal remains of the nameless dead were dissipated into the nothingness of the air from the chimneys of the crematoria. The visitor can find them only in the words of a poet – or in the decaying remains of the hair, cases and shoes that could not be used in time. They can do nothing more than visit the horrors from the safe distance of later generations and their, in one way or another, contemporary interpretation. They have not arrived in the cold stench of a railway cattle wagon, starving and thirsty, cooped up with the sick and dying, almost as near to madness as to death, in order to then die an agonising death by asphyxiation. We, the later generations, have not been subjected to this torture, and

I

Wer dorthin fährt, findet die Ortschaft nicht mehr. Wo immer er sie sucht. Die Begrenzungen seiner Gegenwart trennen ihn von ihr. Hermetisch. Wir nennen sie gleichwohl harmlos Vergangenheit. Als könnten wir sie nach Belieben aufsuchen. Und vergessen dabei, dass sie allein den Toten gehört, den Überwältigten und den wenigen Überlebenden. Menschen, die dort zu Hunderttausenden ermordet wurden. Menschen aus ganz Europa. Sie hatten kein Verbrechen begangen, keine Schuld auf sich geladen, keine Schlacht verloren. Sie mussten sterben, weil ein selbsternanntes „Herrenvolk" es so wollte, sie als „Volksschädlinge" stigmatisierte, als „lebensunwertes Leben", sie, die Juden, eine religiöse Minderheit also. So steht es auch in den Geschichtsbüchern. Viel mehr wird er nirgendwo in Erfahrung bringen.

Doch die Besucherströme halten an. Die Angehörigen und Nachkommen möchten am Leidens- und Sterbeort ihrer Toten gedenken. Und die mobilen Geschichtstouristen unserer Zeit, rastlos auf der Suche nach dem besonderen Erlebnis und angezogen von der negativen Aura des Ortes, dem fernen Ereignis näherkommen, dem Inbegriff menschlicher Bosheit und teuflischer Menschenverachtung. Als könnten sie in der „Metropole des Todes"[1] besser verstehen, was sich 1942 bis 1945 in Auschwitz-Birkenau ereignet hat. Selbst im Zentrum der organisierten Massenvernichtung von Millionen ist die Suche nach der verlorenen Vergangenheit vergeblich. Wie an allen anderen Todesorten ist auch dort die Vergegenwärtigung von Vergangenheit Täuschung und Selbsttäuschung, jede Gedächtnismetapher gegenstandslos, jede Erinnerungsgeste illusionär. Der Zugang, die Rückkehr in jenen Zeitraum nur abstrakt, symbolisch und fiktiv möglich.

Nicht einmal die Überlebenden scheinen ihren Erinnerungen zu trauen. Was offenbar vor allem für jene gilt, die Auschwitz als Kinder erlebt haben. Der fast 80-jährige Holocaust-Historiker und Auschwitz-Überlebende Otto Dov Kulka schreibt jetzt, dass er sich nur an „die Schönheit und Stille" erinnern könne, „den blauen Himmel und die silbernen Spielzeug-Flugzeuge" hoch oben über Birkenau, wenn er sich fragen würde, was „die schönste Erfahrung in den Landschaften"[2] seiner Kindheit war.

Wer nach Auschwitz kommt, findet keine Gräber. Die sterblichen Überreste der namenlosen Toten haben sich durch die Schlote der Verbrennungsöfen im Nirgendwo der Lüfte verflüchtigt. Er begegnet ihnen nur in der Poesie der Dichter – oder in den verfallenen Überresten ihrer nicht mehr verwerteten Haare, Koffer und Schuhe. Er kann dort nicht mehr erreichen als eine Besichtigung des Schreckens aus der geschützten Distanz der Nachlebenden und ihrer so oder so gegenwartsbezogenen Deutungen. Er ist dort nicht nach langem Güterwagentransport angekommen, in Kälte und Gestank, halb verhungert und verdurstet, eingepfercht mit Kranken und Toten, dem Wahnsinn so nah wie dem Tod, um einen qualvollen Erstickungstod zu

3
Reichel, Peter: Glanz und Elend deutscher Selbstdarstellung, Göttingen 2012, p. 281ff.
4
Pelt, R. v./Dwork, D.: Auschwitz. Von 170 bis heute, Zurich and Munich 1998, p. 414ff.; Schlögel, Karl: Im Raume lesen wir die Zeit. Über Zivilisationsgeschichte und Geopolitik, Munich 2003, p. 447f.
5
Reichel, Peter: Nach dem Verbrechen. Nationale Erinnerungen an Weltkrieg und Judenmord, in: Asmuss, B. (Ed.): Holocaust. Der nationalsozialistische Völkermord und die Motive seiner Erinnerung, Berlin 2002, p. 215–238 (exhibition catalogue)

3
Reichel, Peter: Glanz und Elend deutscher Selbstdarstellung, Göttingen 2012, S. 281ff.
4
Pelt, R. v./Dwork, D.: Auschwitz. Von 170 bis heute, Zürich und München 1998, S. 414ff.; Schlögel, Karl: Im Raume lesen wir die Zeit. Über Zivilisationsgeschichte und Geopolitik, München 2003, S. 447f.
5
Reichel, Peter: Nach dem Verbrechen. Nationale Erinnerungen an Weltkrieg und Judenmord, in: Asmuss, B. (Hg.): Holocaust. Der nationalsozialistische Völkermord und die Motive seiner Erinnerung, Berlin 2002, S. 215–238 (Ausstellungskatalog)

we have no estimation of their suffering. For us, the mass murder of millions remains a totally incomprehensible message from another world. It is for us forever inaccessible. Any attempt to recreate that past, however well-meant, can only ever be an illusion, a self-delusion, a pretence. We are – in the actual sense of the word – not affected.

The first Polish architects to address this topic already knew this, displaying a keen sense of sensitive landscape design and the aesthetics of natural materials. Back then, several decades ago, this knowledge led them to adopt an uncompromisingly critical standpoint. Franciszek Duszeńko and Adam Haupt recreated the path that the cattle wagons took on their way into the death camp in Treblinka from the Warsaw Ghetto as a row of large concrete railway sleepers.[3] The Polish Jews, who were driven from the ramp directly into the gas chambers where they died a slow, merciless death of asphyxiation, have been commemorated as a long stretch of large broken shards of granite – as if preserving an image of their last moment under an open sky for all eternity. Zofia and Oskar Hansen even went a step further.[4] In their prize-winning design they proposed closing the Gateway to Death and instead "to remove a few metres of the barbed wire north of the main entrance to create the illusion of an accidental hole in the fence" through which visitors could as it were "creep in" to a time in the past. The earth was not to be walked on, instead a 1,000-metre-long walkway passed through the site to the ruins of the crematorium. No inscription, no monument, no document, no presentation of the remains was to commemorate the dead. Only tranquillity and a view of the place of the throes of death should confront them over and over again with the same question: what happened here and why did it happen? The place would have no answer. The gateway through which the deportation trains passed should be closed forever, signalling to later generations that nothing and no one can return to the space of the past, except in the fictional and virtual world of the media. Nevertheless, this has not prevented the struggle to interpret Auschwitz, and the many other places of suffering and death, from turning these into places of remembrance fully equipped with modern documentation and media technology.[5]

erleiden. Wir, die Nachlebenden, sind keine Gepeinigten, können die Qual nicht ermessen. Die massenhafte Ermordung von Millionen bleibt uns eine gänzlich unverständliche Nachricht aus einer anderen Welt. Sie ist uns für immer verschlossen. Und jeder noch so gut gemeinte Versuch, das Vergangene zu vergegenwärtigen, Illusion, Selbsttäuschung, schöner Schein. Wir sind – im eigentlichen Wortsinn – nicht betroffen. Polnische Architekten der ersten Stunde, mit einem sicheren Gespür für behutsame Landschaftsgestaltung und naturnahe Materialästhetik, wussten das noch. Schon vor Jahrzehnten haben sie aus dieser Erkenntnis eine kompromisslos kritische Konsequenz gezogen. Franciszek Duszeńko und Adam Haupt bildeten in Beton die Schwellen der Gleise nach, auf denen die Güterzüge ihre Menschenfracht aus dem Warschauer Ghetto in das Todeslager Treblinka brachten.[3] Die von der Rampe schnell in die Gaskammern getriebenen polnischen Juden, die dort erbarmungslos langsam erstickten, verewigten sie – als wollten sie für alle Zeit ein Bild vom letzten Augenblick der Todgeweihten unter freiem Himmel schaffen – in einem langen Zug grob behauener Granitbruchsteine. Zofia und Oskar Hansen gingen noch weiter.[4] In ihrem preisgekrönten Entwurf schlugen sie vor, das Tor des Todes zu schließen und stattdessen „nördlich des Haupteingangs zu dem Lager den Stacheldraht auf einigen Metern zu entfernen und damit die Illusion" zu inszenieren, Besucher könnten sich „durch eine zufällige Lücke" in die vergangene Zeit dieses Raumes „einschleichen". Die Erde sollten sie nicht betreten, in den Raum nur über einen 1000 Meter langen Steg gelangen und bis zu den Krematorienruinen gehen können. Keine Inschrift, kein Denkmal, kein Dokument, keine Inszenierung ihrer Überreste sollte an die Toten erinnern. Nur die Stille und der Blick auf den Ort des Todeskampfes sie immer und immer wieder mit der gleichen Frage konfrontieren: Was geschah hier und warum geschah es? Und der Ort ihnen keine Antwort geben. Das Tor aber, durch das die Deportationszüge gefahren waren, sollte für immer verschlossen bleiben und die Nachgeborenen mit der schmerzlichen Wahrheit konfrontiert werden, dass nichts und niemand in den Raum der Vergangenheit vordringen kann, diesseits medialer Fiktionalität und Virtualität. Was nicht verhindern konnte, dass der Deutungskampf um Auschwitz und die vielen anderen Leidens- und Sterbeorte diese in vielbesuchte, mit modernster Dokumentation und Medientechnik ausgestattete Gedenkstätten verwandelt hat.[5]

6
Schlögel, Karl: Im Raume lesen wir die Zeit, passim
7
Freud, Sigmund: Civilisation and Its Discontents (1929), in: The Standard Edition of the Complete Psychological Works of Sigmund Freud, Volume XXI, trans. and ed. James Strachey (1927–1931), London 1953
8
We first presented this scheme and differentiated examination of the notion of memory in: Reichel, P./Schmid, H.: Von der Katastrophe zum Stolperstein. Hamburg und der Nationalsozialismus nach 1945, Hamburg 2005, p.10 ff.

6
Schlögel, Karl: Im Raume lesen wir die Zeit, passim
7
Freud, Sigmund: Das Unbehagen in der Kultur, in: ders., Kulturtheoretische Schriften, Frankfurt a. M. 1986, S. 202f.
8
Erstmals vorgestellt haben wir diese Schemata und Ausdifferenzierungen des Gedächtnisbegriffs in: Reichel, P./Schmid, H.: Von der Katastrophe zum Stolperstein. Hamburg und der Nationalsozialismus nach 1945, Hamburg 2005, S.10ff.

The refusal to open up a space that belongs to a time from the past, to allow people to set foot in it, to exploit it for the flourishing latter-day culture of remembrance, should be accorded respect. Others, however, would also lay claim to this respect – those who examine, describe, document and artistically interpret this space as well as those who exploit its history for political ends. Who, then, does Auschwitz belong to? The Poles, the "Christ among nations", in whose land the crimes took place? The Jews of the world, for whom this place is their largest cemetery? The Germans, as the nation of the perpetrators, who, however, themselves claim to have been the victims of Hitler, and who are stained forever with the blood of anti-Semitism and murderousness? The following generations should not just be informed about what happened. Our tradition of reverence to the dead demands that this also be manifested in culture and incorporated into the self-image and historical portrayal of nations or religions. That in turn is something that raises new conflicts, and creates new hurt which has further consequences.

On the other hand, the "spatial revolution" of 1989 has re-opened and brought back spaces that were previously lost and inaccessible. Even the language of space appears to have been reclaimed. [6] For the present, at least. The spaces of the past, however, remain inaccessible. We should speak here of spatial time frames. The material transformation of spaces leaves traces of their history, invisible walls that make them impassable – and also immensely attractive. Like the dark and grotesque corners of human memory: Sigmund Freud, no less, likened the clearing away of pathogenic psychical material layer by layer with the technique of excavating a buried city and the layers of time, material and meaning it contains. [7] The memory of the city, of its ruins and spaces serves as a kind of magical architectural notepad that can contain an unlimited number of letters, the traces of which remain even after they have been deleted. Freud argued that human memory functions similarly. It is able to absorb ever new impressions and nevertheless creates permanent, but also changeable, memory traces of them. We must think of space as a four-dimensional palimpsest.

From this we can derive some indications and suppositions for cultural memory, its places, functions and spheres of action. [8] Memory is a medium that relates our thinking and perception to *time*. It enables our individual and collective consciousness to both extend across time periods and to differentiate between different time periods. It coordinates and structures the different temporal relationships of our consciousness. For, strictly speaking, there is only one time, namely that which we experience in the present. What was before is the past made present, and what comes after is speculation, prognosis, hope or anxiety. Memory therefore creates a sense of continuity, a fourth dimension of space as it were. Memory is able to bridge breaks and discontinuities in our everyday and political developments. And that is what makes spatial and temporal places of memory so revealing for cultural and historical investigation.

Die Weigerung, den Raum einer vergangenen Zeit zu öffnen, zu betreten, ihn für die florierende Erinnerungskultur unserer Zeit nutzen zu lassen, verdient Respekt. Den werden jedoch auch jene für sich reklamieren wollen, die diesen Ort befragen, beschreiben, dokumentieren, künstlerisch gestalten und nicht zuletzt auch geschichtspolitisch instrumentalisieren. Denn wem gehört Auschwitz? Den Polen, dem „Christus unter den Völkern", in deren Land das Verbrechen geschah? Den Juden der Welt, für die dieser Ort der größte Friedhof ist? Den Deutschen als Nation der Täter, die aber doch Hitlers Opfer gewesen sein wollen und an denen für alle Zeit das Blut des Judenhasses und der Mordlust klebt? Die Nachlebenden sollen nicht nur aufgeklärt werden über das Geschehene. Was dort geschah, muss auch, so verlangen es Pietät und Tradition im Umgang mit den Toten, kulturell manifest und in nationale oder religiöse Geschichts- und Selbstbilder integriert werden. Das geschieht nicht ohne Konflikte, nicht ohne neue Verletzungen und Folgen.

Gewiss, die „Raumrevolution" des Jahres 1989 hat verlorene und verschlossene Räume geöffnet und zurückgebracht. Selbst die Raumsprache scheint rehabilitiert. [6] Für die Gegenwart. Aber die Räume der Vergangenheit bleiben verschlossen. Wir sollten von Raumzeiten sprechen. Materielle Veränderungen der Räume hinterlassen Zeitspuren, die unsichtbaren Mauern machen sie undurchdringlich – und so ungemein anziehend. Wie das abgründig und abseitig Verborgene im menschlichen Gedächtnis. Kein Geringerer als Sigmund Freud verglich die „schichtweise Ausräumung des pathogenen psychischen Materials" mit der „Ausgrabung einer verschütteten Stadt" und den in ihr abgelagerten Zeit-, Material- und Bedeutungsschichten. [7] Das Stadt-, Ruinen- und Raumgedächtnis wäre demnach eine Art architektonischer Wunderblock, der unbegrenzt viele Schriftzeichen aufnimmt und bei ihrer Löschung deren Spuren bewahrt. Ähnlich, so Freud, funktioniere das menschliche Gedächtnis. Es sei aufnahmefähig für immer neue Wahrnehmungen und schaffe doch dauerhafte, wenn auch veränderliche Erinnerungsspuren von ihnen. Wir müssen uns den Raum als vierdimensionales Palimpsest denken.

Daraus ergeben sich Hinweise und Annahmen für das kulturelle Gedächtnis, seine Orte, Funktionen und Handlungsfelder. [8] Gedächtnis ist ein Medium der *Verzeitlichung* unseres Denkens und Empfindens. Es ermöglicht dem individuellen und kollektiven Bewusstsein eine zeitenübergreifende und zwischen verschiedenen Zeiträumen unterscheidende Ausdehnung und Differenzierung. Also eine Strukturierung und Koordination der unterschiedlichen Zeitbezüge unseres Bewusstseins. Denn streng genommen gibt es nur eine Zeit, die der gerade erlebten Gegenwart. Was davor war, ist vergegenwärtigte Vergangenheit, und was danach kommt, Spekulation, Prognose, Hoffnung, Angst. Gedächtnis schafft mithin Kontinuität, also die vierte Raumdimension. Gedächtnis überbrückt Zäsuren, die Diskontinuität von lebensweltlichen und politischen Entwicklungen. Das macht räumliche und zeitliche Gedächtnisorte für die kulturgeschichtliche Erkundung so aufschlussreich.

Given that memory cannot be considered without its medial, personal and social dimension, one should also understand and use it as a medium that relates consciousness to *communities*, and investigate its specific effects. In this process, individual memory passes via family-related or generational places, into group-related memory, contributing to the formation of a group, but is also subject to external influences, such as breaks in social continuity and dramatic political changes such as revolutions and wars. Memory is likewise a medium that links collective consciousness with *spaces* as well as with *objects*, gestures, images or bodies.

Related but not identical to the functions of cultural memory, are the historico-political fields of action that concern our relation to and interest in the past. Our long-term memory is put under exceptional strain at major turning points in history, such as the transition from war and tyranny to democratic conditions. In the 20th century, Germany has been through this transitional process several times over. To put behind and overcome the conditions during the period of Nazi rule after its military defeat, society had to undergo a process of self-reflection. Four aspects of this are relevant and necessary, each of which has a specific conception of the present informed by its relationship to the past:

Firstly: a *normative* democratic re-organisation of the political constitution and political culture, i.e. an abstract, value-related differentiation from the politics of the past. This includes, for example, the prosecution of crimes conducted during dictatorial regimes, the compensation and rehabilitation of the persecuted, the reintegration of groups of people guilty of minor crimes, and the broad area of political consciousness and behaviour.

Secondly: an *affective* policy of commemoration and remembrance, and its cultural manifestations, i.e. a change of direction with respect to the past. This involves public remembrance of the time of dictatorship and its crimes and – from an oppositional standpoint – the painfully long path to democracy, especially in Germany. To this one can count a number of difficult places of remembrance: memorial sites and places of remembrance, commemoration days and monuments through which both victims and perpetrators are remembered. Closely linked with this is

Thirdly: the field of aesthetic culture. Its agents, the producers of artistic representations and interpretations, particularly of National Socialism, do not even pretend to want to recall the past at the authentic sites of crimes or suffering, or to document and explain them using objective evidence and testimony. Their relationship to the past is *subjective*; in *expressing* their

Insofern Gedächtnis gar nicht ohne seine mediale, personale und soziale Dimension zu denken ist, muss man es auch als Medium der Vergemeinschaftung begreifen, nutzen und in seiner Wirkungsweise untersuchen. Jenen Prozess also, in dem das individuelle Gedächtnis, über Familien- und Generationenorte vermittelt, in gruppenbezogener Erinnerung aufgeht, zur Gruppenbildung beiträgt, aber auch externen Einflüssen ausgesetzt ist, gesellschaftlichen Kontinuitätsbrüchen und dramatischen politischen Zäsuren wie Revolutionen und Kriegen. Und natürlich ist Gedächtnis als Medium der *Verräumlichung* von gesellschaftlichem Bewusstsein auch eines der *Vergegenständlichung*, das an Gegenstand und Geste, Bild und Körper haftet.

Mit den Funktionen des kulturellen Gedächtnisses nicht identisch – aber doch verwandt – sind die geschichtspolitischen Handlungsfelder, die Einstellung zur und das Interesse an der Vergangenheit. Das Langzeitgedächtnis wird eminent beansprucht, wenn es um eine so tiefgreifende Zäsur geht wie den Übergang von Krieg und Gewaltherrschaft zu demokratischen Verhältnissen. Deutschland hat diesen transitorischen Prozess im 20. Jahrhundert gleich mehrfach erfahren müssen. Für die Aufhebung und Überwindung der Verhältnisse während der Herrschaft des Nationalsozialismus waren nach seiner militärischen Zerschlagung vier Prozesse gesellschaftlicher Selbstverständigung relevant und notwendig. Für sie ist jeweils ein spezifisches, auf die Vergangenheit bezogenes Gegenwartsinteresse konstitutiv:

Erstens: die von einer *normativen*, also abstrakten, wertbezogenen Abgrenzung ausgehende, heute „Vergangenheitspolitik" genannte, demokratische Reorganisation der politisch-rechtlichen und politisch-kulturellen Verhältnisse. Damit ist die Verfolgung von Straftaten in diktatorischen Unrechtsregimen gemeint, die Entschädigung und Rehabilitierung Verfolgter, die Reintegration minder belasteter Personenkreise und das weite Feld des politischen Bewusstseins und Verhaltens.

Zweitens: die von einer *affektiven* Hinwendung zur Vergangenheit geleitete Gedenk- und Erinnerungspolitik bzw. ihre kulturellen Manifestationen. Hier geht es um die öffentliche Erinnerung an die Zeit der Diktaturen und ihrer Verbrechen bzw. – aus oppositioneller Perspektive – um den, zumal in Deutschland, verlustreichen, langen Weg zur Demokratie. Dazu gehört eine Vielzahl von insofern schwierigen Erinnerungsorten: Gedenk- und Erinnerungsstätten, Gedenktage und Denkmäler, mit denen sowohl der Opfer gedacht wie an die Täter erinnert werden soll. Eng verknüpft damit ist

drittens das Feld der ästhetischen Kultur. Deren Akteure, die Produzenten künstlerischer Darstellungen und Deutungen insbesondere des Nationalsozialismus geben gar nicht erst vor, die vergangene Zeit am authentischen Tat- und Leidensort zurückholen oder sie anhand objektiver Zeugnisse dokumentieren und verständlich machen zu können. Ihr Verhältnis zur Vergangenheit ist *subjektiv, expressiv* und ganz auf die

thoughts and emotions about the past they refer explicitly to the present. Their wish is to reach their public, not a time in the distant past. Their aim is to find images of remembrance that correspond to the time, to give the past a contemporary image. They confront the self-deception of erecting monuments with creative irony. They produce interactive and self-reflective symbols of remembering that highlight the inadequacy of all forms of memorial. No monument is able to commemorate a heroic deed and likewise none a crime. Monuments are public symbols that communicate the interpretation and interests of those who erect them.

Last but not least, there is fourthly: the field of academic research into the past and the politics of interpretation connected with it. Historiographical representation, documentation and interpretation are driven here by a *cognitive* interest in the past. The intention is to gain insight, to understand the past, to explain the origins, development and violent crimes of the Nazi dictatorship – or any other complex and major event with grave consequences – from the context of, or for the benefit of, a new system of governance with a view to using the insights for learning for the future.

All of the places presented in this book are *spaces of sublation* in the threefold sense of the word: 1) What happened there no longer exists, and has been overcome – or, with the exception of isolated physical remains, has been irrevocably lost, removed or destroyed. 2) That which has been overcome or lost, whatever it happens to be, is conserved for the future, whether in the form of remnants and evidence or in subsequent aesthetic reworkings or in scholarly representations and interpretations. In the process of conservation, the place, event or person acquires a "second history" in which the records, tradition and cultural history of a social group, a people or a nation take shape and accumulate. And finally; 3) the process of sublating the past aims to change and to improve the present and the time to come – whatever the reason or method. As such, the place of remembrance is seen as a place of learning, a place in which remembrance and commemoration are (made) self-reflexive, a place that critically views its own history against the background of the controversial tendencies of the day.

The following exploration of projects by sinai for places of remembrance and memorial sites from three different political contexts illustrates what we mean when we speak of "difficult places". It shows what makes auratic spaces so appealing to work with, but also so complex and demanding, and therefore susceptible to misunderstanding and error. The task is all the more formidable given that there is no tradition of close, trusting and critical collaboration among practitioners in the culture of remembrance, in the popular communication of history and in scholarly research. Such collaboration is an experience all three groups of professionals could benefit from – and the general public most of all.

Gegenwart bezogen. Sie wollen ihr Publikum erreichen, aber nicht eine ferne Zeit. Ihr Ziel ist es, zeittypische Erinnerungsbilder zu erfinden, Vergangenem ein gegenwärtiges Gesicht zu geben. Dem Selbstbetrug mit dem Errichten von Denkmalen begegnen sie mit kreativer Ironie. So entstehen interaktive und selbstreflexive Erinnerungszeichen, die das Misslingen allen Gedenkens thematisieren. Denn kein Denkmal vermag an eine Heldentat zu erinnern, keines an ein Verbrechen. Denkmäler sind öffentliche Symbole, die auf das Deutungs- und Machtinteresse ihrer Stifter verweisen. Last but not least ist viertens das Feld der Deutungspolitik und wissenschaftlichen Erforschung der Vergangenheit zu nennen. Historiografische Darstellung, Dokumentation und Deutung sind von einem *kognitiven* Interesse an der Vergangenheit geleitet. Sie wollen Erkenntnis gewinnen, die Vergangenheit verstehen, Entstehung, Selbstbehauptung und Gewaltverbrechen der NS-Diktatur – oder jedes andere komplexe und folgenschwere Großereignis – erklären und aus einem beziehungsweise für einen gewandelten ordnungspolitischen Rahmen deuten und die so gewonnenen Einsichten auch pädagogisch fruchtbar machen.

Alle in diesem Buch vorgestellten Orte sind *Räume der Aufhebung* in der dreifachen Wortbedeutung: Was dort stattfand, existiert nicht mehr, ist überwunden – oder bis auf materielle Überreste unwiederbringlich verloren, beseitigt und zerstört. (1) Das Überwundene oder Verlorene aber wird, was immer es sein mag, dauerhaft aufbewahrt – ob in Überresten und Zeugnissen, ob in später entstandenen ästhetischen Überformungen oder wissenschaftlichen Darstellungen und Deutungen. Im Prozess dieser Aufbewahrung entsteht die „zweite Geschichte" eines Ortes, eines Ereignisses, einer Person; formen und akkumulieren sich Überlieferung, Tradition und kulturelles Gedächtnis eines Sozialverbandes, eines Volkes, einer Nation. (2) Und schließlich will diese Aufhebung der Vergangenheit die Gegenwart und die ihr nachfolgenden Zeiten verändern, verbessern – in welcher Weise, zu welchem Zweck auch immer. Was einschließt, dass der Erinnerungsort, der sich auch als Lernort begreift, als Ort des Erinnerns und Gedenkens selbstreflexiv (gemacht) wird, also seine eigene Geschichte selbstkritisch in den Kontext der kontroversen Zeitgeistströmungen stellt. (3)

Die nachfolgende Besichtigung der von sinai gestalteten Erinnerungsorte und Gedenkstätten aus drei unterschiedlichen politischen Kontexten soll exemplarisch veranschaulichen, was es heißt, wenn wir von „schwierigen Orten" sprechen. Was den Umgang mit den auratischen Räumen so attraktiv macht, aber auch so komplex, so anspruchsvoll und damit eben auch anfällig für Irrtümer und Fehler. Dies wiegt umso schwerer, als hierzulande eine enge, vertrauensvolle und kritische Zusammenarbeit zwischen der erinnerungskulturellen Praxis, der populären Geschichtsvermittlung und der wissenschaftlichen Forschung keine Tradition hat. Die Erfahrung fehlt, dass alle drei Akteure davon profitieren könnten – und die Öffentlichkeit am meisten.

9
Cited in Reichel, Peter: Politik mit der Erinnerung. Gedächtnisorte im Streit um die nationalsozialistische Vergangenheit, Frankfurt a. M. 2nd edition, 1999, p.129
10
Cited in ibid., p.131
11
Cf. Reichel, Peter: Glanz und Elend, p. 270ff. and 279ff.

9
Zit. n. Reichel, Peter: Politik mit der Erinnerung. Gedächtnisorte im Streit um die nationalsozialistische Vergangenheit, Frankfurt a. M. 2. Aufl. 1999, S.129
10
Zit. ebda., S.131

II

Of the concentration camps built in the "Old Reich", i.e. on German territory, the camp near the town of Bergen in Lower Saxony is the most well-known, not least due to the now legendary life story of Anne Frank, the Jewish girl who kept a diary of her days in hiding in an annex on the Prinsengracht in Amsterdam until her family was informed on and she and her relatives were deported. The use of the mythical aura that surrounds Anne Frank's story, which was published all over the world in the 1950s, shows the prominence accorded to the victims in the present day. That was not always the case. To begin with, efforts were made – for a variety of different reasons – to change the nature of the place, in order to put visible distance between the past and the present. Whether the burning down of the barracks in May 1945 by the British military government to curb the spread of disease, the erection of a monument by the survivors to commemorate the dead, or the landscaping of the extensive site in the 1960s and the creation of a first modest archive, all of these actions attempted to assert a new presence that would displace the past of the prisoners' camp and the massive scale of suffering and death that took place there. All were attempts to speed up the passage of time by effecting large-scale physical changes.

Within 20 years of the liquidation of the camp, the Bergen citizens had all but achieved their goal of "burying the sensation of Belsen".[9] Not only had grass grown over the remains of some 50,000 Soviet prisoners of war and almost as many Jews, buried in several mass graves, but an idyllic heathland cemetery had developed, with carefully tended paths, juniper bushes and birch trees – a memorial place that one "enjoys visiting", to use the words with which a German Chancellor was to advertise the Holocaust Memorial in Berlin many years later. In summer 1990, the local press even recommended the memorial to its readers as a "worthwhile day out for those at home over the holidays", an ideal place for a "contemplative walk" between visits to the local zoo, the windmill museum – and, of course, country cafés.

Soon after the war, the second president of the Federal Republic did his best to reassure his people by stating that the number of German casualties was high and that this would "unite our people in sorrow and pain ... also with the Jews from Germany and abroad".[10] But before the incomprehensible reality could be recognised, then endured and eventually accepted in a reinvented version of memory, it had to be either ignored or reinterpreted. Those who had previously constituted the German "people's community" and Hitler's followers, now had to recast themselves as victims of his rule. This self-transformation has meanwhile acquired lasting expression: every year, the Germans – joining their fellow Europeans in a degree of harmony that is not always so easily reached – commemorate the "Day of Holocaust Remembrance" on the 27th January, standing alongside its partners in the EU as if their ancestors had been involved in liberating Auschwitz. The trio of the Neue Wache (New Guard House), the Holocaust Memorial and the Jewish Museum in the German capital function as a correspondingly monumental and spectacular expression of this presumptuous, date-fixated and victim-centred policy of remembrance.[11]

II

Von den im „Altreich", also auf deutschem Territorium errichteten Konzentrationslagern ist das nahe der niedersächsischen Stadt Bergen errichtete Lager das weltweit wohl bekannteste. Seit Mitte der 1950er Jahre die inzwischen legendäre Lebensgeschichte von Anne Frank um die Welt ging, dem jüdischen Mädchen aus der Amsterdamer Prinsengracht, das in seinem Versteck in einem Hinterhaus ein Tagebuch schrieb, bis es verraten und deportiert wurde. Die Verwendung der mythisch stilisierten Aura, die mit Anne Franks Geschichte verbunden ist, signalisiert, wie heute Opferprominenz verwertet wird. Das war nicht immer so. Zunächst wurden – aus durchaus unterschiedlichen Interessen – Anstrengungen zur Veränderung des Ortes unternommen, die sichtbare Distanz schaffen sollten. Ob bereits im Mai 1945 wegen drohender Seuchengefahr auf Veranlassung der britischen Militärregierung sämtliche KZ-Baracken niedergebrannt, durch die Überlebenden Mahnmale zum Gedenken ihrer Toten errichtet wurden, oder in den 1960er Jahren das weitläufige Gelände einer gartenpflegerischen Neugestaltung unterzogen und ein erstes, bescheidenes Dokumentenhaus errichtet wurde, allenthalben machte sich gegenüber der Vergangenheit des Häftlingslagers, dem Massenelend und dem Massensterben Gegenwart breit. Beschleunigung des Zeitverlaufs durch massive Raumveränderung.

So schien schon 20 Jahre nach Liquidierung des Lagers erreicht, was sich die Bergener Bürger früh zum Ziel gesetzt hatten: „Es muss uns gelingen, die Sensation Belsen einzugraben."[9] Über den in mehreren Massengräbern verscharrten Überresten von 50.000 sowjetischen Kriegsgefangenen und etwa ebenso vielen Toten jüdischen Glaubens war nicht nur Gras gewachsen, sondern ein idyllischer Heidepark-Friedhof entstanden, mit gepflegten Wegen, Wacholder und Birken. Ein Gedenkort, an den man „gerne geht" – wie ein Bundeskanzler später das Holocaust-Mahnmal in Berlin anpreisen sollte. Im Urlaubssommer 1990 empfahl ihn jedenfalls eine Lokalzeitung den „Daheimgebliebenen" als „lohnendes Ausflugsziel". Vorzugsweise für „nachdenkliche Spaziergänger", zwischen Besuchen im Tierpark, im Windmühlenmuseum – und in der ländlichen Gastronomie.

Schon früh hatte der zweite Präsident unserer Republik seine Landsleute mit dem Hinweis zu beruhigen gewusst, dass die Zahl der deutschen Opfer groß sei und dies „unser Volk verbinden" würde, in „Leid und Schmerz auch mit den deutschen und ausländischen Juden".[10] Bevor die unverständliche Wirklichkeit erkannt und in erfundenen Erinnerungen ertragen und akzeptiert werden konnte, musste sie ignoriert oder umgedeutet werden. Musste sich die einstige Volksgemeinschaft und Gefolgschaft Hitlers als dessen Opfer ausgeben. Inzwischen manifestiert sich diese Selbstverwandlung in zeitgemäßer Nachhaltigkeit: Jahr für Jahr begehen die Deutschen – in trauter europäischer Eintracht, die nicht immer so preiswert zu haben ist – zusammen mit ihren EU-Partnern den 27. Januar als Holocaust-Gedenktag, als hätten ihre Vorfahren Auschwitz befreit. Das hauptstädtische

12
sinai.exteriors, Neugestaltung der Gedenkstätte Bergen-Belsen. Masterplan, Berlin 2005, p.13

11
Vgl. Reichel, Peter: Glanz und Elend, S. 270 ff. und 279 ff.

12
sinai.exteriors, Neugestaltung der Gedenkstätte Bergen-Belsen. Masterplan, Berlin 2005, S.13

After the first documentation archive was established at Bergen-Belsen in the mid-1960s, the building was extended to accommodate a new permanent exhibition in spring 1990. The prisoner-of-war camp was also included and Bergen-Belsen was described for the first time in the larger context of the Nazi system of terror and extermination. The view of the past had begun to shift and questions were increasingly being asked and demands made. Nevertheless, there was still an obvious discrepancy between the primarily descriptive documentation and the highly controversial debate on the interpretation and evaluation of Hitler's dictatorship – and on its incorporation into modern German history – that was being conducted in scholarly circles and in the press.

All the same, the increasing intensity and polarisation of the debate on Germany's Nazi past led to a shift in thinking in the decade after the reunification. The impact of the debate had reached society as a whole, with lasting consequences for the culture of remembrance and commemoration. Notable points in this context since 1985 include the Bitburg controversy, Weizsäcker's speech on the 40th anniversary of the end of the war, Jenninger's speech on the 50th anniversary of the Kristallnacht, the Holocaust Memorial, the Day of Holocaust Remembrance and *Schindler's List* as well as the Walser-Bubis affair, the Goldhagen debate, the controversy surrounding the Wehrmacht Exhibition, the compensation of forced labourers, the documentation centre about the flight and expulsion of Germans from Eastern Europe and numerous other debates that accompanied book publications, films and television productions. After the end of the GDR, it became necessary to re-examine the presentation of concentration camp memorial sites that lay in East German territories, and the resulting debate prompted comparable sites in West Germany to implement innovations of their own. The memorial and place of remembrance at Bergen-Belsen was once again subject to radical changes: in 2007 a new documentation centre with a new and significantly expanded exhibition was inaugurated and a master plan was drawn up that intended to make the site "legible as a site of historic events" but not to reconstruct it "in the actual sense".[12]

The most obvious new addition is the documentation centre by KSP Architects, an almost 200-metre-long, tunnel-like concrete construction that stretches into the woodland. Where it crosses the perimeter fence of the former camp, the rectangular architecture lifts off the ground, projecting weightlessly over the grass a few metres into the former grounds of the camp. One could see this as a respectful nod to the radical concept mentioned earlier by the Polish architects Zofia and Oskar Hansen, as an expression of the recognition of a boundary that cannot be crossed between the realm of the living and that of the dead. This impression is initially also reinforced by the large panoramic window that looks onto the site, affording visitors a view into the invisible, distant past beyond, establishing a link between the then and now that is solely visual. This impression is undone by the ability to enter and walk around the site. It will take years for the long-term master plan to acquire its full effect. Pathways, corridors and woodland devel-

Ensemble aus Neuer Wache, Holocaust-Mahnmal und Jüdischem Museum gibt der anmaßenden kalendarischen Opfer-Gedenkpolitik den dazu passenden monumentalen und spektakulären Ausdruck.[11]

Nachdem Mitte der 1960er Jahre ein erstes Dokumentenhaus errichtet worden war, konnte im Frühjahr 1990 im erweiterten Bau eine neue ständige Ausstellung präsentiert werden. Das Kriegsgefangenenlager war nun einbezogen. Erstmals wurde Bergen-Belsen in den größeren Zusammenhang des nationalsozialistischen Terror- und Vernichtungssystems gestellt. Der Blick auf die Vergangenheit veränderte sich, die Öffentlichkeit stellte inzwischen Fragen und Forderungen. Aber die Diskrepanz zwischen einer eher bloß deskriptiven Dokumentation und der zeitgleich in Publizistik und Wissenschaft geführten, hochkontroversen Debatte um Deutung, Bewertung und Einordnung der Hitler-Diktatur in die neuere deutsche Geschichte blieb ein offensichtlicher Mangel.

Immerhin hat die Intensivierung, Polarisierung und nun auch gesamtgesellschaftlich geführte Debatte um die NS-Vergangenheit im Jahrzehnt nach der Vereinigung auch der Erinnerungs- und Gedenkkultur nachhaltige Impulse gegeben – Höhepunkte waren seit 1985 der Streit um die Bitburg-Zeremonie, die Weizsäcker-Rede, die Jenninger-Rede, das Holocaust-Mahnmal, der Holocaust-Gedenktag und *Schindlers Liste*, waren die Walser-Bubis-Kontroverse, die Goldhagen-Debatte, die Kontroversen um die Wehrmachtsausstellung, die Zwangsarbeiterentschädigung, das Zentrum gegen Vertreibung und immer wieder Debatten um Buchveröffentlichungen, Filme und TV-Produktionen.

Die nach Auflösung der DDR notwendig gewordene Umgestaltung der auf ihrem Territorium liegenden KZ-Gedenkstätten und die sie begleitenden Debatten haben auch in Westdeutschland vergleichbaren Einrichtungen innovative Impulse gegeben. Der Erinnerungs- und Gedenkort Bergen-Belsen wurde abermals einer einschneidenden Veränderung unterzogen, 2007 wurde ein neues Dokumentationszentrum mit neuer, noch einmal deutlich erweiterter Ausstellung eingeweiht und ein Masterplan erarbeitet, mit dem das Gelände "als Ort historischen Geschehens lesbar" gemacht, aber nicht "im eigentlichen Sinne" rekonstruiert werden soll.[12]

Die markanteste Neuerung ist das Dokumentationszentrum von KSP Architekten, ein fast 200 Meter langer, sich in den Wald tunnelartig streckender Betonbau. Wo sich der Außenzaun des früheren Lagers befand, ragt die kubische Architektur, scheinbar schwerelos über dem Grasboden schwebend, einige Meter in das frühere Gelände hinein. Man mag das als eine respektvolle Erinnerung an das radikale Konzept der polnischen Architekten Zofia und Oskar Hansen lesen. Als Ausdruck der Anerkennung einer unüberschreitbaren Grenze zwischen dem Raum der Lebenden und dem der Toten. Dieser Eindruck wird zunächst verstärkt durch die große Panoramascheibe, die auf das Gelände weist und den Besuchern nur einen Blick in eine unsichtbar ferne Vergangenheit erlaubt, beide Zeiträume also nur visuell verknüpft sehen möchte. Die Begehbarkeit relativiert diesen Blick.

13
Benjamin, Walter: The Arcades Project, trans. Howard Eiland and Kevin McLaughlin, Cambridge 1999, p.447; cf. also Groys, Boris: Topologie der Aura, in: Groys, Boris, Topologie der Kunst, Munich 2003, p.33–46

13
Benjamin, Walter: Das Passagenwerk I, Frankfurt a. M. 1983, S.560; vgl. auch Groys, Boris: Topologie der Aura. in: ders., Topologie der Kunst, München 2003, S.33–46

opment mark the beginning of this process of developing the space. Its aim is to lend visual legibility, to differentiate and to link the two most important time-spaces, the memorial of the present and the camp of the past. It begins with the "stony path" that leads from the entrance to the documentation centre, through the exhibition and onto the site and the grass corridor in its centre where two models of the space are located. It continues with the cleared corridors that reveal the course of the former boundaries of the camp, as well as the wide corridor that runs from north to south down the centre of the site. This connects the former entrance to the camp with the crematorium – and what are now the new points of focus: the memorial area near the mass graves and their memorial stones, plaques, etc. and an area of exploration that comprises the traces of actual built remnants as well as "imaginary places" that are symbolically important but for which there are no material remains. Even though the implementation of the spatial concept of the new landscape architecture is far from complete, one can already see that through the use of sensitive and careful interventions in the natural landscape, it is possible to add clarity as well as subtle differentiation to the impression of the space. Supplemented by a discreet information system that relates back to the flyer and audio guide, the new facilities are well on the way to optimally fulfilling the dual aims of the new design for the memorial.

The perhaps least convincing of the planned new additions is the "place of names". The intention itself already hints at the dangers also present in Bergen-Belsen. However well-meaning it may be to give names and faces to the anonymous mass of victims, and however pressing a need there may be on the part of relatives and descendants, there is a great risk that aestheticisation may falsify the reality of the crime. An essential feature of the terror of the Nazi concentration and extermination camps was that it eradicated the inmates' individual self-perception, supplanting the autonomy and self-determination that characterised their civil lives with despotism, torture and permanent fear.

Ultimately, this place of suffering and death, which with its new combination of abstract symbolism and concrete texture would seem to have attained an almost perfect tension between trace and aura, stands to possibly lose this very quality. Walter Benjamin describes this tension in aphoristic terms in his *Arcades Project*: "The trace is an appearance of a nearness, however far removed the thing that left it behind may be. The aura is the appearance of distance, however close the thing that calls it forth. In the trace we gain possession of the thing, in the aura it takes possession of us."[13]

This place should not and must not be a place of recreational thrill and adventure. It intends to offer its visitors more than just views over a rural landscape, and stories and images of a disturbing world. Its aim is to encourage and enable visitors to understand this world and the unprecedented crime that took place in it, in a manner that they can critically question their own impressions in the context of other contrary opinions or attributions. For this reason, it is important not only that the design and structure of the space of the memorial is of a high quality, but that the exhibition itself also reflects the same level of quality in its conception, content and means of audio-visual presentation. The new, three-part exhi-

Für die Wirksamwerdung des langfristig angelegten Masterplans werden Jahre erforderlich sein. Schneisen, Korridore und Waldentwicklung haben die geplante Raumentwicklung eingeleitet. Sie zielt auf visuelle Transparenz, Differenzierung und Verknüpfung der beiden wichtigsten Zeit-Räume, der Gedenkstättengegenwart und der Lagervergangenheit. Zunächst durch den „Steinernen Weg", der das Gelände vom Eingangsbereich durch das Gebäude und die Ausstellung hindurch erschließt und zum Rasenkorridor führt mit den beiden Raum-Modellen. Ferner durch das Lichtungsband, das die alte Lagergrenze sichtbar macht, und nicht zuletzt durch den in Nord-Süd-Richtung verlaufenden breiten Korridor. Er verbindet den alten Lagereingang mit dem Krematorium – und nun die neuen Schwerpunkte, den Bereich des Gedenkens um die Massengräber und Mahnzeichen mit dem Schwerpunkt der Erkundung entlang der Standorte baulicher Überreste und „gedachter Orte", die hohen Symbolwert haben, für die aber materielle Relikte fehlen. Auch wenn die Realisierung der neuen Raumarchitektur noch längst nicht abgeschlossen ist, aus den Anfängen wird erkennbar, dass durch schonende, aber durchdachte Eingriffe in die natürliche Landschaft ein ebenso transparentes wie differenziertes Raumbild entsteht. Ergänzt durch ein sparsames Infosystem, das an Flyer und Audioguide rückgebunden ist, kann wohl ein Optimum in der schrittweisen Annäherung an das Doppelziel der Neugestaltung der Gedenkstätte erreicht werden.

Die vielleicht am wenigsten überzeugende Neuerung wäre der „Ort der Namen" gewesen. Die Absicht deutet an, welche Gefahr auch in Bergen-Belsen besteht. Mag die Rückgabe von Namen und Gesichtern an die anonymen Opfermassen auch noch so gut gemeint sein und einem drängenden Bedürfnis von Angehörigen und Nachkommen entsprechen, die Gefahr einer die Wirklichkeit des verbrecherischen Geschehens verfälschenden Ästhetisierung ist groß. Wesensmerkmal des Terrors der nationalsozialistischen Konzentrations- und Vernichtungslager war ja gerade die Auslöschung aller Individualität der Häftlinge, die Aufhebung ihres autonom strukturierten, zivilen Lebens durch die Willkür, die Folter, die permanente Angst.

Am Ende könnte diesem Leidens- und Sterbeort das in seiner neuen abstrakten Zeichenhaftigkeit und konkreten Textur als geradezu vorbildlich aufscheinende Spannungsverhältnis von Spur und Aura wieder genommen werden. Jenes Spannungsverhältnis, das Walter Benjamin zuletzt in seinem *Passagenwerk* aphoristisch umschrieben hat: „Die Spur ist Erscheinung einer Nähe, so fern das sein mag, was sie hinterließ. Die Aura ist Erscheinung einer Ferne, so nah das sein mag, was sie hervorruft. In der Spur werden wir der Sache habhaft, in der Aura bemächtigt sie sich unser."[13]

Dieser Ort soll und darf kein Erlebnisort sein. Er will den Besuchern mehr bieten als landschaftliche Impressionen, Geschichten und Bilder aus einer verstörenden Welt. Er will sie ermutigen und befähigen, diese Welt und ein bis dahin unbekanntes Verbrechen zu verstehen, eigenständig und kritisch, also auch im Vergleich konträrer Aussagen und Einordnungen. Deshalb müssen nicht nur an die Gestaltung und Strukturierung des Raumes der Gedenkstätte, sondern auch an die Aus-

14
Lower Saxony Memorials
Foundation (Ed.): Bergen-
Belsen. Wehrmacht POW
Camp, 1940–1945. Concen-
tration Camp, 1943–1945.
Displaced Persons Camp,
1945–1950, Göttingen 2010

14
Stiftung niedersächsische
Gedenkstätten (Hg.): Bergen-
Belsen. Kriegsgefangenen-
lager 1940–1945. Konzen-
trationslager 1943–1945.
Displaced Persons Camp
1945–1950, Göttingen 2009

bition achieves this only partially. It is no longer sufficient to merely relate the history of a place that was
originally a military training ground for the Wehrmacht
with an adjoining construction workers' camp, then a
prisoner-of-war camp, a concentration camp and finally
a Displaced Persons Camp.[14]

At least not when presented as factually as it is in the
current exhibition, without any attempt to embed it in
the preceding history of the Second World War and
persecution of the Jews, and without any attempt to
explain how Hitler rose to power out of a world war, the
revolution and inner divisions of the Weimar Republic.
The general knowledge of most visitors will only cover
isolated facts, without a proper understanding of how
they are interconnected. The need to root and explain
National Socialism in the context of German and European history in the 19th and 20th centuries and not
assume that visitors have adequate prior knowledge has
as yet not been recognised by most German NS-related
places of remembrance and museums of contemporary
history.

Neither has there been sufficient recognition of the fact
that as the happenings at the camps, the Second World
War and the camp's immediate use after the war – and
with it the return of the survivors to their homelands –
recede further and further into the past, people's interest in this period has increased and will continue to rise.
While the first half of the 20th century was a time of
disastrous wars and crimes at a grand scale, the second
half became an age of disaster prevention and disaster
remembrance, but also an age in which new wars and
crimes took place. The younger and future generations
will draw comparisons and ask questions, and that will
happen differently in countries that have experienced
dictatorships twice over than in those that have "only"
had to deal with the consequences of occupation and
exploitation by Hitler's Germany. They will ask questions
about resistance and collaborators, will want to know
how places of terror have become places of remembrance, and how the survivors, forced labourers, concentration camp inmates and soldiers were treated and
reintegrated into society after the war.

That these questions are relevant not only in the context
of one or another specific camp or their later place of
remembrance, but are also of general sociological
interest at transnational levels should be self-evident.
They reveal the mechanisms and underlying patterns of
how cultural memory is formed. To begin with, there
were mostly symbolic manifestations of the survivors,
signs of commemoration and monuments. Gratitude to
the liberators was mixed with sorrow for the dead com-
panions, a sense of guilt at having survived and the
pledge of ever-lasting solidarity in declaring "never
again!" Thereafter followed a period in which the traces
of the past were covered over in an attempt to "make
forgotten" the compromising realities of the past – before a whole generation later they could be recovered
again for assimilation in the present-day communicative
and cultural memory. After a usually short transitional
period in which the camps were used as internment
camps or displaced persons camps, the buildings were
then almost completely removed, creating the conditions necessary for creating a new beginning and a new
face for the place.

stellung hohe Anforderungen gestellt werden, konzeptionell, inhaltlich und in der audio-visuellen Vermittlung. Die neue, nun dreiteilige Ausstellung erfüllt diese
nur bedingt. Es reicht heute nicht mehr, nur die Geschichten eines Ortes zu erzählen, der ursprünglich
einmal Truppenübungsplatz der Wehrmacht war nebst
Bauarbeiter-Barackenlager, dann Kriegsgefangenenlager, Konzentrationslager und schließlich Displaced
Persons Camp.[14]

Jedenfalls dann nicht, wenn dies so unvermittelt geschieht wie in der Ausstellung. Ohne die Einbettung in
die unmittelbare Vorgeschichte des Zweiten Weltkrieges und der Judenverfolgung, ohne den Versuch, dem
Besucher den Aufstieg der Hitler-Bewegung aus
Weltkrieg, Revolution und innerer Spaltung der Weimarer Republik begreifbar zu machen. Zu den punktuellen
Allgemeinkenntnissen gehört solch Zusammenhangs-
wissen meist nicht. Die Einsicht, dass eine Ortsbe-
stimmung des Nationalsozialismus in der deutschen/
europäischen Geschichte des 19. und 20. Jahrhunderts
durchaus auch einer nicht einschlägig vorgebildeten
Öffentlichkeit zu vermitteln ist, hat sich in deutschen
NS-Erinnerungsorten und zeithistorischen Museen
noch zu wenig durchgesetzt.

Ebenso wenig, dass mit wachsender zeitlicher Distanz
zum Lagergeschehen, zum Zweiten Weltkrieg, zur
frühen Nachgeschichte der Lager – und zur Rückfüh-
rung der Überlebenden in ihre Heimatländer – das
Interesse der Besucher an dieser Zeit zugenommen hat
und weiter zunehmen wird. War die erste Hälfte des
20. Jahrhunderts eine Zeit der Großkriege und Großver-
brechen, ist die zweite Hälfte ein Zeitalter der Katastro-
phenvermeidung und Katastrophenerinnerung geworden, aber auch neuer Kriege und Gewaltverbrechen.
Die nachwachsenden Generationen werden verglei-
chen und fragen. In den Ländern mit einer zweifachen
Diktaturerfahrung anders als in solchen, die sich „nur"
mit den Folgen der Besetzung und Ausbeutung durch
Hitler-Deutschland auseinandersetzen müssen.
Werden nach Widerstand und Kollaboration fragen,
werden wissen wollen, wie sich Schreckensorte in
Gedenkstätten verwandelt haben, und wie nach dem
Krieg die Überlebenden, Zwangsarbeiter, KZ-Häftlinge,
Soldaten angesehen und integriert wurden.

Dass diese Fragen nicht nur in jedem anders beschaf-
fenen Einzelfall eines Lagers und der späteren Erinnerungsstätte aufschlussreich sind, sondern auch von
einem länderübergreifenden, soziologisch allgemeinen Interesse, liegt auf der Hand. Sie offenbaren
Mechanismen und Grundmuster kultureller Gedächt-
nisbildung. Zwar standen am Anfang meist symbolische Manifestationen der Überlebenden, Gedenkzeichen und Mahnmale. Der Dank an die Befreier
verband sich mit der Trauer um die toten Häftlings-
gefährten, dem Schuldgefühl, überlebt zu haben, und
dem solidarischen Schwur: „Nie wieder!" Dann aber
wurden die Spuren der Vergangenheit verwischt, das
Kompromittierende vergessen gemacht – bevor es eine
Generation später in das kommunikative und kulturelle
Gedächtnis der Gegenwart zurückgeholt werden
konnte. Nach einer meist kurzen Übergangzeit der
Nutzung als Internierungslager oder Displaced Persons
Camp wurden nicht nur die Bebauungen weitgehend
beseitigt, sondern Voraussetzungen geschaffen für
eine neue Ortsgeschichte, eine neue Ortsansicht.

15
Cited in Skriebeleit, Jörg: Erinnerungsort Flossenbürg. Akteure, Zäsuren und Geschichtsbilder, Göttingen 2009, p. 248
16
Reichel, Peter: Nach Diktatur, Krieg und Gewaltverbrechen. Wiederaufbau, politischer Wandel und Vergangenheitspolitik: die Bundesrepublik in den fünfziger Jahren, in: Nerdinger, W./Florschütz, I. (Ed.): Architektur der Wunderkinder. Aufbruch und Verdrängung in Bayern 1945–1960, Salzburg-Munich 2005, p. 45–57
17
Ibid., p. 238

15
Zit. n. Skriebeleit, Jörg: Erinnerungsort Flossenbürg. Akteure, Zäsuren und Geschichtsbilder, Göttingen 2009, S. 248
16
Reichel, Peter: Nach Diktatur, Krieg und Gewaltverbrechen. Wiederaufbau, politischer Wandel und Vergangenheitspolitik: die Bundesrepublik in den fünfziger Jahren, in: Nerdinger, W./Florschütz, I. (Hg.): Architektur der Wunderkinder. Aufbruch und Verdrängung in Bayern 1945–1960, Salzburg-München 2005, S. 45–57
17
Ebda., S. 238

Neuengamme concentration camp near Hamburg, for example, was turned into the Vollzugsanstalt Vierlande, a prison for young offenders. Bergen-Belsen became an idyllic heathland cemetery, while the "camp of misery at Dachau" was turned temporarily into a refugee camp. On the terraced terrain of the camp in Flossenbürg, the unsightly camp barracks were replaced by pleasant houses built for the settlers expelled from Silesia and the Sudetenland. A "site of suffering" was transformed into "homes of happiness".[15] In Flossenbürg as in Dachau, the building of ecumenical Christian amenities such as chapels, crosses and cemeteries of honour, functioning as meta-political signs of reconciliation and consolation, made it possible to shift the focus of the former site of mass murder and mass death away from the historical perspective of an organised political crime. The towns stigmatised by the camp in their vicinity cast themselves in the role of the victim. West German society followed suit: many whose fate had become uncertain in the wake of the war, the returning servicemen, those whose homes had been destroyed, refugees, as well as civil servants who had been dismissed from service due to their work for the Nazi state (the so-called "131er"), saw themselves for the most part as innocent victims of Hitler, of the war and of the post-war period, as being unfairly held accountable for their crimes.[16] It was easier to deal with the role of the victim, and also better for one's image. No one wants anything to do with perpetrators.

Where the allied liberators, international prisoner-of-war organisations, or individual people had not taken it into their own hands to remember the victims and preserve important buildings, it took a long time for the struggle against forgetting and repression to yield results. Helpful in this respect were impulses provided by events outside the locality. Of particular and lasting importance, not only in the early days, were prominent victims of the camps, among them Anne Frank in Bergen-Belsen in the 1950s or in Flossenbürg, Dietrich Bonhoeffer and Wilhelm Canaris, who had opposed the regime and were executed along with other members of the resistance in April 1945, only weeks before the end of the war. While the efforts of the relatives to honour and commemorate the dead were unable to prevent Flossenbürg from largely eradicating the stain of being the site of a concentration camp, the growing popularisation of the "20 July" plot to assassinate Hitler contributed to paving the way for a memorial. Twenty years after the end of the war, the once poor quarry village in the Upper Palatine Forest was able to rid itself of the stigma of the camp with the help of the camp itself. Making use of former camp buildings, the municipality presented itself in a new guise as a site of industry and recreation. As part of this transformation, the "Valley of Death" became a "Valley of Peace" and the commemoration of those who had died at the camp was rendered politically neutral through the adoption of the by then widely used phrase "the victims of war and tyranny", an expression popularised by the German War Graves Commission that effectively places all fates on the same level.[17] This same formulation can also be found in the Neue Wache in Berlin, Germany's primary national place of remembrance.

In Neuengamme, dem nahe Hamburg gelegenen Konzentrationslager, entstand die Vollzugsanstalt Vierlande, ein Jugendgefängnis. Aus Bergen-Belsen wurde ein idyllischer Heidepark-Friedhof, das „Elendslager Dachau" vorübergehend ein Flüchtlingslager. Und auf dem terrassierten Lagergelände in Flossenbürg verdrängten schmucke Siedlungshäuser für Vertriebene und Flüchtlinge aus Schlesien und dem Sudetenland die hässlichen Baracken. Aus „Stätten des Leides" wurden „Heime des Glücks".[15] In Flossenbürg wie in Dachau gelang es zudem, die einstigen Orte des Massentötens und Massensterbens durch christlich-ökumenische Einrichtungen wie Kapelle, Kreuz und Ehrenfriedhof, durch metapolitische Zeichen der Versöhnung und des Trostes also, aus der historischen Perspektive eines politischen Staatsverbrechens herauszulösen. Die durch die Lager stigmatisierten Orte machten sich den Opferstatus selbst zu eigen. Den sich auch die westdeutsche Gesellschaft zubilligte: Die vielen sogenannten Schicksalsgruppen, die Kriegsheimkehrer und Ausgebombten, Flüchtlinge und aus ihren Ämtern entfernten belasteten Beamten („131er") verstanden sich großenteils als schuldlos-schuldige Opfer Hitlers, des Krieges und der Nachkriegszeit.[16] Der Umgang mit Opfern war und blieb einfacher und fürs eigene Ansehen vorteilhaft. Wer mag schon mit Tätern zu tun haben.

Hatten sich nicht früh die alliierten Befreier, internationale Häftlingsorganisationen oder auch einzelne Personen für das Opfergedenken an den Leidensorten und den denkmalpflegerischen Erhalt wichtiger Gebäude eingesetzt, konnte es lange dauern, bis ihr Kampf gegen das Vergessen und Verdrängen erste Erfolge zeigte. Förderlich waren immer auch Impulse, die aus überlokalen Ereignissen resultierten. Eine frühe und nachhaltige Bedeutung hatte dabei die Prominenz von Lageropfern. So schon in den 1950er Jahren die von Anne Frank in Bergen-Belsen, und in Flossenbürg die von den Regimegegnern Dietrich Bonhoeffer und Wilhelm Canaris. Sie waren dort mit anderen Widerstandskämpfern noch im April 1945 ermordet worden. Mit ihren Initiativen zur ehrenden Erinnerung an ihre Toten konnten die Angehörigen zwar nicht verhindern, dass Flossenbürg sich vom Makel eines KZ-Standortes befreite, aber dank der wachsenden Popularisierung des „20. Juli" doch dazu beitragen, den Weg zur Gedenkstätte zu ebnen. Zwanzig Jahre nach Ende des Krieges war es dem einstigen armen Steinhauerdorf im Oberpfälzer Wald gelungen, das Stigma des Lagers mit Hilfe des Lagers abzustreifen. Nicht zuletzt dank der Nutzung ehemaliger Lagergebäude präsentierte sich die Gemeinde als Industrie- und Erholungsort in neuem Glanz. Passend dazu war aus dem „Tal des Todes" ein „Tal des Friedens" geworden und das Gedenken der KZ-Toten politisch entschärft, in der längst allgemein verbreiteten Volksbund-Nivellierungsformel „Den Opfern von Krieg und Gewaltherrschaft".[17] Auch in der zentralen Gedenkstätte der Nation, der Neuen Wache in Berlin, findet sie sich.

18
Schmitz-Ehmke, Ruth: Bau-
aufgabe und Architektur-
sprache. Zum Problem der
Formfindung im Œuvre des
Clemens Klotz, in: Durth, W./
Nerdinger, W. (Ed.): Architektur und Städtebau der
30er/40er Jahre, Vol. 46 of
the publications of the German National Committee for
the Protection of Historical
Monuments, Bonn 1994,
p. 84 ff. (111 f.)

18
Schmitz-Ehmke, Ruth: Bau-
aufgabe und Architektur-
sprache. Zum Problem der
Formfindung im Œuvre des
Clemens Klotz, in: Durth, W./
Nerdinger, W. (Hg.): Archi-
tektur und Städtebau der
30er/40er Jahre, Bd. 46 der
Schriftenreihe des Deut-
schen Nationalkomitees für
Denkmalschutz, Bonn 1994,
S. 84 ff. (111 f.)

A contemporary design for the memorial site and its im-mediate context – the quarry and the "Valley of Death" – therefore had to place equal emphasis on correcting the commemorative emphasis as on communicating in space the horrors experienced daily by the inmates of the camp on their way from the roll call ground to the quarry and back. sinai have made this path, the path that visitors take to enter the memorial. As in Bergen-Belsen, a pair of models have been placed at a central location – in Flossenbürg on the roll call ground – that show the structure of the site at two points in time: that of the camp and that of the present-day memorial. More suc-cessful than the "Place of Names" in Bergen-Belsen is the "Archive of Names" conceived for Flossenbürg. Between the grounds of the camp and the "Valley of Death", sinai have planned a series of freestanding stone walls for the nameless victims, arranged parallel to one another so that one can pass between them, with the names of the dead inscribed on them – an intervention that remembers the reality of the camp while sensitively respecting the needs of those who wish to be close to the dead.

If the small East Bavarian village of Flossenbürg com-memorated the 50th anniversary of the liberation of the camp as the "rediscovery of a European place of remem-brance", it comes as no surprise that the new Vogelsang Forum in the Eifel region was not content to mark its new function as an international place of education and exchange with the usual programme of activities and food, sport and nature.

The fact that this long inaccessible former military site and ideologically contaminated space has been reha-bilitated and given a new profile as a national park centre must be welcomed. While the planned focus of a docu-mentation centre on National Socialism – on the political education of young Nazi leaders – may seem an obvious choice given that this was the purpose behind the building and the early use of the so-called *Ordensburg*, it is – at best – only suitable for a temporary exhibition; it is not comprehensive enough for a permanent exhibi-tion. Similarly, an exhibition of the architecture of the Nazi period is not a real alternative. The eclectic building designed by Clemens Klotz was not emulated elsewhere in the Third Reich. Hitler found it lacking in monumenta-lity. Journalistic circles criticised the contradiction between the functionalist reinforced concrete building and its conservationist, homeland-eulogising rustic-rural aesthetics.[18] What could potentially make this place an attraction of European importance – after all, it lies closer to the cities of Amsterdam, Brussels and Paris than to Hamburg, Berlin and Munich – would be a comparative documentation of "Fascism in its European Epoch – Origins and Impact". And especially if it were also to document fascist movements and regimes in the inter-war period as well as nationalist, right-wing populist, anti-Semitic and xenophobic political parties and their politico-cultural context in Europe today.

Einer Korrektur des Totengedenkens bei einer Neuge-staltung des Gedenkstättenareals und seines unmittel-baren Kontextes – Steinbruch und Tal des Todes – musste deshalb ebenso große Bedeutung zukommen wie einer räumlichen Vermittlung des täglichen Elends der Häftlinge auf ihrem Weg vom Appellplatz zum Steinbruch und zurück. sinai definiert auf diesem Weg den Besuchereingang ins Lager. Wie in Bergen-Belsen wird er auch in Flossenbürg an zentraler Stelle, eben auf dem Appellplatz, mit einem Doppelmodell über die Strukturen der beiden Raumzeiten des Ortes infor-miert, den lagerzeitlichen und den der gegenwärtigen Gedenkstätte.

Besser durchdacht als in Bergen-Belsen der „Ort der Namen" ist in Flossenbürg das „Archiv der Namen". Die Lagerwirklichkeit bedenkend und zugleich mit großem Gespür für die Bedürfnisse derer, die dort den Toten nahe sein wollen, ist geplant, den namenlos Gemorde-ten am Übergang vom Lagergelände zum „Tal des Todes" lamellenartig, also passierbar, steinerne Wände zu errichten, welche die Namen der Toten tragen.

Wenn schon das ostbayerische Flossenbürg anlässlich des 50. Jahrestages der Lagerbefreiung seine „Wieder-entdeckung als europäischer Erinnerungsort" feierte, dann sollte und wollte das neue Forum Vogelsang in der Eifel seinen Auftrag als internationale Bildungs-und Begegnungsstätte nicht nur mit dem gängigen Erlebnis & Genuss-Programm aus Gastronomie, Sport und Natur anreichern.

Begrüßen muss man, dass der durch militärische Nutzung lange unzugängliche und zuvor ideologisch kontaminierte Raum als Nationalpark rehabilitiert und wieder aufgewertet wird. Der für die NS-Dokumenta-tion zunächst geplante Schwerpunkt zur politischen Erziehung des nationalsozialistischen Führungsnach-wuchses mag durch die Entstehung und frühere Nut-zung der sogenannten Ordensburg naheliegen. Er taugt – bestenfalls – für eine temporäre Ausstellung, für eine Dauerausstellung trägt das Thema nicht. Auch eine NS-Architekturschau wäre dort keine wirkliche Alternative. Der eklektizistische Clemens-Klotz-Bau hat im Dritten Reich keine Nachahmer gefunden. Hitler monierte die fehlende Monumentalität. Die Kunstpubli-zistik kritisierte den Widerspruch von funktionalisti-schem Stahlbetonbau und rustikalem Heimatschutz-stil.[18] Was den Ort, der den europäischen Metropolen Amsterdam, Brüssel und Paris näher liegt als Hamburg, Berlin und München, aber zu einer europaweiten At-traktion machen könnte, wäre eine vergleichende Dokumentation „Der Faschismus in seiner europä-ischen Epoche – Entstehung und Folgen". Jedenfalls dann, wenn sie über die faschistischen Bewegungen und Regime der Zwischenkriegszeit ebenso Auskunft geben würde wie über die nationalistischen, rechts-populistischen, antisemitischen und xenophoben Parteien und ihren politisch-kulturellen Kontext im Europa heute.

19
Kaminsky, A. (Ed.): Orte des Erinnerns, Gedenkzeichen, Gedenkstätten und Museen zur Diktatur in SBZ und DDR, Bonn, 2nd edition, 2007
20
In an essay of the same name by W. Sofsky. In: Prigge, W. (Ed.): Bauhaus. Brasilia. Auschwitz. Hiroshima. Weltkulturerbe des 20. Jh.: Modernität und Barbarei, Berlin 2003, p. 122ff.
21
Detjen, M.: Die Mauer, in: Sabrow, M. (Ed.): Erinnerungsorte der DDR, Munich 2009, p. 389ff.

19
Kaminsky, A. (Hg.): Orte des Erinnerns, Gedenkzeichen, Gedenkstätten und Museen zur Diktatur in SBZ und DDR, Bonn 2. Aufl. 2007
20
Der gleichnamige Aufsatz von W. Sofsky. In: W. Prigge (Hg.): Bauhaus. Brasilia. Auschwitz. Hiroshima. Weltkulturerbe des 20. Jh.: Modernität und Barbarei, Berlin 2003, S. 122ff.
21
Detjen, M.: Die Mauer, in: Sabrow, M. (Hg.): Erinnerungsorte der DDR, München 2009, S. 389ff.

III

On the territory of the new Federal Republic of Germany, the dominant culture of remembrance still concerns the history of National Socialism, the Second World War and the war crimes. The not inconsiderable difference to the German Democratic Republic can be seen in the different positions that both dictatorships and their crimes occupy in national and global history. However, the number of places and their manifestations has risen considerably over the last 20 years. A representative publication in 2007 identified over 600 places of remembrance.[19] For the most part, these are dedicated to the victims of Stalinist repression and the SED regime. A not inconsiderable number of these are memorial plaques commemorating the 17 June 1953 and the 9 November 1989, events that reveal the essential difference between the regimes of both German dictatorships but also the power of protest, resistance and uprising.

The National Socialist regime was founded on a utopian vision of a biologically superior society. It employed the means of breeding and extermination, selection and elimination, with the members of the "Aryan people's community" on the one hand and the ideologically and politically as well as ethnically and biologically stigmatised "strangers to the community" on the other. While the former were integrated into society negatively through the restriction of political freedom, coercive measures and intimidation, and positively through ideological valorisation, a politics of appearances, the leadership cult, media propaganda and mass organisation, the latter were subject to exclusion, exploitation, persecution and liquidation. The places and means of this form of politics were the camp barracks in all their variants, now emblematic symbol of an authoritarian "Führer State", an organised "people's community" and a regime of dictatorship. For the outcasts, however, the camp was in its ambivalence, a "block", a "concentrated space of terror".[20]

The socialist SED, the governing party in East Germany, defined itself as a revolutionary avant-garde on the path to a utopian vision of a classless and conflict-free society. It was based on a belief in historical materialism as a principle of development. And because questions of belief are not always easily reconcilable with politics, the party laid claim to a monopoly of power and ideology – choosing not to rely on the incalculability of the voters but on the military backing of the communist Soviet Union to reinforce this claim. Those who did not subscribe to this model of society and claim to power due to a lack of democratic and constitutional values, sought their chances in the West. Faced with flight and depopulation, the regime responded by locking up its territories. In 1961, the Wall became the symbolic structure of this regime.[21]

Instead of tens of thousands of inaccessible enclaves inside a country, as was the case during the Nazi dictatorship, an entire section of the nation, equivalent to the former Soviet-occupied zone, became a vast, prison-like enclave within the Soviet empire. To hermetically seal it off from its Western "brother state", a primitive barrier in the form of a wall and barbed wire was initially erected, followed later by the construction of an ultra-modern border security system with two sets of walls, automatic firing devices and electronic surveillance systems.

III

Auf dem Territorium der neuen Bundesrepublik dominiert weiterhin die Erinnerungskultur für die Auseinandersetzung mit der Geschichte des Nationalsozialismus, des Zweiten Weltkrieges und seiner Gewaltverbrechen. Die nicht geringe Differenz zur DDR spiegelt den unterschiedlichen national- und weltgeschichtlichen Ort beider Diktaturen und ihrer Verbrechen. Allerdings ist die Zahl der Orte und Manifestationen in den vergangenen 20 Jahren erheblich gewachsen. Eine repräsentative Veröffentlichung hat 2007 über 600 Einrichtungen dokumentiert.[19] Sie sind vor allem den stalinistischen Opfern und den Opfern der SED-Herrschaft gewidmet. In nicht geringer Zahl finden sich darunter auch Gedenktafeln und Erinnerungszeichen für die Ereignisse um den 17. Juni 1953 und den 9. November 1989. Ereignisse, in denen sich der Wesensunterschied der Gewaltherrschaft beider deutscher Diktaturen offenbart, aber auch die Kraft des Protestes, des Widerstands, der Erhebung.

Das NS-Regime beruhte auf einer biologischen Gesellschaftsutopie. Es stützte sich auf Züchtung und Vernichtung, auf Auslese und Ausmerzung. Der „arischen Volksgemeinschaft" standen die weltanschaulichpolitisch und ethnisch-biologisch stigmatisierten „Gemeinschaftsfremden" gegenüber. Während jene negativ durch politischen Freiheitsentzug, Zwangsmaßnahmen und Einschüchterung, positiv aber durch ideologische Aufwertung, eine Politik des schönen Scheins, Führerkult, Medienmobilisierung und Massenorganisation integriert wurde, trafen die anderen Maßnahmen der Ausgrenzung, Ausbeutung, Verfolgung und Liquidierung. Ort und Mittel dieser Politik war die Lagerbaracke in all ihren Varianten. Symbol eines autoritären Führerstaates, einer organisierten Volksgemeinschaft und Gewaltherrschaft. Für die Ausgestoßenen war das Lager in seiner Ambivalenz der „Block", der „Nahraum des Terrors".[20]

Die sozialistische SED definierte sich als revolutionäre Avantgarde auf dem Weg zur Utopie einer klassen- und konfliktlosen Gesellschaft. Sie stützte sich auf den Glauben an das Entwicklungsgesetz des Historischen Materialismus. Und weil das mit Glaubensfragen in der Politik so eine Sache ist, beanspruchte sie ein Weltanschauungs- und Machtmonopol – und stützte sich mit diesem Anspruch sicherheitshalber nicht auf ein unberechenbares Wählervotum, sondern auf den militärischen Rückhalt der kommunistischen Sowjetunion. Jenen, die sich diesem Gesellschaftsmodell und Herrschaftsanspruch wegen seiner fehlenden demokratisch-rechtsstaatlichen Ausstattung verweigerten, um im Westen nach Lebenschancen zu suchen, begegnete das durch Flucht und Entvölkerung bedrohte Regime durch die Selbstabschließung seines Territoriums. Das symbolische Bauwerk dafür wurde 1961 die Mauer.[21]

Nicht Zehntausende Lager wie in der NS-Diktatur waren unzugängliche Enklaven im eigenen Land. Das ganze teilstaatliche Gebilde, hervorgegangen aus der einstigen sowjetischen Besatzungszone, verwandelte sich in eine gefängnisähnliche Großenklave innerhalb des sowjetischen Imperiums. Hermetisch abgetrennt vom westlichen „Bruderstaat", anfangs durch eine

22
Düwell, F. J. (Ed.): Licht und Schatten. Der 9. November in der deutschen Geschichte, Baden-Baden 2000; Reichel, P.: Glanz und Elend, p. 207ff.
23
Schulze, W.: Der 14. Juli 1789. Biographie eines Tages, Stuttgart 1989
24
Verein Berliner Mauer (Ed.): Gedenkstätte, Dokumentationszentrum und Versöhnungskapelle in der Bernauer Straße, Berlin 1999

22
Düwell, F. J. (Hg.): Licht und Schatten. Der 9. November in der deutschen Geschichte, Baden-Baden 2000; Reichel, P.: Glanz und Elend, S. 207ff.
23
Schulze, W.: Der 14. Juli 1789. Biographie eines Tages, Stuttgart 1989
24
Verein Berliner Mauer (Hg.): Gedenkstätte, Dokumentationszentrum und Versöhnungskapelle in der Bernauer Straße, Berlin 1999

The breaching of the Wall on the 9 November 1989 and its subsequent near-complete demolition not only eradicated a territorial division. The removal of the Wall transformed the most famous as well as notorious physical symbol of the self-liquidating GDR into a date on the calendar. Or more rightly: the popular uprising could have done that. In the now legendary moment of its fall, the Wall was simultaneously an object of hate, of triumph, of transfiguration – as well as an object to rid oneself of, to be sold and marketed. For the people of Germany, the day the Wall came down was a day of celebration in their often thorny history of democracy. Had the national parliament of the now united Germany not heeded the concerns of the political sceptics, as happens all too often, the national holiday might have been on this day and not on the 3rd October. This date marks the parliamentary declaration of the dissolution of the GDR but is for most people not as momentous as the events that preceded it. The 9 November 1989 could then have been the "Day of the German Revolution" which would proudly commemorate (with thanks to Mr Gorbatchev) the third attempt, after 1848 and 1918, to achieve a state of freedom and unity for all Germans. And also one that might prevail in the long term. [22] Let us look briefly beyond the Rhine to recall with admiration a historical precursor: on the 14 July 1789, after the insurgent citizens of Paris had stormed the Bastille, Pierre-François Palloy – a supporter of the revolution as well as an entrepreneurial building contractor sensitive to the marketability of political symbolism – began the very same day with the dismantling of the state prison and hated symbol of the monarchy, out of which he made stone souvenirs of the revolution, honouring the friends of the revolution. A year later the wealthy patriot arranged a celebratory festival for the people at his own cost – laying the foundation for what later became a national holiday. Nevertheless, it took almost a century for the three symbols of the new French Republic – the Tricolore, the Marseillaise and the 14 July – to be adopted with the founding of the Third Republic. Palloy is today all but forgotten, but his deed is immortalized in the national symbolism of the French Republic. [23] The extension of the Berlin Wall Memorial could have become Germany's "Place de la Bastille" and the 9 November, Germany's 14 July.
The memorial on the Bernauer Strasse keeps alive the memory of the erection, successive expansion and operation of the 155-kilometre-long Berlin Wall – with which the GDR effectively transformed its territory into a prison of national dimensions. [24] The extension to the memorial achieves this in a manner that is both simple and sparing in its means and considered and sensitive in its choice of materials, adding traces made of rusted steel that re-chart the events of the past. For the first time, a section of the former Wall – a 1.4-kilometre-long broad corridor between the Nordbahnhof and the Mauerpark, originally cleared by the GDR to make space for the death strip between the inner and outer walls of the border – has been dedicated to the creation of a subtly differentiated topography of places for commemorating events and incidents and for remembering the victims of the Wall. In the stretches between the still

primitive Absperrung aus Mauer und Stacheldraht, später durch den Bau eines hochmodernen Grenzsicherungssystems, mit doppelter Mauer, Selbstschussanlagen und elektronischer Überwachung. Die Öffnung der Mauer am 9. November und ihr weitgehender Abriss danach, hoben nicht nur die räumliche Trennung auf. Die Beseitigung der Mauer verwandelte auch das weltweit bekannteste und berüchtigtste Architektursymbol der sich selbst liquidierenden DDR in ein kalendarisch-zeitliches. Oder richtiger: Die Volkserhebung hätte es tun können. Die Mauer war im nachhaltigen Augenblick ihres Abrisses gleichermaßen Objekt des Hasses, des Triumphes, der Verklärung – und der Veräußerung. Der Tag des Mauerfalls ein Volksfesttag in unserer dornigen Demokratiegeschichte. Wäre das nationale Parlament des nun vereinten Deutschlands, wie so oft hierzulande, nicht allein den politischen Bedenkenträgern gefolgt, unser Nationalfeiertag müsste nicht der 3. Oktober sein. Als parlamentarische Beurkundung der Selbstauflösung der DDR ein eher bedeutungsblasses Datum. Der 9. November 1989 wäre dann heute der „Tag der deutschen Revolution", an dem wir uns stolz – und mit Dank an Herrn Gorbatschow – an den nach 1848 und 1918 dritten Versuch erinnern, für alle Deutschen Freiheit und Einheit zu erreichen. Und nun vielleicht dauerhaft erfolgreich. [22]
Mit einem bewundernden Blick über den Rhein sei kurz an das historische Vorbild erinnert: Schon am 14. Juli 1789, als die aufständischen Pariser Bürger die Bastille stürmen, das verhasste Staatsgefängnis der Monarchie, beginnt der so revolutionsbegeisterte wie symbolpolitisch fantasievolle und geschäftstüchtige Bauunternehmer Pierre-François Palloy mit dem Abriss des monumentalen Verlieses, macht aus den Steinen Revolutionsreliquien und ehrt damit die Freunde der Revolution. Ein Jahr später veranstaltet der vermögende Patriot auf seine Kosten an diesem Ort ein Volks- und Erinnerungsfest – und legt den Grundstein für den späteren Nationalfeiertag. Es dauert allerdings ein Jahrhundert, bis die drei zentralen Symbole des neuen Frankreich, die Trikolore, die Marseillaise und der 14. Juli, durchgesetzt sind. Das gelingt erst zu Beginn der III. Republik. Palloy ist heute nahezu vergessen. Seine Tat hat sich in der Nationalsymbolik der französischen Republik verewigt. [23] Die Erweiterung der Gedenkstätte Berliner Mauer hätte die deutsche „Place de la Bastille" werden können, der 9. November der deutsche 14. Juli.
Die Gedenkstätte an der Bernauer Straße trägt zunächst der Erinnerung an Entstehung, Perfektionierung und Nutzung der 155 Kilometer langen Berliner Mauer Rechnung – mit ihr verwandelte sich die DDR endgültig in ein territoriales Staatsgefängnis. [24] Bei der Erweiterung der Gedenkstätte tut dies in so einfacher wie sparsamer, aber materialästhetisch durchdachter Weise durch eine „Nachzeichnung" (Rekartierung) mit rostigem Baustahl. Erstmals wurde nun, zwischen Nordbahnhof und Mauerpark, auf einer 1,4 Kilometer langen, breiten Schneise, dem zu DDR-Zeiten in die Stadt gesprengten Todesstreifen zwischen Grenz- und Hinterlandmauer, eine hochdifferenzierte Topografie der Zeitorte und des Totengedenkens geschaffen. Wo die Grenzmauer verlief, die dort teilweise noch erhalten ist, reihen sich in dichter Folge Rundstäbe – ein

25
Paul, G. (Ed.): Das Jahr-
hundert der Bilder, Göttingen
2009, Vol. 2, p. 258 ff.

25
Paul, G. (Hg.): Das Jahrhundert der Bilder, Göttingen
2009, Bd. 2, S. 258 ff.

existent sections of the Wall, a row of clustered vertical round rods mark the line of the former border wall – a sign that can be read as both a symbol of the division as well as of its removal. It can also be read as a humorous reference to the industrious "wall peckers" whose commercially motivated removal of pieces of the Wall left the iron reinforcement rods exposed. The same materiality is employed in the tracing of the sentry path, signal fence and watchtower and for marking the positions of the former buildings demolished along the south side of the Bernauer Strasse. In this once densely-populated area in which the burgeoning middle-class area of Berlin-Mitte met the working-class district of Berlin-Wedding, green grass predominates, interleaved with rusted steel elements – strips in the ground, rods, columns and towers – that serve as abstract and unpretentious markers in an area of the city that was particularly drastically effected by the division. They are the scars in a new urban space – now open in both senses of the word – that has begun to fill with new urban vitality. The outlines of the former buildings along the border, in particular, are an especially striking symbol that is unique in Berlin. For a while the division between East and West ran along the same line that separated the private living quarters of neighbours. This would become the site of images that went around the world and are now part of our visual memory of the 20th century. [25] They show people jumping out of the windows in an attempt to reach freedom in the West. Soon after, the windows and doors were bricked in and the façades of the houses themselves became part of the boundary wall. The houses too were eventually demolished to make space for the Wall.

The "Window of Remembrance" as well as the "Steles of Death" commemorate people who died at the Bernauer Strasse or elsewhere trying to cross the border in Berlin. "Soundings" showing the excavated remains and markings delineating the path of escape tunnels have been introduced as well as information panels and incidence markers that, in a manner reminiscent of the "Stumbling Blocks" used to remember the deported and murdered Jews, have been set into the different surfacing materials of the ground. Part of this open-air exhibition consists of the large-format images on the firewalls of the houses bordering the site. These are part of an effort, born out of the specific history of the memorial, to incorporate the disparate existing fragments of the landscape of remembrance that had been implemented in the 1990s.

Among the architectural elements that existed prior to the extension of this open-air memorial are the new information pavilion, the documentation centre with its lookout tower, the Chapel of Reconciliation and the so-called "Monument", a 70-metre-long stretch (designed by Kohlhoff & Kohlhoff) of the former border installations framed between a pair of high steel walls. It looks not unlike the real courtyard of a prison, and if one did not know better, one could mistake it for a convincing outdoor film set for the studios in Babelsberg. All that is missing are the actors enacting night-time escape scenes in the manner of reality-tv documentary soaps.

doppelt lesbares Zeichen: als Symbol der Teilung und ihrer Überwindung. Zudem eine augenzwinkernde Erinnerung an das phasenweise kommerziell motivierte Werk der emsigen „Mauerspechte", die in den Eisenstäben der Betonsegmente an ihre Grenze kamen. „Nachgezeichnet" in dieser materialästhetischen Formensprache sind auch „Postenweg", „Signalzaun", „Wachturm" und die Standorte der einstigen Grenzhäuser an der Südseite der Bernauer Straße. In diesem einst dicht bevölkerten Areal, in dem die wachsende bürgerliche Stadtmitte auf das Arbeitermilieu des Wedding traf, dominieren das Grasgrün des Bodenbelages und der rostige Stahl eingelassener Bänder, Stäbe, Säulen und Türme – abstrakte, unpathetische Markierungen einer dort besonders schwer gezeichneten Stadt. Narben eines im doppelten Wortsinn neuen Freiraumes, den eine neue, urbane Vitalität zu füllen begonnen hat.

Gerade die Grundrissmarkierungen der Grenzhäuser müssen deshalb als ein besonders markantes und in Berlin einmaliges Symbol hervorgehoben werden. War doch an diesem Ort die Grenze der Ost-West-Teilung der Welt identisch mit der Teilung der privaten, nachbarschaftlichen Lebenswelt. Dort entstanden Bilder, die um den Globus gingen und zum visuellen Gedächtnis des 20. Jahrhunderts gehören. [25] Sie zeigen, dass und wie sich Menschen durch einen Sprung in den freien Westen zu retten suchten. Bald wurden Fenster und Türen zugemauert, die Hausfassaden zur „Grenzsicherung". Später mussten auch sie der Mauer weichen.

Das „Fenster des Gedenkens" und die „Todesstelen" erinnern an die Toten der Bernauer Straße bzw. die Maueropfer in Berlin. Sondagen mit freigelegten Überresten und Markierungen für den Verlauf der Fluchttunnel fehlen so wenig wie Info-Stelen, Ereignismarken, die, analog den „Stolpersteinen" zur Erinnerung an die deportierten und ermordeten Juden, in die unterschiedlichen Bodenbeläge eingelassen sind. Teil dieser Open-Air-Ausstellung sind auch die großflächigen Informationen an Brandmauern von Häusern in unmittelbarer Nähe. Es gehört zur Entstehungsgeschichte und Eigenart der Gedenkstätte, dass die Erweiterung die bereits in den 1990er Jahren angelegten Fragmente einer Erinnerungslandschaft zusammenführt.

Zu den bereits vor der Erweiterung vorhandenen architektonischen Fixpunkten dieser Freiraumausstellung gehören das Dokumentationszentrum mit Aussichtsturm, die Kapelle der Versöhnung und das „Denkmal" genannte, von Kohlhoff & Kohlhoff geplante 70 Meter lange Stück des einstigen Grenzsicherungssystems, das durch hohe Stahlwände rahmenartig eingefasst ist. Einem realen Gefängnisinnenhof nicht unähnlich. Eine Filmkulisse, die sich als Außenstelle für Babelsberg empfiehlt. Es fehlte nur noch, dass hier bei Nacht spektakuläre Flucht-Szenen nachgespielt werden, im Stil der Doku-*soaps* des die Zuschauer verdummenden *Reality-TV*. Künstlerisch das wohl am wenigsten überzeugende Element der weiträumigen Gedenkstätte, und nicht grundlos schon während seiner Entstehung

26
Senatsverwaltung für Stadtentwicklung: Erweiterung der
Gedenkstätte Berliner Mauer,
Berlin 2007, p. 93 f.
27
Ibid., p. 99
28
Cited in Loy, Thomas: Lücken
der Erinnerung, in: Der Tagesspiegel, 23–24 May 2010

26
Senatsverwaltung für Stadt-
entwicklung: Erweiterung der
Gedenkstätte Berliner Mauer,
Berlin 2007, S. 93 f.
27
Ebda., S. 99
28
Zit. n. Loy, Thomas:
Lücken der Erinnerung, in:
Der Tagesspiegel, Berlin,
23./24.5.2010

Artistically, it is the least convincing element of the whole memorial site, and it is not without reason that its original creation in 1997/98 was highly contentious. Here, if not before, one becomes aware of a misunderstanding, one that the abstract concept of marking thankfully does its best to avoid in the rest of the site. In the competition brief from July 2007, the Senate Administration of Berlin stated that a central aspect of the design task would be to "communicate the brutal character of the border facilities as a sensory experience" – a rather unfortunate choice of words. Presumably this meant that one should attempt to recreate the real, physical and emotional experience of knowing that "people trying to escape to West Berlin would be deliberately shot". The designers were faced with the problem – unfortunately, or perhaps thankfully – of showing something that no longer existed. [26] And, of course, while that cannot work, the monument and chapel, and the open-air exhibition and documentation centre are overburdened with "functional requirements". As the visitor makes their way around the site, they progress around a veritable circuit of information panels and experiences. By the end of the audio-visual tour of discovery, visitors should have "visualised, internalised and consolidated" [27] their knowledge of the site. Interested tourists who feel the need to take up this challenge could conceivably, given good physical condition and cognitive faculties, spend days taking in the "Berlin Wall History Mile". Then again, they may soon have felt exhausted by the Disney-Park-like [28] remembrance landscape of Berlin, and taken a break perhaps at the German Currywurst Museum near the Wall Exhibition at Checkpoint Charlie, or a meal at the Peking Ente Restaurant where Hitler's monumental Reich Chancellery, built by Speer, once stood. One would hope that they have not strayed so far from their original intended path of discovery to have succumbed to taking a trip around the city in noisy, colourfully-painted Trabis, as were offered in the first "days after" – or even a round-trip flight in a raisin bomber. Or that they have been dragged in front of a camera at the Pariser Platz to be photographed together with people dressed up as soldiers of the Red Army or policemen from the People's Police.

While that may sound like a more or less amusing and somewhat exaggerated story, it is actually more of an approximation of the daily satire of life in Berlin. On their long and convoluted path from the Bernauer Strasse to the Tränenpalast, the Reichstag Parliament, Brandenburg Gate, Holocaust Memorial, the Topography of Terror and the Jewish Museum, visitors have no means of orientation unless they have good background knowledge of the layout of the city and its national and global history – or a series of well-thumbed tour guides in their backpacks.

1997/98 hochumstritten. Denn spätestens an diesem Ort wird man auf ein Missverständnis aufmerksam, das zu erzeugen das abstrakte Markierungskonzept im erweiterten Bereich glücklicherweise tunlichst vermeidet.
Die Auslobung der Senatsverwaltung vom Juli 2007 hatte, wenn auch in offensichtlich widersprüchlicher Diktion, ins Zentrum ihrer Wettbewerbsaufgabe gestellt, dass die „sinnliche Erfahrung des Gewaltcharakters der Grenzanlagen" erreicht werden müsse. Was wohl heißen soll, die physisch und emotional reale Erfahrbarkeit, dass „Menschen auf der Flucht nach West-Berlin gezielt getötet wurden". Man stehe allerdings – bedauerlicher- oder glücklicherweise?, möchte man ergänzen – vor dem Problem, etwas zeigen zu wollen, was nicht mehr existiere. [26] Ach so. Und weil das eben nicht gelingen kann, werden Denkmal und Kapelle, Open-Air-Ausstellung und Doku-Zentrum plakativ mit „funktionalen Anforderungen" überfrachtet. In seinem Rundgang durchläuft der Besucher der Gedenkstätte einen komplexen Informations- und Erlebnis-Parcours. Am Ende seiner audiovisuellen Erkundungstour soll dann ein dreifaches Bildungsziel erreicht werden: „Veranschaulichung, Verinnerlichung und Vertiefung". [27]
Vielleicht ist der so ge- und überforderte Geschichtstourist, gute konditionelle und kognitive Fähigkeiten vorausgesetzt, schon Tage unterwegs, entlang der „Geschichtsmeile Mauer". Vielleicht hat er sich zwischenzeitlich auch im „Disney-Park" [28] der Erinnerungslandschaft Berlin entspannt mit einem Abstecher ins Deutsche Currywurst Museum nahe der Mauerausstellung am Checkpoint Charlie oder gestärkt mit einem Imbiss in der Peking-Ente, dort wo einst Hitler in Speers monumentaler Reichskanzlei residierte. Dass er so vom rechten Erkundungsweg abgekommen ist und sich zu einer knatternden Stadtrundfahrt mit den bunt bemalten Trabis, wie am ersten Tag „danach", hat hinreißen lassen – oder gar zu einem Rundflug mit dem Rosinenbomber, wird man nicht befürchten müssen. Noch weniger, dass er von den gierigen Fotografen auf dem Pariser Platz zusammen mit kostümierten „Rotarmisten" oder „Volkspolizisten" vor die Kamera gezerrt worden ist.
Man mag das für eine mehr oder weniger amüsante Spekulation und Übertreibung halten. Es ist eher die Annäherung an eine Berliner Realsatire. Auf seinem langen und komplizierten Weg von der Bernauer Straße über den Tränenpalast, das Reichstagsgebäude, Brandenburger Tor, das Holocaust-Mahnmal, die Topografie des Terrors und das Jüdische Museum ist er ohne Orientierung, sofern er nicht die stadträumliche, national- und weltgeschichtliche Navigation im Kopf oder in mehreren markierten Büchern im Rucksack hat. Die seinerzeit von Reinhard Rürup erfundene Freiraumausstellung „Geschichtsmeile Wilhelmstraße" fand jedenfalls eine Nachahmung nur in der „Geschichtsmeile Berliner Mauer". Nach einer entsprechenden Strecke „Erster Weltkrieg, Revolution und Weimarer

29
Riehl, W.H., cited after
Schlögel, Karl: Im Raume
lesen wir die Zeit, p.305

29
Riehl, W. H., zit. n. Schlögel,
Karl: Im Raume lesen wir die
Zeit, S. 305

The first open-air exhibition entitled "Wilhelmstrasse History Mile", devised by Reinhard Rürup, has as yet only been continued once with the "Berlin Wall History Mile". There is no trail covering the "First World War, Revolution and Weimar Republic", and no corresponding path to provide orientation on "National Socialism, the Murder of the Jews, the Second World War and Resistance". The "Berlin Wall Trail", on the other hand, has over 100 signboards with maps and provides a twin row of cobblestones for pedestrians and cyclists that inscribes the path into the city.

The way in which the Bornholmer Brücke, just 1.5 kilometres from the Mauerpark, connects conceptually as well as aesthetically in its use of materials with the Memorial on the Bernauer Strasse provides an indication of what a "GDR History Mile" could look like.

It is surprising that the dramatic escalation of the conflict of power between the party and state leadership and the people striving for freedom, which was nowhere more apparent than here at the Bornholmer Brücke, has not been celebrated with anything more than a few exhibition panels with large-format photographs. More disappointing, by contrast, is the fact that no other artistic expression could be found at this place for the surge of the masses and the final and most beautiful utterance of the GDR's inhuman bureaucratic jargon: "We're flooding now!" – in other words "we're letting the drive for freedom run its course" – than a delicate grove of cherry trees and an inconspicuous inscription on the floor citing this final distress call with which the GDR finally dropped its mask.

It is a shameful fact, however, that the authorities have not seen fit to officially recognise the dedication of this stretch of road leading up to the Bornholmer Brücke to the day of the opening of the Wall on the 9 November 1989. A road sign with the inscription "Platz des 9. November 1989" is nowhere to be found, and there is likewise no entry in the map of the city, the cartographic reference grid in the memory of every city. In this comparatively quiet stretch between the railway lines, ring road and allotment gardens, this omission goes largely unnoticed, but it remains a scandal all the same. There was, after all, an alternative: a place that would have been a better match for the symbolic and political significance of the 9 November, namely the urban space between the Reichstag, the Tiergarten and the Brandenburg Gate. It would have also been an opportunity to correct a misconception: for the city is not only "a mirror image of its social structure" [29]; its cartography and especially the correction of its entries also provide an indication of social movements, conflicts, catastrophes, successes and progress. If it makes any sense at all to commemorate particular occurrences in place and time in the organic structure of the city, then, for major events at least, these should be entered into the plan of the city where they have happened.

Republik" sucht der Tourist ebenso vergeblich wie nach einem Orientierungspfad „Nationalsozialismus, Judenmord, Weltkrieg und Widerstand". Der „Berliner Mauerweg" hat mit seinen rund 100 Übersichtstafeln und einer doppelten Pflastersteinreihe für Fuß- und Radwanderer die Wegeführung in den Stadtplan eingezeichnet.

Dass die Bornholmer Brücke, nur anderthalb Kilometer vom Mauerpark entfernt, konzeptionell und materialästhetisch an die Gedenkstätte Bernauer Straße anschließt, deutet an, wie die „Geschichtsmeile DDR" einmal innerstädtisch aussehen könnte. Dass die dramatische Zuspitzung des Machtkonfliktes zwischen Partei- und Staatsführung und dem an der Bornholmer Brücke so kraftvoll wie nirgendwo sonst zur Freiheit drängenden Volk keinen anderen Ausdruck gefunden hat als den großformatiger Foto-Ausstellungstafeln, überrascht. Enttäuschend aber, dass dort, wo für den Ansturm der Massen und die letzte und schönste Anordnung der menschenverachtenden Bürokratensprache der DDR kreiert wurde: „Wir fluten jetzt!" – was ja nichts anderes hieß als: Wir lassen dem Freiheitsdrang seinen Lauf! – keine andere künstlerische Zeichensprache zu finden war als die eines spärlichen Zierkirschenhains und einer unauffälligen Bodeneinschreibung dieses Notrufs, mit dem sich die DDR selbst demaskierte.

Als Hohn aber muss man empfinden, dass dieser Straßenabschnitt vor der Bornholmer Brücke zwar dem Mauer öffnenden Freiheitstag des 9. November 1989 gewidmet ist, aber offenbar nur informell. Ein Straßenschild mit der Aufschrift „Platz des 9. November 1989" sucht man jedenfalls ebenso vergeblich wie einen Eintrag im Stadtplan, dem kartografischen Orientierungsraster in jedem Stadtgedächtnis. Das fällt dort, in dieser heute wenig frequentierten Gegend zwischen Bahngleisen, Ringstraße und Kleingartenkolonien, nicht weiter auf, aber ein Skandal bleibt es.

Immerhin gab es eine Alternative, einen Ort, der dem symbolpolitischen Rang des 9. November sehr viel besser gerecht geworden wäre, den Platz zwischen Reichstag, Tiergarten und Brandenburger Tor. Damit hätte man zugleich einen Irrtum korrigieren können. Die Stadt ist ja nicht nur das „Spiegelbild ihres gesellschaftlichen Gefüges" [29], ihre Kartografie, vor allem die Korrekturen der Einträge, geben auch Auskunft über die sozialen Bewegungen, Konflikte, Katastrophen, Erfolge und Fortschritte. Wenn es denn erinnerungspolitisch irgendeinen Sinn ergibt, unterschiedliche Zeitorte im gewachsenen Stadtbau zu markieren, dann sollten doch, zumindest bei Großereignissen, diese dort im Stadtplan eingetragen werden, wo sie sich zugetragen haben.

The Reichstag would be the place for a permanent exhibition on 9 November, a date that was deemed contentious for a national holiday due to its multiple references (1848: Robert Blum; 1918; 1923: Beer Hall Putsch, 1938: Reichskristallnacht – "Night of Broken Glass"; 1939: Hans Georg Elser; 1989

30
Im Reichstag wäre der Ort für eine Dauerausstellung zum 9. November, der als Nationalfeiertag wegen seiner Mehrfachbezüge umstritten ist (1848: Robert Blum; 1918; 1923: Hitler-Putsch; 1938: Reichskristallnacht; 1939: Hans Georg Elser; 1989)

The revolts against the King's soldiers on the night of barricades on the 18 March 1848 did not take place in front of the Brandenburg Gate but in front of the Schloss, the City Palace. When the time came to reverse the naming of the Marx-Engels-Platz back to the Schlossplatz, another choice of name would therefore also have been conceivable. At this ugly square that symbolised the hypocritical and much-hated "People's Democracy" of the GDR, one could have recalled the beginnings of democracy during the pre-March era of the 19th century. As the "Platz des 18. März" this square would have reminded everyone of those who took part in the initially peaceful rally and later lost their lives in their struggle for civil rights.

The space in front of the western face of the Brandenburg Gate would have been at least as worthy a site for the "Platz des 9. November". Not only because Berliners from the East and West danced in front of the Brandenburg Gate on the night of the fall of the Wall, but also because on this day 71 years previously, the social-democratic Reichstag member and Secretary of State to the Kaiser, Philipp Scheidemann, announced the abdication of the Kaiser and proclaimed the first German Republic, and because shortly after soldiers of the government secured the Brandenburg Gate to defend the Republic against the contending interests of communist counter-revolutionaries.[30]

Die Revolte gegen das königliche Militär in der Barrikadennacht des 18. März 1848 nahm nicht vor dem Brandenburger Tor, sondern vor dem Schloss ihren Ausgang. Es hätte naheliegen können, bei der Rückbenennung des Marx-Engels-Platzes in Schlossplatz einen anderen Namen zu wählen. Und an diesem verkommenen Ort einer verlogenen und zuletzt verhassten „Volksdemokratie" von den vormärzlichen Anfängen der Demokratie zu erzählen. Als „Platz des 18. März" würde er heute an jene erinnern können, die an dieser zunächst gewaltlosen Volksversammlung teilnahmen und im Kampf um ihre Bürgerrechte ihr Leben ließen.

Der westliche Vorplatz des Brandenburger Tores aber hieße mit sehr viel größerer Berechtigung „Platz des 9. November". Nicht nur, weil dort Berliner aus Ost und West in der Nacht des Mauerfalls vor dem Brandenburger Tor tanzten. Sondern auch weil vom benachbarten Reichstag aus, an diesem Tag, 71 Jahre zuvor, der sozialdemokratische Reichstagsabgeordnete und kaiserliche Staatssekretär Philipp Scheidemann den Rücktritt des Kaisers verkündete, die erste deutsche Republik ausrief und wenig später Regierungssoldaten, vom Brandenburger Tor aus, die umkämpfte Republik gegen kommunistische Gegenrevolutionäre verteidigten.[30]

31
Abraham, H.: Der Friedrichshain. Die Geschichte eines
Berliner Parks von 1840 bis
zur Gegenwart, Berlin (GDR)
1988

31
Abraham, H.: Der Friedrichshain. Die Geschichte eines
Berliner Parks von 1840 bis
zur Gegenwart, Berlin (DDR)
1988

IV

It was not their heroic deed but their death that con-
ferred them immortality. They gave their lives for a hope,
a vision, they fought for freedom, equality, the rule of law
and a decent life – but had none of their own. In the eyes
of their contemporaries and of later generations, those
who fought at the barricades on the night of the 18 March
1848 were therefore martyrs – champions of democracy
who deserve to be remembered accordingly. But which
democracy do people mean when they cite the "March
Revolutionaries"? The struggle to enlist them for the
legitimation of different political orders, to appropriate
the past for contemporary ideological and political
interests, means that they have remained the object of
interpretation and cultic glamourisation to the present
day. The images and the interpretation of the events of
March 1848 by later generations stand between us and
what actually happened. We cannot bring these events
back from the past; our only access is through the
testimonies of those living at the time and of subsequent
generations. As such, the actual obstacle to accessing
the space of the Cemetery of the March Revolution is its
semantic-idealistic overdetermination: a dense weave
of words, representations, interpretations and visual-
isations that has accumulated over a period of over 150
years. Furthermore, the landscape of the Friedrichshain
underwent extraordinary changes following the war.
In order to be able to read time in space, we first need
to decode it as an abstract space of interpretation, to
uncover its essential aspects, as well as to know its
concrete spatial morphology. Finally, the site is also a
space within a space, a cemetery in a park, each of which
has its own historical pattern of use. [31]
The decision to construct an expansive park in the east
of the city fell on the occasion of the centennial of
Friedrich II's accession to the throne in May 1840, in
which the City of Berlin also laid the foundation stone
for an equestrian statue of the king by Christian Daniel
Rauch to be erected on Unter den Linden. The Friedrichshain was intended as a middle class counterpoint
to the Tiergarten in the west that had originally been
created by Berlin's aristocracy outside the city gates.
The park in Friedrichshain was designed by Gustav
Meyer, a student and close assistant of Peter Joseph
Lenné, who laid it out in the manner of Lenné's earlier
Klosterberggarten in Magdeburg (1823). Like its pre-
decessor, the park was to serve the purposes of prome-
nading and leisure for the middle classes. Towards the
end of the century, however, the increasingly bad living
conditions in the area led it to be opened to the people
as a *Volkspark* (people's park). Alongside parkland for
playing and recreation, sports facilities, an open-air
theatre, restaurants and meeting places were created
to give the workers an active space for leisure, cultural
activities and further education.

IV

Nicht schon ihre tapfere Tat – erst der Tod verlieh ihnen
Unsterblichkeit. Dass sie ihr Leben gaben für eine
Hoffnung, eine Vision, dass sie kämpften für Freiheit,
Gleichheit, Recht, ein menschenwürdiges Leben – und
ein eigenes nicht hatten, diese Interpretation der Mit-
und Nachlebenden machte die Berliner Barrikadenkämpfer in der Nacht des 18. März 1848 zu Märtyrern,
zu erinnerungswürdigen Vorkämpfern der Demokratie.
Aber welche Demokratie meinen jene vielen, die sich
auf die „Märzgefallenen" berufen? Der Streit um sie zur
Legitimation unterschiedlicher politischer Ordnungen,
die ideologie- und interessegeleitete Instrumentali-
sierung der Vergangenheit für gegenwärtige Zwecke,
macht sie bis in unsere Tage zum Objekt des Deutungs-
kampfes und der kultischen Verklärung. Die Bilder und
Bewertungen der Märzereignisse durch die Nachlebenden stehen zwischen uns und dem einstigen Geschehen. Ereignisse, die unwiederbringlich vergangen sind,
uns nur durch die Zeugnisse der Mit- und Nachlebenden zugänglich. Insofern liegt der eigentliche Raum-
widerstand auch des Friedhofs der Märzgefallenen im
semantisch-ideellen Überbau dieses Ortes. Einem in
über 150 Jahren gewachsenen Dickicht der Wörter,
Darstellungen, Deutungen und Visualisierungen.
Außerordentliche, kriegsbedingte landschaftliche
Veränderungen des Friedrichshains kommen hinzu.
Wollen wir die Zeit im Raum lesen, müssen wir ihn als
abstrakten Deutungsraum entziffern, in Grundzügen
aber natürlich auch die konkrete Raummorphologie
kennen. Zumal es sich um eine Raum-in-Raum-Gestalt
handelt, den Friedhof im Parkgelände, mit je eigenen
Nutzungsgeschichten. [31]
Zur Hundertjahrfeier der Thronbesteigung Friedrichs II.
beschloss der Berliner Magistrat im Mai 1840, einen
weiträumigen Park im Osten der Stadt anzulegen – zusammen mit der Grundsteinlegung für das Reiterstand-
bild des Königs von Christian Daniel Rauch Unter den
Linden. Der Friedrichshain war gedacht als das bürgerliche Gegenstück zum westlichen Tiergarten, den sich
das aristokratische Berlin vor der Stadt geschaffen
hatte. Gustav Meyer, ein Schüler und enger Mitarbeiter
von Peter Joseph Lenné, hat ihn nach seinem Magde-
burger Klosterberggarten (1823) konzipiert und war wie
der Tiergarten auf den Zweck des Promenierens und
der Erholung der bürgerlichen Bevölkerung zuge-
schnitten. Gegen Ende des Jahrhunderts hat sich
dieses Konzept unter dem Druck der schlechten Wohn-
verhältnisse öffnen und zum Volkspark erweitern
müssen. Neben Spiel- und Liegewiesen wurden auch
Sportanlagen, Freilichttheater, Gaststätten und Ver-
sammlungsräume bereitgestellt und insbesondere den
Arbeitern Räume aktiver Erholung, kultureller Betäti-
gung und weiterführender Bildung geboten.

The Cemetery of the March Revolution was created in March 1848 on the southwest-facing Lindenberg ("Kanonenberg") hill. On the 21 March, the city assembly agreed the erection of two monuments, the demolition of the windmills and the burial of the dead for the following day. The assembly initially decreed that all who died on the 18 March – soldiers and protestors – should be buried together in the cemetery. But the majority of the people of Berlin wanted the heroic battle of the barricades to be marked as the beginning of political change – and not played down as "an unfortunate twist of fate" or "misunderstanding". To avoid foreseeable conflicts, the "perpetrators" were then indeed separated from the "victims" and buried without ceremony or details of numbers in the Invaliden Cemetery.

From the very beginning, the 254 barricade protestors buried in Friedrichshain became the object of embittered wrangling. While the liberal middle class and social democrats glorified them as heroes, using commemorative ceremonies as a way to establish a tradition of political protest, the imperial police and military aggressively suppressed all forms of remembrance in their honour. But whatever the city or the state devised to hinder the annual commemorations – picket fences, thorny hedges, physical force or the planning of a railway station, even the secret transferral of the dead to another grave – none of this plans or measures were powerful or ingenious enough to have any effect. In 1873, celebrations commemorated two uprisings and their dead: the March Revolutions and the uprising of the Paris Commune. The "red" demonstrators had long been perceived as a new revolutionary threat, and after they started to sing revolutionary songs, the police cleared the park by force. In 1898 the city assembly wanted to finally carry out what had been obstructed for a half a century. Once again, the erection of a memorial stone for "The Fallen of the 18 March 1848" was forbidden by the state authorities – not even a wrought-iron gateway for "The last resting place of the March Revolutionaries" was permitted. Two years later, the leaders of the social-democratic movement circumvented renewed conflict with a cleverly worded gesture. In an ironic sideswipe at the authorities, they printed their wreath ribbon with the words "You yourselves have created your monument".

Dort, genauer auf dem südwestlich gelegenen Lindenberg ("Kanonenberg") entstand im März 1848 der Friedhof der Märzgefallenen. Am 21. März beschloss die Stadtverordnetenversammlung die Errichtung von zwei Denkmälern, den Abriss der beiden Windmühlen und das Begräbnis für den kommenden Tag. Beschlossen wurde zudem, alle Toten der Nacht des 18. März, also auch die Soldaten, auf dem Friedhof gemeinsam zu bestatten. Aber die Berliner wollten mehrheitlich den heldenhaften Barrikadenkampf als Beginn eines politischen Wandels gedeutet sehen – und nicht als "unglücklichen Zufall", als "Missverständnis" bagatellisieren lassen. Tatsächlich trennte man "Opfer" und "Täter", um diese, ohne nähere Angaben zur Zahl und ohne Aufhebens, auf dem innerstädtischen Invalidenfriedhof beizusetzen – und sie zugleich dem Ort absehbarer Konflikte zu entziehen.

Von Anfang an waren die 254 im Friedrichshain beigesetzten Barrikadenkämpfer das Objekt erbitterter Auseinandersetzung. Zunächst als Vorbilder der sie verklärenden Traditionspflege durch liberales Bürgertum und Sozialdemokraten einerseits und der aggressiven Unterdrückung aller ehrenden Erinnerung durch Polizei und Militär der kaiserlichen Obrigkeit andererseits. Aber was Stadt und Staat sich auch einfielen ließen, ob Bretterzaun oder Dornenhecke, physische Gewalt oder die Planung eines Bahnhofs und die heimliche Umbettung der Toten, kein Mittel war stark und raffiniert genug, das jährliche Gedenken zu unterbinden. 1873 wurde an zwei Erhebungen erinnert und ihrer Toten feierlich gedacht, an die Märzrevolte und den Aufstand der Pariser Commune. Längst galten die "roten" Demonstranten als neue revolutionäre Gefahr. Als sie Revolutionslieder sangen, räumte die Polizei den Hain gewaltsam. 1898 wollten die Stadtverordneten endlich nachholen, was ein halbes Jahrhundert lang beständig verhindert worden war. Abermals wurde ihnen ein Gedenkstein für die "Gefallenen des 18. März 1848" untersagt. Nicht einmal ein schmiedeeisernes Eingangsportal für die "Ruhestätte der Märzgefallenen" fand die Zustimmung der staatlichen Behörden. Zwei Jahre später wich die Sozialdemokratie einem neuerlichen Konflikt durch eine überlegene verbale Geste aus. Ihre Kranzschleifen bedruckte sie mit einem ironischen Seitenhieb und der Widmung für die Märzkämpfer: "Euer Denkmal habt ihr Euch selbst gesetzt."

32
Valentin, V.: Geschichte der deutschen Revolution von 1848–1849, Weinheim 1998 (1931); Vossler, O.: Die Revolution von 1848 in Deutschland, Frankfurt a. M. 1967; Hachtmann, R.: Berlin 1848, Bonn 1997
33
Koselleck, R.: Revolution, in: Brunner, O./Conze, W./Koselleck, R. (Ed.): Geschichtliche Grundbegriffe, Stuttgart 1984, Vol. 5, p. 653ff.

32
Valentin, V.: Geschichte der deutschen Revolution von 1848–1849, Weinheim 1998 (1931); Vossler, O.: Die Revolution von 1848 in Deutschland, Frankfurt a.M. 1967; Hachtmann, R.: Berlin 1848, Bonn 1997
33
Koselleck, R.: Revolution, in: Brunner, O./Conze, W./Koselleck, R. (Hg.): Geschichtliche Grundbegriffe, Stuttgart 1984, Bd. 5, S. 653ff

During the Second World War, the park underwent many changes. Two flak bunkers gave the site a bizarre appearance. A few years later, they disappeared into huge heaps of rubble, which over time gradually transformed into greened over bunker-hills, giving the Berliners something they don't normally have: toboggan runs and ski slopes. Only later did the first memorial treatment of the park take place – put in place by people with quite other intentions and interests. In addition to a large memorial stone commemorating simply "The Dead of 1848 and 1918", in the process amalgamating two events into one, a series of sculptural memorial elements were erected. They include memorials to the Spanish Civil War, the German members of the International Brigade, the comradeship-in-arms between Polish soldiers and German anti-fascists during the Second World War, and the "Red Sailor" statue by Hans Kies (1960) that refers to the sailors' revolt in the early days of November 1918, generally regarded as the beginning of the November revolution. The events of March 1848 are treated here merely as a prologue to the anti-fascist battles of the communists in the 20th century. The place has therefore long been in need of an intervention providing correction and commentary.

The ongoing critique of textual sources, language and ideology has, in the meantime, made inroads into the thicket of interpretations and reinterpretations which could help to overcome the habitual use of language and narrow-sightedness. The changes following the spectacularly visible fall of the Wall were much easier to put into effect than the breaking through of imaginary barriers between the ideologies of divergent worlds. Even in the new "maerz_baustelle" – an exhibition in a building site container installed on the site of the cemetery in May 2011 that aims, through interactive communication with the visitor, to explore the future design of the place of remembrance – reference is still made throughout to "revolution" without any qualifying explanation. This terminology, as used to describe the happenings of March 1848, has a typifying effect and has, in non-communist historical research at least, long been called into question.[32] Similarly, 1848/49 and 1918/19, two major events in Germany's history of democracy, are labelled with the same illustrious-sounding but polarising and emotive term: "revolution". This wilfully ignores the danger that words that are used differently in different political and cultural contexts cannot adequately describe what is meant without additional qualification.[33] Uprising, rebellion, revolution, revolt, counter-revolution (left-wing or right-wing), and civil war: all highly abstract terms that we believe adequately represent complex circumstances, all the while forgetting to question what actually happened. However engaging the concept of making the message of the place ("A foundation stone of democracy") into a medium of communication between the organisers (Paul Singer e.V. Berlin) and the public, if its intentions are vague and ambiguous from the outset, perhaps even misleading, the results are likely to be viewed with scepticism.

Erhebliche Veränderungen erfuhr das Parkgelände während des Zweiten Weltkrieges. Zunächst gaben ihm zwei Flakbunker ein bizarres Aussehen. Wenige Jahre später verschwanden sie unter gewaltigen Trümmerschutthalden, die sich nach und nach in begrünte Bunkerberge verwandelten und den Berlinern bescherten, was sie sonst nicht haben: Rodelbahn und Skipiste. Nun erst fand auch die denkmalkünstlerische Überbauung des Friedhofs ihren Abschluss – durch Akteure ganz anderer Intentionen und Interessen. Mit einem großen Gedenkstein, der umstandslos die „Toten von 1848 und 1918" gleichsetzt, und einer Reihe von skulpturalen Erinnerungszeichen. Sie verweisen auf den Spanischen Bürgerkrieg, die deutschen „Interbrigadisten", auf die deutsch-polnische Kampfgemeinschaft im Zweiten Weltkrieg, und mit dem „Roten Matrosen" von Hans Kies (1960) auch auf die Matrosenrevolte in den frühen Novembertagen 1918, im allgemeinen Sprachgebrauch der Beginn der Novemberrevolution. Die Märzereignisse des Jahres 1848 werden dort zur bloßen Vorgeschichte des antifaschistischen Kampfes der Kommunisten des 20. Jahrhunderts. Der Ort macht eine korrigierende und kommentierende Intervention längst unabweisbar.

Quellen-, Sprach- und Ideologiekritik haben in das Dickicht der Deutungen und Umdeutungen längst Öffnungen geschnitten, die überkommene Sprachgewohnheiten und Blickverengungen überwinden könnten. Der so spektakulär sichtbare Mauerfall war sehr viel leichter zu vollziehen als die Durchbrechung der imaginären Barriere zwischen weltanschaulich divergenten Welten. Noch in der seit Mai 2011 eingerichteten maerz_baustelle – sie soll in interaktiver Kommunikation mit den Besuchern der Container-Ausstellung die zukünftige Gestaltung der Erinnerungsstätte finden – ist durchgängig und unkommentiert von „Revolution" die Rede. Wird also eine das Märzgeschehen 1848 typisierend kennzeichnende Begrifflichkeit benutzt, die zumindest die nichtkommunistische Forschung seit langem in Frage stellt.[32] Wird über beide Großereignisse unserer Demokratiegeschichte, 1848/49 und 1918/19, gleichermaßen die vieldeutig schillernde und polarisierende Pathosformel „Revolution" gestülpt. Als bestünde nicht die Gefahr, dass der in unterschiedlichen politisch-kulturellen Kontexten verschieden gebrauchte Begriff die gemeinte Sache ohne Kommentierung gar nicht angemessen kennzeichnen kann.[33] Aufruhr, Rebellion, Revolution, Revolte, Gegenrevolution – von links, von rechts, Bürgerkrieg? Wir glauben, komplexe Sachverhalte mit hochabstrakten Begriffen angemessen beschreiben zu können, und vergessen, Fragen nach dem konkreten Geschehen zu stellen. Und so sympathisch ein Verfahren ist, das die Botschaft des Ortes („Grundstein der Demokratie") zum Medium zwischen Auslober bzw. Bauherr (Paul Singer e.V. Berlin) und Publikum macht: Wenn die Vorgaben ungenau und vieldeutig sind, also irreführend, wird man das Ergebnis von vornherein skeptisch beurteilen.

34
Roth, C.: Das trennende Erbe.
Die Revolution von 1848 im
deutsch-deutschen Erinne-
rungsstreit 100 Jahre danach,
in: Winkler, H. A. (Ed.): Griff
nach der Deutungsmacht.
Zur Geschichte der Ge-
schichtspolitik in Deutschland, Göttingen 2004,
p. 209 ff.
35
Cited in Hettling, M.: Totenkult statt Revolution. 1848
und seine Opfer, Frank-
furt a. M. 1998, p. 21 and 44 ff.

34
Roth, C.: Das trennende Erbe.
Die Revolution von 1848 im
deutsch-deutschen Erinne-
rungsstreit 100 Jahre danach,
in: Winkler, H. A. (Hg.): Griff
nach der Deutungsmacht.
Zur Geschichte der Ge-
schichtspolitik in Deutschland, Göttingen 2004,
S. 209 ff.
35
Zit. n. Hettling, M.: Totenkult
statt Revolution. 1848 und
seine Opfer, Frankfurt a. M.
1998, S. 21 und 44 ff.

Today, all that we can be sure of is that the night of the barricades on the 18 March 1848 in Berlin was a social protest, a forceful uprising against the Prussian military. For weeks, the presence of soldiers in the streets and their use of force had been a continual provocation for the people peacefully demonstrating for the March rights (most notably freedom of speech and of the press, freedom of assembly and association, the arming of the people, and the earliest possible convention of the national assembly). This tension flared up as the infamous shots were fired – who fired them and whether by accident or on orders no one knows – and the first dead lay on the Schlossplatz amid the throngs of people who were waiting expectantly and loyally, after the king's concessions of the days before, for their monarch to appear. The mood swung to panic and anger and the latent conflict escalated. The battle of the barricades erected around the City Palace continued all night, the bloodbath only ending as the king withdrew his artillery in the early hours of the morning. Nearly 200 people lost their lives. But as the notoriously indecisive king turned to making verbal and symbolic pseudo-concessions, he was once again – temporarily – more popular than ever. The greater majority of the people did not want his throne, or his head, likewise no bloodshed, no *terreur* – all it wanted was rights and the chance to contribute: a *constitution*.

The Marxist concept of revolution aims to overthrow the structures of power and property ownership, thereby blurring the above differentiation. While the GDR laid claim to the 18 March as being representative of its supposedly democratic-revolutionary past history,[34] the Federal Republic did not assertively ground its democratic tradition on the entire pre-March develop-ments but instead on the Frankfurt Parliament in St. Paul's Church and its pioneering constitution. As a result of these divergent politics of history, the 18 March has come to be labelled as a revolutionary day that it never was, and – unlike the 14 July in France – never could be, and at the time was never intended to be by the majority of the citizens.

Commentators at the time called the boycott by the middle classes of Gustav Julius' left-liberal democratic newspaper *Zeitungshalle* a "parody of the Tennis Court Oath", an ironic reference to the happenings in France.[35] After the 18 March, it could be heard in many of the spontaneous gatherings in the city that "what happened in Berlin was no revolution, just an unfortu-nate twist of fate". The National Assembly skirted using the term at all costs. The bloody protest against the military might of the monarchy was merely "an incident". For the students of Berlin and the Democratic Club in particular, it seemed therefore all the more important to lend this the shine of a revolutionary event. From the very beginning, however, the left-wing tradition of com-memorating this day with the dead, the funeral proces-sion, the burial place and the memorial ceremony for the night of the barricades that had started that very same year, was divided. "Have we had a revolution" or just a

Unstrittig ist heute nur, dass die Berliner Barrikaden-nacht des 18. März ein sozialer Protest war, eine gewalt-same Erhebung gegen das Preußische Militär. Seit Wochen war seine innerstädtische Präsenz und Gewalt eine fortwährende Provokation für die friedlichen De-monstrationen der Bevölkerung für ihre Märzforderun-gen (das waren insbesondere Presse- und Meinungs-freiheit, Versammlungs- und Vereinigungsfreiheit, Volksbewaffnung, vorgezogene Einberufung des Land-tages). Dieses Spannungsverhältnis eskalierte, als die berühmt-berüchtigten Schüsse fielen – versehentlich oder befohlen, und von wem? Und Tote auf dem Schlossplatz lagen, in einer Menge, die durch Zuge-ständnisse der königlichen Regierung vom Vormittag erwartungsvoll erregt und unbedingt loyal auf das Erscheinen ihres Monarchen wartete. Nun schlug die Stimmung in Panik und Wut um, der latente Konflikt eskalierte. Die ganze Nacht tobten Barrikadenkämpfe um das Schloss. Erst als der König am frühen Morgen seine Artillerie zurückzog, endete das Blutbad, in dem fast 200 Menschen ihr Leben verloren hatten. Friedrich Wilhelm IV. wankte in seiner Machtstellung. Aber als der notorisch entscheidungsschwache König in verba-le und symbolische Schein-Zugeständnisse flüchtete, war er – vorübergehend – beliebter denn je. Das Volk wollte mit übergroßer Mehrheit nicht seinen Thron, schon gar nicht seinen Kopf, es wollte kein Blut, keine *terreur*, es wollte Rechte und Mitbestimmung – eine *Constitution*.

Der auf die Umwälzung der gesellschaftlichen Macht-und Eigentumsverhältnisse zielende marxistische Revolutionsbegriff verwischt diese Differenz. Und dass die DDR den 18. März geschichtspolitisch für ihre an-geblich demokratisch-revolutionäre Vorgeschichte vereinnahmte,[34] die Bundesrepublik ihr demokrati-sches Traditionsverständnis aber nicht offensiv auf den ganzen Vormärz gründete, sondern vor allem auf das Paulskirchenparlament und dessen wegweisende Verfassung, hat den 18. März zu einem Revolutionstag gestempelt, der er nicht war, der er – anders als der 14. Juli – nicht werden konnte und von der bürgerlichen Mehrheit aus gesehen auch nicht werden sollte.

Schon Beobachter des Geschehens nannten den bürgerlichen Boykott gegen die linksliberale demokra-tische *Zeitungshalle* von Gustav Julius mit einem ironi-schen Seitenblick auf die französischen Verhältnisse eine „Parodie des Ballhausschwurs".[35] Nicht wenige erklärten auf den vielen spontanen Versammlungen in der Stadt nach dem 18. März, „Berlin habe keine Revo-lution gemacht, sondern ein unglücklicher Zufall habe stattgefunden". Und die Nationalversammlung mied den Begriff wie der Teufel das Weihwasser. Den bluti-gen Protest gegen die monarchische Gewalt tat sie als bloße „Begebenheit" ab.

Umso wichtiger erschien es insbesondere den Berliner Studenten, dem Demokratischen Klub und – ihnen nachfolgend – der von Anfang an gespaltenen linken Traditionspflege dieses Tages mit den Toten, dem Trauerzug, dem Begräbnisort und den noch im selben Jahr beginnenden Gedenkfeiern die Barrikadennacht im Glanz eines revolutionären Ereignisses zu über-

36
Müller, H.: Die November-
Revolution. Erinnerungen,
Berlin 1928, p. 7 f.
37
Hofmann, J.: Berlin-Fried-
richsfelde. Ein deutscher
Nationalfriedhof, Berlin 2001,
p. 22 ff.

36
Müller, H.: Die November-
Revolution. Erinnerungen,
Berlin 1928, S. 7 f.
37
Hofmann, J.: Berlin-Fried-
richsfelde. Ein deutscher
Nationalfriedhof, Berlin 2001,
S. 22 ff.

"revolt" could be read in one flyer. And a poem published for the memorial celebration at the beginning of June asked:
"Hardly is Spring upon us, do you deny
the great deed, the revolution?"
The idea proposed in the documentation in the maerz_baustelle container that the funeral procession to the cemetery in Friedrichshain be made the decisive event of the uprising is consequently understandable, but more than questionable.

That applies to an even greater degree to the unconditional equating of the dead from the night of the barricades in 1848 with the dead from the so-called November Revolution in 1918. If one takes a closer look at the constitutional situation and political distribution of power in this confusing transitional period between the monarchy and the republic, one can see that some of those in responsible positions at the time had already recognised that "a revolution is no longer necessary".[36] The sailors' revolt and the ensuing uprisings of the workers' and soldiers' councils were nothing other than a violent communist revolt against the parliamentary democracy in Germany that had existed constitutionally since the 28 October 1918 and politically since the abdication of the Kaiser and the proclamation of Friedrich Ebert to the position of Reich Chancellor on the 9 November 1918. This fact, so crucial to the founding of the Federal Republic, is still not anchored in the general historical consciousness of the people of Germany to the present day!

In a document published by the Berlin Foundation for Historic Churchyards and Cemeteries, for example, it states: "In 1918, 33 victims of the revolutionary clashes in Berlin in November and December were buried." No further explanation is given. Likewise, there is no mention of the fact that, or why, the Berlin City Council and the Council of People's Deputies refused to allow the dead of the anti-revolutionary, left-wing socialist Spartacist Uprising to be buried in Friedrichshain, declaring that the more than 150 bodies be buried in a collective grave in a corner of the comparatively new Friedrichsfelde Central Cemetery (the so-called "criminals' corner"), which had been founded in the 1890s. In 1900 a prominent social democrat, Wilhelm Liebknecht, had been buried there.[36] Later Ignaz Auer, Paul Singer and other prominent social democrats were also buried in what became popularly known as the "Cemetery of the Socialists". Since the early 1920s, the memorial to the KPD (Communist Party of Germany) has grown around the misleadingly named "Revolution Monument", designed in brick by Ludwig Mies van der Rohe, and includes grave slabs for Rosa Luxemburg, Karl Liebknecht, Wilhelm Pieck, Ernst Thälmann and others. That Hermann Müller, the last social-democratic (SPD) Reich Chancellor of Germany, and Rudolf Breitscheid, who switched back from the Independent Social Democratic Party (USPD) to join the leadership committee of the Social Democratic Party (SPD), are both also buried in Friedrichsfelde alongside precisely those communist leaders who had previously defamed them as "social fascists" is a scandalous misrepresentation in the public portrayal of German history. An impression that is reinforced year after year when the supporters and members of the successor to the GDR's SED party march every 15 January to their place of pilgrimage.

höhen. „Haben wir eine Revolution gehabt" oder nur eine „Revolte", hieß es in einem Flugblatt. Und in einem Gedicht zur Gedenkfeier Anfang Juni
„Kaum Frühling ist's und Ihr verleugnet schon
Die große Tat, die Revolution?"
Der Vorschlag der Container-Dokumentation in der maerz_baustelle, den Trauerzug zum Friedhof Friedrichshain zum entscheidenden Ereignis der Erhebung zu machen, erscheint insoweit verständlich, aber mehr als bedenklich.

Das gilt in noch größerem Maße für die umstandslose Gleichsetzung der Toten der Barrikadennacht 1848 mit den Toten der sogenannten Novemberrevolution 1918. Sieht man sich die staatsrechtlichen und machtpolitischen Verhältnisse in dieser unübersichtlichen Übergangszeit zwischen Monarchie und Republik genauer an, wird erkennbar, was verantwortlich beteiligte Personen schon früh erkannten, dass „eine Revolution nicht mehr nötig gewesen sei."[36] Die Matrosenrebellion und nachfolgenden Kämpfe der Arbeiter- und Soldatenräte waren nichts anderes als eine gewaltsame kommunistische Revolte gegen die parlamentarische Demokratie in Deutschland, die seit dem 28. 10. 1918 verfassungsrechtlich bestand und mit der Abdankung des Kaisers und der Ernennung Friedrich Eberts zum Reichskanzler seit dem 9. 11. 1918 auch verfassungspolitisch. Im allgemeinen historischen Bewusstsein ist dieses für unsere Republikgeschichte zentrale gründungspolitische Faktum bis heute nicht verankert!
So heißt es im Papier der Berliner Stiftung Historische Kirch- und Friedhöfe – ohne jede weitere Kommentierung: „Im Jahre 1918 erfolgte die Zubettung von 33 Opfern der revolutionären Auseinandersetzungen in Berlin im November und Dezember." Und auch ohne jeden Hinweis, dass und warum der Berliner Magistrat und der Rat der Volksbeauftragten die Beisetzung der Toten des gegenrevolutionären, linkssozialistischen Spartakusaufstandes im Friedrichshain untersagte und für die mehr als 150 Toten am Rande des erst in den 1890er Jahren eingerichteten Friedhofs Friedrichsfelde ein Sammelgrab („Verbrecherecke") anordnete. 1900 war dort erstmals ein prominenter Sozialdemokrat beerdigt worden, Wilhelm Liebknecht.[37] Später kamen Ignaz Auer, Paul Singer und andere prominente Sozialdemokraten hinzu. Im Volksmund hieß der Ort bald „Sozialistenfriedhof". Seit den frühen 1920er Jahren entstand um das – irreführend – „Revolutionsdenkmal" genannte Klinkermonument von Ludwig Mies van der Rohe die Gedenkstätte der KPD mit den Grabplatten für Rosa Luxemburg, Karl Liebknecht, Wilhelm Pieck, Ernst Thälmann und anderen. Dass in Friedrichsfelde auch der letzte SPD-Reichskanzler Hermann Müller und der über die USPD in die SPD-Führung zurückgekehrte Rudolf Breitscheid neben jenen Kommunistenführern liegen, die ihre vormaligen Genossen als „Sozialfaschisten" diffamierten, bleibt ein Skandal der öffentlichen Geschichtsvermittlung in unserem Land. Der Jahr für Jahr in die Medien rückt, wenn an jedem 15. Januar die Anhänger und Mitglieder der SED-Nachfolgerin zu ihrem Wallfahrtsort marschieren.

38
Müller, H.: Die November-
Revolution, p. 255

38
Müller, H.: Die November-
Revolution, S. 255

It is high time to resolve this confusing and difficult-to-grasp situation in the historical tradition and commemoration rituals of socialist and social-democratic circles and parties. Friedrichshain should be reserved exclusively for remembering those who died on 18 March 1848, and in Friedrichsfelde the arrangement of the graves and memorial plaques should be re-organised to differentiate between the supporters and opponents of the Weimar Republic, some of whom died naturally and some of whom were killed. The objective must be to avoid mixing the supporters of parliamentary democracy together with the opponents without any means of differentiation. At present, those who called "Down with Scheidemann! Down with Ebert! Long live the World Revolution!" are commemorated in the same breath as those who marched against them calling "Down with Liebknecht! Down with Spartacus! Long live Democracy!", blocking their attempts to occupy the government quarter.[38] Later generations need to be able to learn about the protracted and mostly bloody history of conflict between revolutionary and counter-revolutionary movements of left-wing or right-wing origin, that was formative for Germany's present-day system of democracy.

To properly honour and appreciate the different freedom and democracy movements in Germany since the pre-March period, not only do we need several places of remembrance, but we must also make their inner spatial and temporal relationships legible. An exemplary case in this respect is the "Democracy Trail" that has been developed in what was known as the "Third Germany", the actual cradle of modern multi-party parliamentary democracy. In Berlin, the places of democracy still need to be linked together to form a landscape of remembrance of the democratisation of Prussian Germany. The memorials at the Cemetery of the March Revolution and the Cemetery of the Socialists in Friedrichsfelde have the makings of a beginning. This is where the maerz_baustelle can perhaps play a role in this discourse.

The past is for us inaccessible, a place we cannot reach. What we can achieve, however, is accurate differentiation, a more precise use of terminology and honest intellectual discourse in our ongoing endeavours to communicate the past. That we continue to strive for this is vital, as is the need to cultivate a public culture of remembrance, one that makes Germany visible as a nation that has grown over a century of wars, revolution, violent crimes and division, that has matured into a republic and to a nation state that stands – to paraphrase Brecht – not above, and not below its neighbours.

Es ist hoch an der Zeit, dieses schwer durchschaubare Durcheinander in der sozialistischen und sozialdemokratischen Traditionspflege und Totenehrung aufzuheben, den Friedrichshain ausschließlich den Toten des 18. März 1848 vorzubehalten. Und in Friedrichsfelde die Anordnung der Gräber bzw. Gedenktafeln für die gewaltsam und eines natürlichen Todes gestorbenen Anhänger und Gegner der Weimarer Republik so zu reorganisieren, dass nicht die Verfechter und Verächter der parlamentarischen Demokratie bis zur völligen Unkenntlichkeit des historischen Geschehens vermischt werden. Und jene, die auf Berlins Straßen im Januar schrien: „Nieder mit Scheidemann! Nieder mit Ebert! Hoch die Weltrevolution!", im gleichen Atemzug mit jenen geehrt werden, die ihnen entgegenmarschierten und mit dem Ruf: „Nieder mit Liebknecht! Nieder mit Spartakus! Hoch die Demokratie!" die Besetzung des Regierungsviertels verwehrten.[38] Und wir, die Nachlebenden lernen könnten, aus welcher zumeist blutigen und langen Konfliktgeschichte revolutionärer und gegenrevolutionärer Bewegungen links- und rechtsextremistischer Provenienz die deutsche Demokratie der Gegenwart hervorgegangen ist.

Für eine Würdigung der verschiedenen Freiheits- und Demokratiebewegungen seit dem Vormärz sind nicht nur viele Erinnerungsorte erforderlich – auch ihr innerer, räumlicher wie zeitlicher Zusammenhang ist sichtbar zu machen. Vorbildlich scheint dies im „Dritten Deutschland" gelungen, der eigentlichen Wiege der modernen parlamentarischen Parteiendemokratie, mit der „Straße der Demokratie". In Berlin steht diese stadträumliche Verknüpfung der Orte der Demokratie zu einer Erinnerungslandschaft der Demokratisierung Preußen-Deutschlands noch aus. Mit den Gedenkstätten des Friedhofs der Märzgefallenen und des Sozialistenfriedhofs Friedrichsfelde könnte der Anfang gemacht werden. Vielleicht lässt sich die maerz_baustelle im Sinne eines solchen Diskurses verstehen. Die Vergangenheit ist für uns ein unerreichbarer Ort. Differenzierende Genauigkeit, begriffliche Präzision und intellektuelle Redlichkeit im fortdauernden Versuch ihrer Darstellung, sind es nicht. Das kompromisslose Bemühen darum ist so unverzichtbar wie der Kampf um eine öffentliche Erinnerungskultur, die Deutschland als eine Nation sichtbar macht, die in einem Jahrhundert der Kriege, Revolutionen, Gewaltverbrechen und Teilung politisch erwachsen wurde, zur Republik gereift ist und zu einem Staat, der – mit Brecht – nicht über und nicht unter seinen Nachbarn stehen will.

Grounds of the Bergen-Belsen Memorial,
Lohheide, 2003–2012

Außengelände der Gedenkstätte Bergen-Belsen,
Lohheide, 2003–2012

**Bergen-Belsen
– The Art of Drawing
Distinctions**

Bergen-Belsen
– Die Kunst der
Unterscheidbarkeit

The perimeter fence and main entrance are the key symbols of a concentration camp. The entrance marks the transition from a world of normality, of everyday life, to a realm of barbarism. This is at least how it is commonly portrayed in the historiography of a tyrannical regime. The horrors began behind the fence and gate.

But the camps in National Socialism were also everyday places, not just for those interned within them but also for those living nearby, a realisation that only becomes clear when one marks these boundaries rather than mythologising them. sinai landscape architects have taken this approach in their design for the grounds of the Bergen-Belsen Concentration Camp Memorial. Approximately 60 kilometres northeast of Hanover in the area known as the Lüneburg Heath lies the site of the former prisoner-of-war and concentration camp at Bergen-Belsen. In 1936, as Nazi Germany was intensifying its military preparations, a camp of huts was set up to house 300 Polish and German prisoners who were made to construct barracks for the military base at Belsen. After the invasion of France in 1940, 600 French and Belgian prisoners were forced to work in the camp, and in 1941 the Wehrmacht cleared a larger enclosure surrounded with barbed wire fences and watchtowers to extend the camp: it became one of many prisoner-of-war camps known as *Stammlager*, or *Stalag* for short. In preparation for the invasion of the Soviet Union, the Wehrmacht established three such camps in the Lüneburg Heath alone, in the military training areas in Bergen and Munster.

Zaun und Tor gelten als Schlüsselsymbole eines Konzentrationslagers. Markierte das Tor doch den Übergang vom Reich der Normalität, des Alltags, in einen Bereich der Barbarei. So zumindest legt es die Geschichtsschreibung, die Vermittlung der Geschichte eines Unrechtsregimes nahe. Hinter Tor und Zaun begann das Grauen.

Wie sehr jedoch die Lager im Nationalsozialismus auch Orte des Alltags waren, für Internierte wie für die Nachbarn, wird erst deutlich, wenn man die Grenzen kennzeichnet, statt sie zum Mythos zu erheben. sinai Landschaftsarchitekten bauen darauf ihren Entwurf für die Gedenkstätte Bergen-Belsen auf.

Etwa 60 Kilometer nordöstlich von Hannover liegt in der Lüneburger Heide das Gelände des ehemaligen Kriegsgefangenen- und Konzentrationslagers Bergen-Belsen. Während der Aufrüstung des nationalsozialistischen Deutschlands entstand dort 1936 ein Barackenlager für 300 gefangene polnische und deutsche Arbeiter, die für das Truppenlager Belsen Kasernen bauen mussten. Nach dem Frankreichfeldzug 1940 wurden an diesem Ort 600 inhaftierte Franzosen und Belgier zur Arbeit gezwungen, und ab 1941 wurde durch die Wehrmacht eine große Erweiterungsfläche mit Stacheldraht und Wachtürmen umzäunt: eines von vielen Kriegsgefangenen-Mannschafts-Stammlagern, Stalag genannt. Von denen wurden in Vorbereitung auf den Überfall auf die Sowjetunion allein drei auf den Truppenübungsplätzen Bergen und Munster in der Lüneburger Heide angelegt.

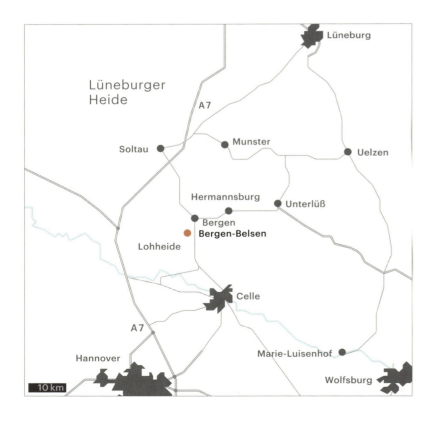

The order and chaos of extermination

The first prisoners of war from the Soviet Union arrived at the camp in July 1941 and by November more than 20,000 captives were interned in the camp. Only then were the first improvised huts built, while most of the prisoners vegetated in burrows or the most simple form of tents. Lacking sufficient food, over 18,000 Soviet prisoners of war had died of starvation and disease in Bergen-Belsen by spring 1942. A typhus epidemic led to the area being sealed off and the establishment of a quarantine zone for the entire military area.

The Wehrmacht's prisoner-of-war camp, in which survival was barely possible, ceased operation in 1943 although a hospital for soviet prisoners of war remained until 1944, in which a further 11,000 soldiers died. The site was handed over to the SS, who turned it into a camp for Jews and had a crematorium constructed among other facilities. The first Jews to be interned in Bergen-Belsen were transported from Poland in 1943.

In addition to Italian military internees and members of the Warsaw Uprising, Jews from a variety of countries were held in the so-called *Aufenthaltslager* ("holding camp"), which came to be known as the concentration camp at Bergen-Belsen. The Jews in the "holding camp" were kept for "possible exchange purposes" and were held in separate, isolated subsections of the camp: in the "star camp", the "neutrals camp", the "Hungarian camp", the "special camp" and the "prisoners camp". The number of internees rose from approximately 6,400 to over 15,000 between July and December 1944. One thousand inmates suffering from tuberculosis were

Ordnung und Chaos der Vernichtung

Erste Kriegsgefangene aus der Sowjetunion trafen im Juli 1941 ein, bis zum November waren bereits über 20.000 Gefangene interniert. Erst zu dieser Zeit begann man mit dem Bau von provisorischen Unterkünften, während die meisten Gefangenen in Erdhöhlen oder einfachsten Zelten vegetierten. Ohne ausreichende Ernährung starben bis zum Frühjahr 1942 in Bergen-Belsen über 18.000 sowjetische Kriegsgefangene an Hunger und Seuchen. Wegen einer Fleckfieber-Epidemie wurde das Lager weiträumig gesperrt und eine Quarantäne für den gesamten Truppenübungsplatz verhängt.

Das Kriegsgefangenenlager der Wehrmacht, in dem ein Überleben kaum möglich war, wurde 1943 aufgelöst, ein Lazarett für sowjetische Kriegsgefangene, in dem wohl weitere 11.000 Soldaten starben, blieb bis 1944 bestehen. Die SS hatte derweil die Flächen übernommen und dort ein Lager für Juden vorbereitet, wofür unter anderem ein Krematorium errichtet wurde. Ab 1943 wurden erste Juden aus Polen nach Bergen-Belsen transportiert.

Neben italienischen Militärinternierten und polnischen Teilnehmern am Warschauer Aufstand wurden Juden aus unterschiedlichen Staaten in das „Aufenthaltslager" genannte KZ Bergen-Belsen gebracht. Sie sollten für „eventuelle Austauschzwecke" zur Verfügung stehen und waren in unterschiedlichen, voneinander isolierten Lagerbereichen, so im „Sternlager", im „Neutralenlager", im „Ungarnlager", im „Sonderlager" oder im „Häftlingslager" untergebracht. Die Zahl der Lagerbewohner stieg vom Juli bis zum Dezember 1944 von etwa 6.400 auf über 15.000. Allein aus dem KZ Mittelbau-Dora bei Nordhausen wurden etwa 1.000 an Tuberkulose Erkrankte gemeinsam mit nicht mehr zur Zwangsarbeit fähigen Häftlingen anderer Lager in Bergen-Belsen interniert. In einem von der SS als

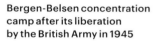

Bergen-Belsen concentration camp after its liberation by the British Army in 1945

Konzentrationslager Bergen Belsen nach der Befreiung durch die Britische Armee 1945

1
Puvogel, Ulrike and Stankowski, Martin: Gedenkstätten für die Opfer des Nationalsozialismus, Eine Dokumentation, published by the bpb Federal Agency for Civic Education, Bonn 1995, p. 383
2
Ibid., p. 380

1
Puvogel, Ulrike und Stankowski, Martin: Gedenkstätten für die Opfer des Nationalsozialismus, Eine Dokumentation, hrsg. von der Bundeszentrale für Politische Bildung, Bonn 1995, S. 383
2
Ebda., S. 384

transferred from the concentration camp at Mittelbau-Dora near Nordhausen together with inmates from other camps that were too sick to work. In a section of the camp designated by the SS as an *Erholungslager* ("recovery camp"), only some 50 of the inmates from the "Dora Transport" were still alive when the concentration camp was liberated in April 1945.

Beginning in August 1944 with the advance of the Red Army, many Polish and Hungarian Jewish women held in camps and ghettos in the east were transported to Bergen-Belsen and from there "on to numerous sub-camps of the concentration camps in Neuengamme, Buchenwald and Flossenbürg, who from Summer 1944 were put to work in several large factories."[1] One of the 8,000 women transported in October and November 1944 from the concentration camp at Auschwitz-Birkenau to Bergen-Belsen was the 15-year-old Anne Frank, whose diary of her time in hiding in Amsterdam was published after the war. Anne Frank died in Bergen-Belsen in the final months of the war as the situation grew ever more chaotic. "Since the end of 1944, tens of thousands of inmates held by the SS in concentration camps near the front were 'evacuated' towards the interior of the Reich", including 7,000 from Sachsenhausen and nearly 30,000 from Dora-Mittelbau. "Many of them were transported to Bergen-Belsen. Those who survived the death marches on foot or were not shot beforehand found themselves interned in a hastily extended but nevertheless catastrophically overcrowded camp. Between the beginning of January and mid-April 1945, in what became known as the 'Inferno of Bergen-Belsen', some 35,000 people died as a result of the dramatic medical conditions, epidemics and starvation. [...] The name Bergen-Belsen became synonymous with the horrors of the National Socialist system of concentration camps and with the terror and German crimes of the Nazi period."[2]

What makes the horrors of Bergen-Belsen so incomprehensible to this very day is the chilling degree of organisation and bureaucracy applied to dealing with the inmates, which had its own logic and logistical infrastructure and became ever harder to maintain in the final months of the war. The consequence was that people died even more quickly than they would have at the hands of the Nazi apparatus of destruction.

"The conditions in the camp were really indescribable; no description nor photograph could really bring home the horrors that were there outside the huts, and the frightful scenes inside were much worse," recounted the British medical officer Glyn Hughes at the Bergen-Belsen trial in late 1945. "There were various sizes of piles of corpses lying all over the camp, some in between the huts. The compounds themselves had bodies lying about in them. The gutters were full and within the huts there were uncountable numbers of bodies, some even in the same bunks as the living. Near the crematorium were signs of filled-in mass graves, and outside to the

„Erholungslager" bezeichneten Teil des Konzentrationslagers waren bei der Befreiung des KZ im April 1945 nur noch etwa 50 Häftlinge des „Dora-Transportes" am Leben.

Mit dem Vormarsch der Roten Armee wurden seit August 1944 viele polnische und ungarische Jüdinnen aus den weiter östlich gelegenen Arbeitslagern und Ghettos nach Bergen-Belsen und von dort aus „weiter zu zahlreichen Außenkommandos der Konzentrationslager Neuengamme, Buchenwald und Flossenbürg, die ab Sommer 1944 in vielen großen Fabrikbetrieben eingerichtet wurden",[1] transportiert. Unter den 8.000 Frauen, die im Oktober und November 1944 aus dem Konzentrationslager Auschwitz-Birkenau in Bergen-Belsen eintrafen, war auch die 15-jährige Anne Frank, deren Tagebuch aus ihrem Amsterdamer Versteck nach Kriegsende veröffentlicht wurde. Anne Frank starb in Bergen-Belsen, wo die Situation in den letzten Monaten vor Kriegsende immer chaotischer wurde. „Seit Ende 1944 wurden Zehntausende von Häftlingen von der SS aus frontnahen Konzentrationslagern ins Reichsinnere ‚evakuiert'", darunter 7.000 aus Sachsenhausen und bis zu 30.000 aus dem KZ Dora-Mittelbau. „Ziel vieler dieser Transporte war Bergen-Belsen. Wer nicht schon auf den Fußmärschen starb oder erschossen wurde, kam in ein notdürftig erweitertes und dennoch katastrophal überfülltes Lager. Aufgrund dramatischer medizinischer Umstände, Epidemien und Hunger starben im Inferno von Bergen-Belsen zwischen Anfang Januar und Mitte April 1945 etwa 35.000 Menschen. [...] Der Name Bergen-Belsen wurde zu einem Symbol für die Gräuel des nationalsozialistischen Konzentrationslagersystems, für den Terror und die deutschen Verbrechen der NS-Zeit."[2]

Was Bergen-Belsen heute so unbegreiflich sein lässt, ist dieser Eindruck von einer wahnwitzigen Ordnung und bürokratischen Struktur, einer eigenen Logik und Logistik im Umgang mit den Inhaftierten, die im Verlauf der letzten Kriegsmonate immer weniger aufrechterhalten werden konnte und so den Tod der Menschen noch beschleunigte, der sowieso immer Ziel dieser geordneten Vernichtung war.

„Die Zustände im Lager waren wirklich unbeschreiblich; kein Bericht und keine Fotografie kann den grauenhaften Anblick des Lagergeländes hinreichend wiedergeben; die furchtbaren Bilder im Inneren der Baracken waren noch viel schrecklicher." So schilderte der britische Sanitätsoffizier Glyn Hughes im Bergen-Belsen-Prozess Ende 1945 seine Eindrücke beim Betreten des Lagers. „An zahlreichen Stellen [...] waren die Leichen zu Stapeln von unterschiedlicher Höhe aufgeschichtet; einige dieser Leichenstapel befanden sich außerhalb des Stacheldrahtzaunes, andere innerhalb der Umzäunung zwischen den Baracken. Überall im Lager verstreut lagen verwesende menschliche Körper. Die Gräben der Kanalisation waren mit Leichen gefüllt, und in den Baracken selbst lagen zahllose Tote, manche sogar zusammen mit den Lebenden auf einer einzigen Bettstelle. In der Nähe des Krematoriums sah man Spuren von hastig gefüllten Massengräbern.

3
Cited in Puvogel and Stankowski, op. cit., p. 384; English quotations in www.scrapbookpages.com/BergenBelsen/BergenBelsen05.html, and www.bergenbelsen.co.uk/pages/Trial/Trial/TrialProsecutionCase/Trial_006_GlynHughes.html
4
Reichel, Peter: Politik mit der Erinnerung, Gedächtnisorte im Streit um die nationalsozialistische Vergangenheit, Munich 1995, p. 162

3
Zitiert nach Puvogel und Stankowski, a.a.O., S. 384
4
Reichel, Peter: Politik mit der Erinnerung, Gedächtnisorte im Streit um die nationalsozialistische Vergangenheit, München 1995, S. 162

left of the bottom compound was an open pit half-full of corpses. It had just begun to be filled."[3] The BBC filmed the liberation of the concentration camp by the British Army, and the scenes that met the soldiers on 15 April 1945 were broadcast around the world. To the present day, Bergen-Belsen represents the visible embodiment of mass death and suffering in a concentration camp. All the huts were burned down in May 1945 to prevent the further spread of disease.

The memorial at Bergen-Belsen has officially existed since 1952. A wooden memorial cross was erected just after the war in 1945, a Jewish monument in 1946, and an obelisk in 1947 as a memorial to the atrocities of the camp. Around these first memorials a kind of cemetery arose, but it was not until the mid-1960s that a place of remembrance was successively established in several small steps, and with it the documentation of hundreds of thousands of crimes. History "first had to be repressed before it could be remembered."[4]

Hinter dem letzten Lagerabteil befand sich eine offene Grube, halb mit Leichen gefüllt; man hatte gerade mit der Bestattungsarbeit begonnen."[3] Die Befreiung des Konzentrationslagers durch die britische Armee war von der BBC gefilmt worden. Die Bilder, die sich den Soldaten am 15. April 1945 boten, gingen um die Welt. Sie machen Bergen-Belsen bis heute zum sichtbaren Inbegriff des massenhaften Sterbens und Leidens in einem Konzentrationslager. Vor Ort dagegen wurden sämtliche Baracken noch im Mai 1945 niedergebrannt, um Seuchen zu vermeiden.

Die Gedenkstätte Bergen-Belsen existiert offiziell seit 1952. Schon seit 1945 erinnert ein hölzernes Totenkreuz, seit 1946 ein jüdisches Mahnmal und seit 1947 ein Obelisk an das Grauen dieses Lagers. Rund um diese Zeichen der Erinnerung entstand eine Art Friedhof. Erst Mitte der 1960er Jahre begann in kleinen Schritten der Ausbau eines Erinnerungsortes und mit ihm die Dokumentation der hunderttausendfachen Verbrechen. Die Geschichte „musste erst einmal verdrängt werden, bevor sie wieder erinnert werden konnte".[4]

The memorial from the post-war years: mass graves, obelisk and inscription plaque in amongst the heather

Gestaltung der Nachkriegsjahre: Massengräber, Obelisk mit Inschriftenwand, Heide

5
Pohle, Albrecht: "Zur Ent-
wicklung der Gedenkstätte
Bergen-Belsen", in: Wiede-
mann, Wilfried and Wolschke-
Bulmann, Joachim (Ed.):
Landschaft und Gedächtnis,
Munich 2011, p. 33.

5
Pohle, Albrecht: „Zur Ent-
wicklung der Gedenkstätte
Bergen-Belsen", in: Wiede-
mann, Wilfried und Wolsch-
ke-Bulmann, Joachim (Hg.):
Landschaft und Gedächtnis,
München 2011, S. 33

Burying the "sensation"

This repression of history also employed the means of landscape architecture. Within the boundaries of the concentration camp at Bergen-Belsen, a memorial landscape was created in the image of a cemetery. The British military administration entrusted the German authorities with the task of landscaping this site on which, until the end of 1946, "some 6,000 Polish survivors and around 12,000 mostly Eastern European Jews still lived before the dissolution of the Displaced Persons (DP) Camp in 1950." For the Jews, "the memorial was not only a place of sorrow; Bergen-Belsen also represented the legitimation of political demands for an own state in Palestine where they would be protected and free from persecution and defenceless incarceration in extermination camps. The DP Camp next to the place of torment and death was a unique place for the revival of Jewish life. In the DP Camp, people married and some 1,500 Jewish children were born. For the survivors, Bergen-Belsen was also a place of self-assertion. And this remained after the last survivors left the DP Camp. To the very end they tried to effect the transfer of the memorial into the custody of an international organisation because they did not trust the Germans." [5] As a consequence, different expressions of sorrow, commemoration and remembrance existed alongside one another for several years on the grounds of Bergen-Belsen. In 1952, responsibility for the site passed to the State of

Die ‚Sensation' eingraben

Diese Verdrängung der Geschichte wurde mit den Mitteln der Landschaftsarchitektur betrieben. Im Bereich des KZ Bergen-Belsen entstand eine nach dem Bild eines Friedhofs gestaltete Gedenklandschaft. Die britische Militäradministration hatte den deutschen Behörden die Aufgabe der gärtnerischen Gestaltung dieses Geländes übergeben, auf dem bis Ende 1946 noch „rund 6.000 polnische Überlebende und bis zur Auflösung des DP [displaced persons] Camp im Jahr 1950 etwa 12.000 zumeist osteuropäische Juden" lebten. „Für die Juden war die Gedenkstätte nicht nur ein Ort der Trauer, Bergen-Belsen trug für sie auch die Bedeutung einer politischen Forderung nach einem eigenen Staat in Palästina, der sie schützt und der verhindert, dass sie je wieder von Antisemiten verfolgt und wehrlos in Vernichtungslager getrieben werden. Das DP Camp neben dem Ort der Qualen und des Todes war ein einzigartiger Ort der Wiedererstehung jüdischen Lebens. Im DP Camp wurden Ehen geschlossen und etwa 1.500 jüdische Kinder geboren. So war Bergen-Belsen für die Überlebenden ein Ort der Selbstvergewisserung. Er blieb es auch, nachdem die letzten Überlebenden das DP Camp verlassen hatten. Bis zuletzt hatten sie noch versucht, die Gedenkstätte in die Obhut einer internationalen Organisation gelangen zu lassen, weil sie den Deutschen nicht trauten." [5] So existierten einige Jahre verschiedene Ausdrucksweisen der Trauer und des Gedenkens und Erinnerns

An unsettling pastoral scene: a cemetery in a landscape of heather

Verstörende Idylle: Friedhofsgestaltung als Heidelandschaft

6
Wiedemann, Wilfried and Wolschke-Bulmann, Joachim: "Landschaft und Gedächtnis – eine persönliche Einführung", in: Wiedemann and Wolschke-Bulmahn, op. cit., p. 19. Built ostensibly to commemorate the death of 4,500 Saxons at the hands of Charlemagne, the Grove of the Saxons (Sachsenhain) was appropriated by Himmler as a gathering place for the SS. See Nature and Ideology: Nature and Garden Design in the Twentieth Century, Wolschke-Bulmahn, Joachim (Ed.), Washington 1997, p. 211
7
Pohle, op. cit., p. 34
8
Wiedemann and Wolschke-Bulmahn: "Landschaft und Gedächtnis – eine persönliche Einführung", in: Wiedemann and Wolschke-Bulmahn, op. cit., p. 11

6
Wiedemann, Wilfried und Wolschke-Bulmann, Joachim: „Landschaft und Gedächtnis – eine persönliche Einführung", in: Wiedemann und Wolschke-Bulmahn, a.a.O., S. 19
7
Pohle, a.a.O., S. 34
8
Wiedemann und Wolschke-Bulmahn: „Landschaft und Gedächtnis – eine persönliche Einführung", in: Wiedemann und Wolschke-Bulmahn, a.a.O, S. 11

Lower Saxony, more specifically, the Cemetery Administration of the State Ministry of the Interior. The interpretation of this place as a cemetery, as reflected in its design, was now also officially institutionalised as such. That this "cemetery" was designed according to plans by the landscape architect Wilhelm Hübotter, who "ten years earlier had designed the Sachsenhain near Verden an der Aller for Heinrich Himmler,"[6] first became an issue in the 1980s. Research into the work of Hübotter began at the same school for horticulture and landscape planning in Hanover that he himself had founded after the war together with Professor Heinrich Friedrich Wiepking-Jürgensmann – who during the war had been a Special Representative on matters of landscape design to the head of the SS, Heinrich Himmler. Joachim Wolschke-Bulmahn, who together with Gerd Gröning and others conducted much research into the relationship between landscape architecture and National Socialism, was inspired during a period spent at Harvard University to examine the topic of memorial landscapes on the grounds of former concentration camps more closely. Around the same time in the mid-1980s, a shift in the perception of memorial landscapes began to take place among historians. Local history workshops, citizens' initiatives and associations began to revisit their respective local history from the Nazi era. In Bergen-Belsen too, local citizens and young people founded the Bergen-Belsen Working Group in 1985. By contacting survivors, visiting other places of remembrance and providing information and guided tours of Bergen-Belsen, the working group was able to compensate for "at least some of the deficits resulting from the State of Lower Saxony's custody of the memorial site."[7] At this time, the first political initiatives for redesigning the memorial at Bergen-Belsen were also submitted to the State Parliament of Lower Saxony.

Historians, among them Wilfried Wiedemann who later headed the redesign of the memorial at Bergen-Belsen, had discovered through research conducted in London and Jerusalem at the beginning of the 1980s that far more material was available on the concentration camp at Bergen-Belsen "than was available in the documentation archives of the Bergen-Belsen Memorial, or elsewhere in Germany. [...] It soon became clear to me that the studies available in Germany, and contained in the document archives at Bergen-Belsen reflected the state of research from the early 1960s and left much unanswered – for example what happened to the Soviet prisoners of war or the Sinti and Roma in Bergen-Belsen." At that time Wiedemann "had not yet considered the chain of decisions that had led to the specific cemetery-influenced design of the memorial at Bergen-Belsen". He felt that "the existing solution was both ethically as well as aesthetically appropriate and saw absolutely no need for it to be changed."[8]

nebeneinander auf dem Gelände Bergen-Belsen. 1952 wurde das Land Niedersachsen, und zwar die beim Innenministerium angesiedelte Friedhofsverwaltung, zuständig für das Gelände. Die Interpretation des Ortes als Friedhof hatte sich nicht nur gestalterisch, sondern auch institutionell durchgesetzt.

Dass dieser „Friedhof" gestaltet wurde nach Plänen des Landschaftsarchitekten Wilhelm Hübotter, der „zehn Jahre vorher für Heinrich Himmler den Sachsenhain bei Verden an der Aller geplant hatte",[6] wurde erst in den 1980er Jahren zum Thema. Die Erforschung der Arbeiten Hübotters, der nach dem Zweiten Weltkrieg gemeinsam mit Professor Heinrich Friedrich Wiepking-Jürgensmann – während des Krieges Sonderbeauftragter des Reichsführers SS, Heinrich Himmler, für Fragen der Landschaftsgestaltung – die Gründung einer Hochschule für Gartenbau und Landeskultur in Hannover betrieb, begann an eben dieser Hochschule. Joachim Wolschke-Bulmahn, der gemeinsam mit Gerd Gröning und weiteren zu den Zusammenhängen zwischen Landschaftsarchitektur und Nationalsozialismus forschte, wurde anlässlich eines Aufenthaltes an der Harvard-Universität angeregt, dieses Thema der Gedenkstättenlandschaften auf den Geländen ehemaliger Konzentrationslager näher zu untersuchen. Etwa zeitgleich begann sich Mitte der 1980er Jahre unter Historikern ein neuer Blick auf die Gedenkstättenlandschaft durchzusetzen. In Geschichtswerkstätten, Bürgerinitiativen und Vereinen wurde die jeweilige Lokalgeschichte während der NS-Zeit neu aufgearbeitet. So auch in Bergen-Belsen, wo 1985 durch Bürgerinnen und Bürger sowie Jugendliche die Arbeitsgemeinschaft Bergen-Belsen gegründet wurde. Diese Arbeitsgemeinschaft glich durch Kontakte zu Überlebenden, durch Studienfahrten zu anderen Gedenkorten und durch Führungen und Informationsmaterial zu Bergen-Belsen „wenigstens teilweise die Defizite aus, die das Land Niedersachsen als Trägerin der Gedenkstätte offen ließ".[7] Erste politische Initiativen zur Umgestaltung der Gedenkstätte Bergen-Belsen erreichten in dieser Zeit den niedersächsischen Landtag.

Die Historiker, allen voran der spätere Leiter der Neugestaltung der Gedenkstätte Bergen-Belsen, Wilfried Wiedemann, hatten durch Recherchen in London und Jerusalem zu Beginn der 1980er Jahre erfahren, dass es zum KZ Bergen-Belsen weit umfangreicheres Material gab, „als es im Dokumentenhaus der Gedenkstätte Bergen-Belsen vorhanden noch in Deutschland bekannt" war. „Mir wurde rasch klar, dass die in Deutschland vorliegenden Untersuchungen ebenso wie auch das Dokumentenhaus in Bergen-Belsen den Forschungsstand der frühen 1960er Jahre repräsentierten und viele Fragen offen ließen – zum Beispiel die nach den sowjetischen Kriegsgefangenen oder den Sinti und Roma in Bergen-Belsen." Wiedemann stellte sich zu diesem Zeitpunkt „noch nicht die Frage, welche Entscheidungsprozesse zu der spezifischen Friedhofsgestaltung von Bergen-Belsen geführt hatten". Er „hielt die gefundene Lösung ethisch wie ästhetisch für angemessen und sah überhaupt keinen Handlungsbedarf".[8]

9
Letter from Wilhelm Hübotter to the District Administrator Wentker, 28 November 1945, Celle District Archives, cited in Wiedemann, Wilfried and Wolschke-Bulmann, Joachim: "Bergen-Belsen. Zur Entwicklung der Gedenk-Landschaft", in: Wiedemann and Wolschke-Bulmann, op. cit., p. 81

10
Wilhelm Hübotter, Belsen Memorial, Description, 4 December 1945, Celle District Archives, cited in ibid., p. 86

11
Wiedemann, Wilfried and Wolschke-Bulmann, Joachim: "Bergen-Belsen. Zur Entwicklung der Gedenk-Landschaft", in: Wiedemann and Wolschke-Bulmann, op. cit., p. 93

9
Schreiben von Wilhelm Hübotter an Landrat Wentker, 28. November 1945, Kreisarchiv Celle, zit. n. Wiedemann, Wilfried und Wolschke-Bulmann, Joachim: „Bergen-Belsen. Zur Entwicklung der Gedenk-Landschaft," in: Wiedemann und Wolschke-Bulmann, a.a.O., S. 81

10
Wilhelm Hübotter, Belsen-Gedenkstätte, Erläuterung, 4. Dezember 1945, Kreisarchiv Celle, zit. n. ebda., S. 86

11
Wiedemann, Wilfried und Wolschke-Bulmann, Joachim: „Bergen-Belsen. Zur Entwicklung der Gedenk-Landschaft", in: Wiedemann und Wolschke-Bulmann, a.a.O., S. 93

Following the work of the commission led by Wiedemann, which culminated in the presentation of a concept for a permanent exhibition in 1987, and the discovery of a previously unknown aerial photograph taken by the Royal Air Force on 13 September 1944 that showed the entire camp complex including the prisoner-of-war camp and the concentration camp, both historians as well as landscape architects began to question Hübotter's conception of the memorial site as the definitive solution to the task.

"Never in the history of mankind has there been anything comparable, and it is absolutely necessary through a memorial of this kind to place a final stone so to speak, to mark the end of a time that must never be allowed to repeat. For this reason, I am of the conviction that the idea and its manifestation must be large, not necessarily in a material sense, but in the way it is presented. We must succeed in burying the 'sensation' of Belsen and transform it into a monument of lasting effect. [...] The meaning of Belsen as the end point of an epoch is beyond doubt and requires a sufficiently imposing means of expression."[9] The critical examination of Hübotter's project that influenced the design of the memorial at Bergen-Belsen in the 1960s culminated in a highly personal debate on his work and the moral evaluation of his activities, an argument that also fuelled discourse on the meaning of landscape in the ideology of National Socialism. This debate within the profession was to prove fundamental for the later landscape architecture competition for Bergen-Belsen.

On the one hand, there was Hübotter's understanding of landscape architecture as a means to shape the landscape: "Any approach that employs only gardening means (as is typical for a cemetery) [cannot] fulfil the task at hand. [...] For this reason, the intention was to find a fundamentally more generous manner of expressing this memorial [...]. The expansiveness of the landscape that the visitor sees must be heightened using the means of design."[10] On the other hand, there was a call for a landscape architecture that does not "subordinate the aesthetics of a place of suffering for tens of thousands of people to the surrounding landscape, to an 'ideal landscape' as seen through the eyes of the perpetrators", a landscape architecture that instead accords respect to the victims, to their different political and religious convictions, their different nationalities and ethnic origins and that does not elevate a "primarily ideologically-based image of the landscape" to its "guiding principle" but instead calls this into question. "The ideal of the heath landscape was not adequate for the landscape design of the memorial at Bergen-Belsen. The landscaping of the memorial at Bergen-Belsen as experienced by visitors over decades was more suited to a process of forgetting than to remembering and reminding."[11] In spite of this, any new design concept could not and should not disregard this history of remembrance.

Erst die Arbeit einer von Wiedemann geleiteten Kommission, die 1987 die inhaltliche Konzeption für eine neue Dauerausstellung vorlegte, sowie im Jahr 1990 das Auffinden einer bis dahin nicht bekannten Luftaufnahme der Royal Air Force vom 13. September 1944, die den gesamten Lagerkomplex aus Kriegsgefangenenlager und Konzentrationslager zeigte, bestärkte die Historiker wie die Landschaftsarchitekten, die Auffassung Hübotters von einer Gedächtnisstätte als Schlussstein zu hinterfragen.

„Wohl noch niemals in der Menschheitsgeschichte hat es derartiges gegeben, und es ergibt sich die zwingenden Notwendigkeit mit einer solchen Gedächtnisstätte einen SCHLUSS-STEIN zu setzen hinter eine Zeit, die niemals wiederkehren darf. Aus diesem Grunde bin ich der Überzeugung, dass die Idee und die Gestaltungsmittel gross sein müssen, d. h. nicht gross im Sinne des Materiellen, sondern in ihrer Art. Es muss uns gelingen, die ‚Sensation' Belsen einzugraben und in eine ständig wirksame Mahnung umzuwandeln. [...] Die Bedeutung von Belsen als Schlussstein für eine Epoche ist ohne Zweifel und verlangt eine Ausdrucksform eindrucksvoller Art."[9] Die Auseinandersetzung mit der Planung Hübotters, wie sie die Gestaltung der Gedenkstätte Bergen-Belsen in den 1960er Jahren beeinflusste, mündete einerseits in eine sehr persönlich geführte Auseinandersetzung über das Werk Hübotters und die moralische Wertung seines Tuns, andererseits beflügelte dieser Streit den Diskurs um die Bedeutung der Landschaft in der Ideologie des Nationalsozialismus. Für den späteren landschaftsarchitektonischen Wettbewerb zu Bergen-Belsen ist dieser Streit der Profession grundlegend.

Auf der einen Seite steht die Landschaftsarchitektur mit ihren Mitteln der landschaftlichen Inszenierung, wie Hübotter sie verstand: „[J]ede nur rein gärtnerische Gestaltung (Friedhofsmässige Auffassung) [kann] die hier gestellte Aufgabe nicht erfüllen [...] Aus diesem Grunde ist versucht worden, eine grundlegendere Idee grosszügiger Art für diese Gedenkstätte zu finden [...]. Die grosszügige Weite der Landschaft, die sich dem Beschauer darbietet, muss durch die Gestaltungsmittel noch gesteigert werden."[10] Auf der anderen Seite steht die Forderung an eine Landschaftsarchitektur, die keine „Unterordnung der Ästhetik dieses Ortes des Leids für Zehntausende von Menschen unter die umgebende Landschaft, unter die ‚Ideallandschaft' der Täter" propagiert, die stattdessen im Respekt vor den Opfern, ihren anderen politischen und religiösen Überzeugungen, ihren anderen Nationalitäten und ethnischen Abstammungen das „überwiegend ideologisch begründete Landschaftsideal" gerade nicht „zur Richtschnur" macht, sondern in Frage stellt. „Das Ideal der Heidelandschaft war für die landschaftliche Ausgestaltung der Gedenkstätte Bergen-Belsen nicht adäquat. Die Landschaftsgestaltung der Gedenkstätte Bergen-Belsen, wie sie sich über Jahrzehnte den Besuchenden darbot, war geeignet, tendenziell eher den Prozess des Vergessens als den des Erinnerns und Mahnens zu fördern."[11] Eine neue Gestaltung konnte und sollte sich über diese Geschichte des Gedenkens zugleich aber nicht hinwegsetzen.

12
Krebs, Stefanie: "Wo kein
Gras darüberwächst",
Deutsches Architektenblatt,
5/2012, p. 32

12
Krebs, Stefanie: „Wo kein
Gras darüberwächst", in:
Deutsches Architektenblatt,
5/2012, S. 32

Dimensions and limits

In response to the political debate and new research findings, the German Federal Government decided to fund the memorial at Bergen-Belsen due to its national and international significance. Further international support was obtained with the help of the historian Sybil Milton who had set up the United States Holocaust Memorial Museum. A competition followed in 2002 for a new concept for the memorial and its grounds. The first prize was awarded to sinai landscape architects in 2003, who had submitted their competition entry together with the architects Sigel Dubbers. Project construction began in 2007, undertaken as a cooperation between sinai and the architects KSP Engel & Zimmermann, who designed the new exhibition centre, Hans Dieter Schaal, who designed the exhibition architecture and Weidner Händle Atelier who were responsible for the exhibition graphics.

"In Bergen-Belsen the redesign of the camp grounds meant finding a position with respect to the landscaping that had taken place after the war. [...] The proposal that was realised is characterised by a sense of respect and restraint towards the historic site."[12] Through the introduction of a few interventions, sinai's design calls Hübotter's earlier design into question without eradicating this layer of the site's development. The most important changes regard reconfiguring the entrance to the grounds, and providing a more differentiated understanding of the site: Bergen-Belsen was a prisoner-of-war camp, a labour camp, a concentration camp but not a typical extermination camp, and yet still an "inferno" that is only eclipsed by Auschwitz as an international symbol of the inhumanity of National Socialism. While this complex history does not need to be shown in detail, just the cemetery on its own, and the emphasis it places on the mass graves, was felt by A. W. Faust to be insufficient. The guiding idea for the redesign of the memorial is orientation: "orientation" in terms of making the history individually relatable by rendering visible the large number of developments and fates, as well as orientation in the landscape. While the mass graves deliberately sought not to commemorate individual victims, but simultaneously transport the central message, the new interventions in the landscape highlight the development of the camp further and further into the wood as an additional layer of meaning. This approach provides a means of remembering the acts of extermination, of the establishment and the extension of the camp and of its dimensions.

Dimensionen und Grenzen

Auf Grundlage der politischen Debatte und der neuen Forschungen entschied im Jahr 2000 die Bundesregierung, die Gedenkstätte Bergen-Belsen wegen ihrer nationalen und internationalen Bedeutung zu fördern. Mit der Historikerin Sybil Milton, die das United States Holocaust Memorial Museum mit aufgebaut hatte, konnte internationale Unterstützung gewonnen werden. 2002 wurde ein Wettbewerb zur Neukonzeptionierung der Gedenkstätte und der Gedenkstätten-Landschaft ausgelobt. Der 1. Preis in diesem Wettbewerb wurde 2003 sinai Landschaftsarchitekten zuerkannt, die einen Entwurf gemeinsam mit den Architekten Sigel Dubbers eingereicht hatten. Die Realisierung seit 2007 erfolgte dann in Kooperation von sinai mit den Architekten KSP Engel & Zimmermann, die für das neue Ausstellungszentrum verantwortlich zeichneten, sowie mit Hans Dieter Schaal für die Ausstellungsarchitektur und mit Weidner Händle Atelier für die Ausstellungsgrafik.

„[I]n Bergen-Belsen erforderte [...] die Neugestaltung des Lagergeländes eine Haltung gegenüber der landschaftlichen Überformung der Nachkriegszeit [...] Umgesetzt wurde ein Vorschlag, der durch Respekt und Zurückhaltung gegenüber dem historischen Ort geprägt ist."[12] Durch einige Eingriffe stellt der Entwurf von sinai die Planung Hübotters in Frage, ohne diese Schicht der Entwicklung des Geländes zu beseitigen. Die wichtigsten Veränderungen betreffen den Zugang auf das Gelände, und auch der inhaltliche Zugang wurde differenzierter möglich: Bergen-Belsen war ein Kriegsgefangenenlager, ein Arbeitslager, auch als KZ kein typisches Vernichtungslager, und dennoch ein Ort des „Infernos", der wie nur noch Auschwitz weltweit für die nationalsozialistische Unmenschlichkeit steht. Diese komplexe Geschichte ist nicht detailliert abzubilden. Doch allein den Friedhof mit der Betonung der Massengräber empfand A. W. Faust als ebenfalls nicht angemessen. „Orientierung" durch Individualisierung, durch ein Aufzeigen der großen Anzahl der Entwicklungen und der Schicksale, ebenso als Orientierung in der Landschaft, wurde zur Leitidee für die Neugestaltung der Gedenkstätte. Während die Massengräber eine Erinnerung an die einzelnen Opfer bewusst vermieden, zugleich aber die wesentliche Botschaft trugen, wird nun der Eingriff in die Landschaft, die Entwicklung des Lagers in den Wald hinein, ebenfalls thematisiert. Auf diesem Weg wird ein Erinnern auch an die Taten der Vernichtung möglich, an die Anlage und die Erweiterungen des Lagers und an seine Dimensionen.

13
Reichel, op. cit., p. 158 ff.

13
Reichel, a.a.O., S. 158 f.

For the design, orientation could be gleaned from the aforementioned aerial photograph taken by the British forces, which was rediscovered in 1990. It provides the best document of the condition of the camp in September 1944, and sinai used it to establish and mark the positions of corridors and camp boundaries on the site. Cleared areas in the now regrown woodlands provide the intended orientation; the boundaries of the camp are made visible as cleared corridors of grass, providing a means of comprehending the dimensions and structure of the camp at Bergen-Belsen.

By overlaying this structure of the camp onto the site, sinai were able to respect the large cemetery and avoid violating it in any way while simultaneously revealing the presence of the camp. In addition, the landscape architecture of the new design provides orientation by helping to clarify the two phases of the history of the place: "Like other concentration and extermination camps, [Bergen-Belsen has] long become a memorial with two histories: that of the camp where the survivors later said that those who were brought to Bergen-Belsen, fell 'out of life and out of time' (Renata Laqueur), and that significantly longer history of the camp as a place of memorial".[13]

Orientierung für den Entwurf bot die erwähnte Luftaufnahme der britischen Streitkräfte, die 1990 entdeckt wurde. In ihr ist der Zustand des Lagers vom September 1944 am besten dokumentiert. sinai legten dieses Luftbild einer neuen Einmessung und Markierung der Korridore und Lagergrenzen zugrunde. Rodungen in dem in den letzten Jahrzehnten aufgewachsenen Wald schaffen die angestrebten Orientierungen; die Lagergrenzen wurden mit Hilfe dieser durch Rodung entstehenden Rasenkorridore wieder sichtbar, und damit auch die Dimensionen und die Strukturen des Lagers Bergen-Belsen.

Es gelang sinai, die Überlagerung der Lagerstruktur durch den großen Friedhof zu respektieren, auch im Sinne der Totenruhe, zugleich aber das Lager wieder erkennbar zu machen. Außerdem ermöglicht der neue Entwurf eine orientierende Auseinandersetzung der Landschaftsarchitektur mit zwei Phasen der Geschichte dieses Ortes: Denn Bergen-Belsen ist, „wie die anderen Konzentrations- und Vernichtungslager auch, längst ein Gedächtnisort mit einer doppelten Geschichte: jener der Lager, von der Überlebende später sagten, wer nach Bergen-Belsen kam, der fiel ‚aus dem Leben und der Zeit heraus' (Renata Laqueur), und jener sehr viel längeren Geschichte, in der aus dem Lager ein Gedächtnisort wurde".[13]

Aerial photograph taken by the Royal Air Force on 13 September 1944. The discovery of this photo in 1990 made it possible to determine the boundaries and structure of the camp.

Luftbild der Royal Air Force vom 13. September 1944. Mit der Entdeckung dieser Aufnahme 1990 wurden Grenzen und Struktur des Lagers nachgewiesen.

Aerial photograph taken in 2001, the situation prior to the competition: the memorial site looks like a large clearing. The contours of the former camp are no longer visible.

Luftbild von 2001, Bestand vor dem Wettbewerb: Das Gedenkstättengelände wirkt als große Lichtung. Die Kontur des vormaligen Lagers ist nicht mehr zu erkennen.

Spatial distribution of the master plan from 2005: overlay with cleared strips that reveal the perimeter and internal divisions of the camp.

Raumbild des Masterplans 2005: Überlagerung durch Rodung. Lagergrenzen und die Organisation des Lagers werden sichtbar.

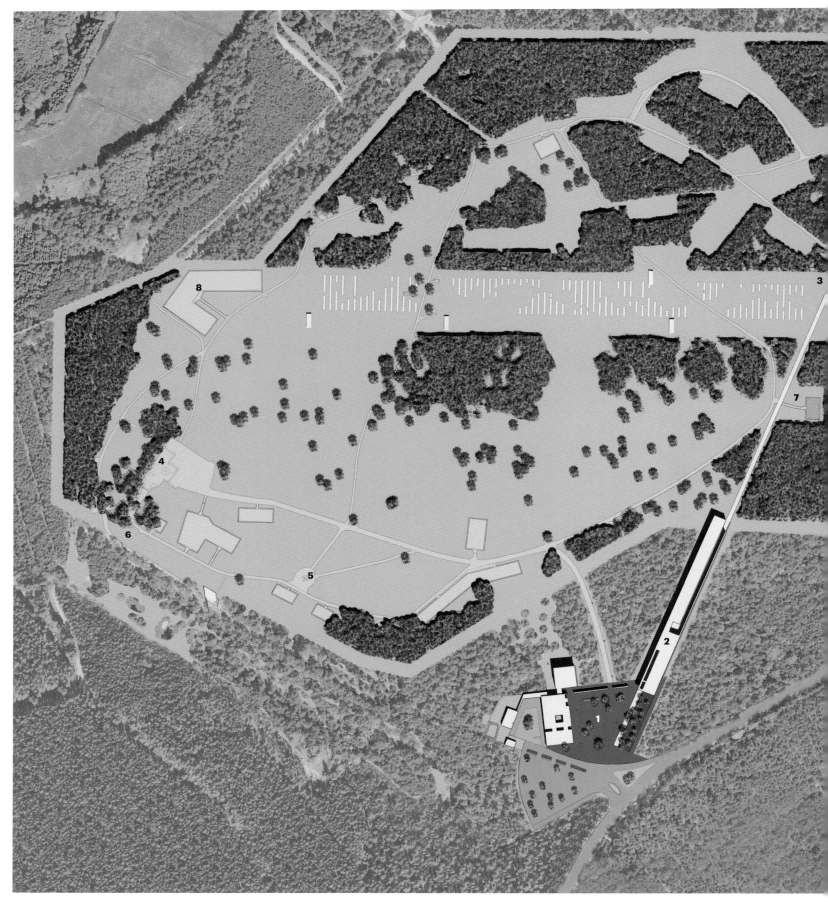

Design for the master plan from 2005

1 Anne-Frank-Platz
2 Documentation centre
3 Plateau

4 Obelisk and
  inscription plaque
5 Jewish monument
6 Polish wooden cross

7 Roll call ground
8 Crematorium

9 Relics: disinfection station
10 Relics: foundations
   of barracks
11 Main camp road

Entwurfsplan
zum Masterplan 2005

1 Anne-Frank-Platz
2 Dokumentationszentrum
3 Plateau

4 Obelisk und Inschriftenwand
5 Jüdisches Mahnmal
6 Polnisches Holzkreuz

7 Appellplatz
8 Krematorium

9 Relikte Desinfektions-
gebäude
10 Relikte Barackenfundamente
11 Lagerstraße

14
Assmann, Aleida: Geschichte im Gedächtnis, Munich 2007, p. 29

14
Assmann, Aleida 2007: Geschichte im Gedächtnis, München 2007, S. 29

A new approach

"If the Germans wish to remember history, they have no choice but to remember how history is remembered."[14] Which historical instance could and should the design for this place of memory – this place with two histories – relate to? All traces of the camp were virtually eradicated in 1945 and the landscaping of the post-war period heavily modified the grounds. Could this design correspond to the images of the situation at the time of the camp's liberation, in which Bergen-Belsen was broadcast around the world? And can one use the means of landscape architecture to communicate the moral and spatial dimensions of the site, as revealed in the aerial photograph found in 1990, after these same means have failed to provide clarification in the past?

Reading eyewitness accounts makes it clear, as A. W. Faust has described, that "in the final phase of the Second World War [this place was] above all a place of chaos, and of suffering and death in this chaos". To a certain extent, it is understandable that directly after the conquest there was an almost reflex-like urge to impose a new order and shape to the site and, on the instructions of the British Allied Forces, to reclaim the place for humanity. Today, almost 70 years after this reclamation, we need another, more differentiated view of this place.

sinai landscape architects were guided primarily by the idea of facilitating a new approach to the site and its history. Consequently, sinai redesigned the entrance situation to the memorial site at Bergen-Belsen.

This entrance area is a key to the design. A stipulation was that the site no longer be entered via the large gateway in the cemetery wall, but instead through the new building for the documentation centre. This building acts as a hinge linking the visitor and the expectations and information they bring with them to the impressions that await them on the site. The path leads through the exhibition, giving each visitor a better impression and understanding of the site of the former camp before they

Ein neuer Zugang

„Wenn die Deutschen Geschichte erinnern wollen, kommen sie nicht umhin, sich auch zu erinnern, wie Geschichte erinnert worden ist."[14]

Auf welchen historischen Ort konnte und sollte sich der Entwurf für diesen Gedächtnisort, diesen Ort mit doppelter Geschichte beziehen? Spuren der Lager waren schon 1945 kaum mehr vorhanden, die Landschaftsgestaltung der Nachkriegszeit hatte den Raum dann weitgehend überformt. Konnte diese Gestaltung den Bildern von der Situation der Befreiung des Lagers, in denen Bergen-Belsen weltweit präsent war, entsprechen? Und kann man die moralischen wie die räumlichen Dimensionen, die in dem 1990 aufgefundenen Luftbild erneut vor Augen geführt wurden, mit den Mitteln der Landschaft zum Ausdruck bringen, nachdem diese schon einmal so wenig aufklärend eingesetzt worden waren?

Die Lektüre der Augenzeugenberichte zeigt, dass dieser Ort, wie A.W. Faust es beschreibt, „in der Schlussphase des Zweiten Weltkrieges vor allem ein Ort des Chaos, des Leidens und Sterbens in diesem Chaos war". In gewisser Hinsicht ist es verständlich, dass unmittelbar nach der Eroberung beinahe reflexartig nach einer neuen Ordnung und Gestaltung gesucht wurde und auf Veranlassung der britischen Alliierten quasi eine Wiederaneignung dieses Ortes durch die Menschlichkeit erreicht werden sollte. Heute, fast 70 Jahre nach dieser Wiederaneignung, ist nun eine andere, differenziertere Haltung zu diesem Ort notwendig. sinai Landschaftsarchitekten ließen sich von der Idee leiten, einen neuen Zugang zum Lager und zu seiner Geschichte zu ermöglichen. Konsequent ist es daher, dass sinai den Eingangsbereich zum Gedenkort Bergen-Belsen neu gestalteten. Dieser Eingangsbereich ist ein Schlüssel zum Entwurf. Vorgegeben war, das Gelände nicht mehr durch das große Tor in der Friedhofsmauer zu betreten, sondern durch das neu errichtete Informationsgebäude. Dieses Gebäude dient als Scharnier zwischen dem Besucher mit seinen Erwartungen und Informationen und dem Eindruck, der diesen Besucher auf dem Gelände

pass into the present-day landscape of the memorial. The building itself is a functional and deliberately understated concrete building in which the path leading through the information rises gradually. The building appears to hover over the ground of the camp, a sign of respect with regard to the Jewish cemetery, which shall never be built over.

The historical documentation is also presented in advance of experiencing the site because the documentation centre informs about aspects of the site that are otherwise hard to imagine when visiting the grounds because the gentle heathland landscape so effectively veils the horrors of the site. The landscape architecture is less demonstrative in its role than other media that communicate the history of the site, among these in particular also seemingly unspectacular exhibits that have a story to tell about the people behind the numbers of those who died. For A. W. Faust, Yvonne Koch's gloves are an especially powerful example: they are the gloves of an eleven-year-old child deported to the camp without relatives in November 1944, where she meets a Russian inmate whom she grows close to and who presents her one winter day with a pair of self-knitted gloves. Today, this exhibit – a pair of gloves – stands for kindness and humanity, and is the antithesis of the horrors of the history of this place. Such exhibits are "stronger than anything that can be achieved with the means of design, whether for the purpose of reconciliation or stirring one's conscience," concedes A. W. Faust, "but the landscape architecture must be open to accommodating such stories and narratives, and be receptive to the emotional power they exert." Of that he is convinced.

The design by sinai landscape architects, together with Sigel Dubbers architects and the designer collective stoebo – Oliver Störmer & Cisca Bogman – is therefore a specific response to this place and cannot be seen as the contribution to a typological approach to memorial sites. The management of the memorial site has also been very supportive in this shift of focus from a culture of burial to a culture of remembering at Bergen-Belsen.

erwartet. Die Führung des Weges durch die Ausstellung ermöglicht es, dass jeder Besucher mit einem erweiterten Eindruck und Verständnis für den Ort das eigentliche Lagergelände, die heutige Gedenklandschaft betritt. Das Gebäude selbst ist ein funktionaler, betont schlichter Betonbau, der leicht ansteigend den Informationsweg umfasst. Über dem Lagergelände selbst schwebt dieser Bau im Respekt gegenüber dem Ort als einem jüdischen Friedhof, der eine Überbauung auf ewig verbietet.

Die Dokumentation der Geschichte ist dem Erleben des Areals auch deshalb vorgeschaltet, weil dort im Dokumentationszentrum die Inhalte und Themen des Ortes vermittelt werden, deren Verständnis auf dem Gelände selbst so schwerfällt, da die liebliche Heidelandschaft dem Grauen so massiv entgegensteht.

Die Landschaftsarchitektur tritt in ihrer Rolle zurück hinter andere Medien, die der Geschichtsaufbereitung dienen, insbesondere auch unscheinbare Exponate, die die individuellen Geschichten hinter den Zahlen des Todes verstehen lassen. Es sind die Handschuhe der Yvonne Koch, die A.W. Faust besonders beeindruckt haben, die Handschuhe eines elfjährigen Kindes, im November 1944 allein ins Lager deportiert, wo sie eine russische Mitgefangene trifft, die zur Bezugsperson wird und Yvonne im Winter eines Tages die selbstgestrickten Handschuhe schenkt. Heute stehen diese Handschuhe als Ausstellungsstück für Menschlichkeit und Antithese zur Grausamkeit der Geschichte dieses Ortes. „Stärker als alles, da kann Gestaltung – weder versöhnliche noch aufrüttelnde – nicht mithalten. Die Landschaftsarchitektur muss aber berührbar sein durch solche Geschichten und Erzählungen, und Raum für dieses Berühren lassen", davon ist A.W. Faust überzeugt.

Daher ist der Entwurf von sinai Landschaftsarchitekten zusammen mit Sigel Dubbers Architekten und stoebo – Oliver Störmer & Cisca Bogman als Gestaltung speziell für diesen Ort und nicht als Beitrag zur Entwicklung einer Gestaltungstypologie „Gedenkstätte" zu lesen. Diesen Wechsel von einer Begräbniskultur zur Erinnerungsarbeit am Ort Bergen-Belsen hat die Leitung der Gedenkstätte bis heute sehr unterstützt.

Approach: the Anne-Frank-Platz in front of the documentation centre gives visitors space to adjust. The stony path is visible as a trace.

Annäherung: Der Anne-Frank-Platz ist Distanzraum vor dem Dokumentationszentrum. Der steinerne Weg wird als Spur erkennbar.

The path onto the site leads first through the exhibition in the documentation centre. Panorama window at the far end of the building with the historic aerial photograph

Der Weg auf das Gelände führt zunächst in das Ausstellungsgebäude. Panoramafenster am Gebäudekopf mit historischem Luftbild

Reduction

In the grounds of the memorial, the landscape architects have responded to the complex history and extensive landscape of the site by practicing the art of leaving out. Instead of making insertions, the memory of the camp has been made legible through the marking of its dimensions in space and by emphasising a specific sense of space. This – oppressive – feeling begins to set in as the visitor makes their way through the in-depth sections of the information in the exhibition before arriving at a large window with a panoramic view of the grounds of the camp. How does one reconcile the horrors of the situation with the beauty of the landscape? Mindful of this struggle, the landscape architects leave space for the visitor to turn over these questions in their minds, creating a conducive atmosphere of tranquillity and dignity.

The design of the landscape architecture of the site does not attempt to explain so as not to "disturb" this sense of incomprehension the visitor feels as they move around the site. A plain concrete path leads from the new entrance building into the site and a few concrete info-steles and floor-mounted panels engraved with a site plan of the former concentration camp are all that provide orientation and information.

For sinai, it was clear that there was little that landscape architecture could have done to counteract or otherwise alter the beauty of the natural landscape with its birch trees, meadows, heather and birdsong. As such, not only the designer but also the visitor must tolerate this mismatch of impressions during their visit.

Reduktion

Auf dem Gelände reagieren die Landschaftsarchitekten mittels der Kunst des Weglassens auf die komplexe Geschichte und das weiträumige Landschaftsbild. Nicht durch Hinzufügungen wird die Erinnerung an die Lager gestärkt, sondern durch die Markierung der Raumdimensionen und durch die Betonung eines spezifischen Raumgefühls. Dieses – beklemmende – Gefühl stellt sich für den Besucher spätestens dann ein, wenn er den Informationsweg der Ausstellung mit ihren vertiefenden Abschnitten passiert hat und abschließend vor einer Panoramascheibe steht, die den Blick auf das Gelände freigibt. Wie sind Schrecken und Schönheit in dieser Situation in Übereinstimmung zu bringen? Eine Frage im Kopf des Besuchers, der die Landschaftsarchitekten einen angemessenen Raum gewähren, eine Stille und Würde, die diese Fragen zulässt und bestärkt.

In seiner Fassungslosigkeit wird der Besucher auf dem Gelände nicht durch eine erklärende Landschaftsarchitektur „gestört". Ein schlichter Betonweg führt vom Eingangsgebäude auf das Gelände, wenige Informationsstelen in Beton sowie Bodenreliefs mit den Lageplänen des ehemaligen KZ geben Orientierung und Informationen.

Gegen die starken Eindrücke, die aus der Landschaft selbst entstehen, gegen die Schönheit der Birken, der Wiesen und Heiden, der Vogelstimmen hätte keine Landschaftsarchitektur bestehen und etwas anderes ausrichten können, da waren sich sinai sicher. Insofern muss nun nicht nur der Gestalter, sondern auch der Besucher diesen Kontrast fassungslos ertragen.

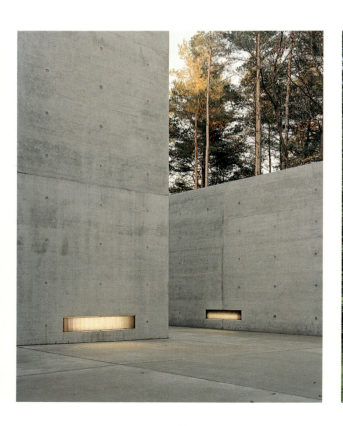

Visitors reach the grounds of the former camp via a 120-metre-long stony corridor.

Über einen 120 Meter langen steinernen Korridor erreicht der Besucher das Lagerareal.

A. W. Faust sees space not so much as a frame of reference for the viewer but rather as a container, as an individual context for each individual's perception. For him, this means that landscape architecture is not primarily about designing an objective space in which functions and the way it is experienced are predetermined, but that it should provide opportunities and atmospheres for accommodating the viewers' respective individual expectations. This approach of "designing atmospheres" led Faust to the idea of adding only a single element to the memorial at Bergen-Belsen: the broad concrete path, which leads from the exhibition into the site.

For the landscape architects, "the space actually begins before the space": by this they underline the need to reinterpret the entrance to the site. This has partly functional reasons, as a range of functional requirements – parking spaces for visitors and buses and initial information – had to be provided economically on a small site in the woods outside the memorial site. At the same time, this place of arrival should not be made too important; it should provide the functions necessary in a neutral manner.

A.W. Faust versteht Raum weniger als Rahmensetzung für den Betrachter, sondern vielmehr als „Container", als individuelles Umfeld des individuell Wahrnehmenden. Daraus leitet der Landschaftsarchitekt ab, dass es in der Landschaftsarchitektur nicht vordringlich darum gehe, einen objektiven Raum zu entwerfen, seine Funktionen und Erlebnisstrukturen vorzugeben, sondern den individuell unterschiedlichen Erwartungen Anhaltspunkte und Atmosphären anzubieten. Dieses „atmosphärische Entwerfen" brachte Faust im Falle der Gedenkstätte Bergen-Belsen zu der Idee, dem Gelände selbst nur den breiten Betonweg, der aus der Ausstellung heraus in das Gelände führt, hinzuzusetzen. Eigentlich „beginnt der Raum vor dem Raum". Die Landschaftsarchitekten begründen so, dass sie einen Schwerpunkt auf die Neuinterpretation der Eingangssituation legten. Zunächst einmal hat dies einfache funktionale Gründe, denn vor der Gedenkstätte musste mit geringem Budget eine hohe Funktionalität erreicht werden, um Besucherparkplätze, Busparkplätze und die ersten Informationen auf geringer Fläche im Wald unterzubringen. Zugleich sollte dieser Ort des Ankommens nicht zu wichtig werden, sondern eine Neutralität der puren Funktion ausstrahlen.

The end of the building with the window is raised to float above the boundary of the camp.

Der Gebäudekopf mit dem Fenster schwebt über der Lagergrenze.

The stony path leads visitors into the centre of the historic grounds of the camp.

Der steinerne Weg bringt den Besucher ins Zentrum des historischen Lagergeländes.

The landscape architecture creates an opening situation, a moment of concentration, an atmosphere of readiness. The materials used in this area reinforce the neutrality of this preliminary situation: gritted asphalt is a surface that is straightforward and demands no special attention. Visitors do not need to think about where they are walking and are free to gather themselves and their thoughts. At the same time, the stone chippings rolled into the surface make it clear that this is neither a road nor a supermarket car park. There is a sense of character and dignity, but one that does not yet demand any special attention – all this is reflected in the choice of materials for the surfacing. Similarly, the placement of solitary trees in the entrance area, each encircled by a ring of crushed stone, signifies that this visit is not simply a walk in the woods.

That leads to the second principal idea of the design concept: the cut-outs. By clearing sections in the prevailing character of the landscape, cut-outs are formed that create interruptions in our perception of the landscape and simultaneously mark the spatial boundaries of the former camp.

These few measures achieve a culture of remembrance without overburdening the landscape with a new strong image or even a counter-image that competes with the existing cemetery landscape. sinai adopt a different approach and at the same time signal that one should not have too high expectations of what landscape architecture is able to achieve. This landscape design cannot correspond to the history of the place, but it can help create an atmosphere of concentration in which one can take in information and so confer the victims a sense of dignity that was lost in the barbarism of the past.

Die Landschaftsarchitektur schafft ein Entree, eine Konzentration, eine aufnahmebereite Stimmung. Diese Stimmung der Neutralität des Ortes findet ihren Ausdruck in den gewählten Materialien dieser Vorzone. Abgestreuter Asphalt als Bodenbelag ermöglicht eine einfache Zuwegung, die selbst keine Konzentration verlangt. Der Besucher muss hier seine Schritte nicht gezielt setzen, nichts besonders beachten, sondern er kann sich in Gedanken vorbereiten. Zugleich vermittelt der Splitt auf dem Asphalt, dass wir uns nicht auf einer asphaltierten Straße oder auf einem Parkplatz vor einem Supermarkt befinden. Charakter und Würde, aber noch nicht eine zu frühe Bindung von Aufmerksamkeit – diese Ansprüche spiegeln sich wider in der Wahl des Bodenbelages. Freigestellte Baumsolitäre auf diesem Vorplatz, jeder gefasst durch einen Schotterring, vermitteln, dass es sich beim Besuch der Gedenkstätte nicht um einen Waldspaziergang handelt.

Das führt zur zweiten Schlüsselidee, der Ausstanzung, die den Entwurf trägt. Indem Rodungen den vorherrschenden Landschaftscharakter aufbrechen, schaffen die Ausstanzungen eine Irritation und zugleich eine Markierung der räumlichen Dimensionen der ehemaligen Lager.

Landschaft wird hier als Erinnerungsraum nicht durch neue starke Bilder, gar durch Gegenbilder zum Landschaftsfriedhof überlastet. sinai vertreten eine Position, und sie warnen zugleich vor zu hohen Erwartungen an die Möglichkeiten der Landschaftsgestaltung. Der Geschichte des Ortes kann die Landschaftsgestaltung nicht entsprechen. Aber sie kann die Atmosphäre der konzentrierten Informationsaufnahme unterstützen und den Opfern so eine Würde zuerkennen, die in der Barbarei verloren ging.

A 60-metre-wide and 1,000-metre-long mown corridor forms the principal space of orientation on the site. The internment areas lay to the north and south of this axis.

Ein 60 Meter breiter und 1.000 Meter langer Rasenkorridor als wichtigster Orientierungsraum auf dem Gelände. Die Häftlingsbereiche lagen nördlich und südlich dieser Achse.

**Bookmarks with visualisation
and description of individual
sections of the camp**

Lesezeichen mit Darstellung
und Erläuterung einzelner
Lagerteile

Charting and marking

Just as there is no objective view of history, there can also be no objectively adequate design of historical spaces. Starting from this standpoint, sinai landscape architects begin by analysing the respective situation of each place and its historical development. What can be seen on the site? What effect does it have on the viewer? What effect is desired, how should its effect change as a result of a new design or redesign? What expectations does society have? The landscape architects discuss these questions using very concrete, visual ideas. For A. W. Faust, "the more complex the history of a place, the more challenging it is for one's power of imagination."

The landscape architects draw a distinction between the space and the exhibition: the two are designed in conjunction with one another but serve different purposes. Space is clarified, usually by making markings that trace historical references or functions. These markings can have different material, visual or haptic qualities or, as in Bergen-Belsen, be the product of selective removal. The exhibition, on the other hand, is dedicated to providing information. It is important to differentiate between a historical place and a place of remembrance. For the landscape architects, the aura of a historically significant place is on its own not clear enough to make this distinction; in places of remembrance, the designers underline and offer guidance through the conscious use of strategies of reinforcement, reduction as well as irritation.

Kartierung und Markierung

Eine objektive Geschichtsschreibung gibt es nicht, also kann es auch keine objektiv stimmige Gestaltung von Geschichtsräumen geben. Ausgehend von dieser Annahme beginnen sinai Landschaftsarchitekten mit der Analyse der jeweiligen Situation des Ortes und seiner Entwicklungsgeschichte. Was ist vor Ort zu sehen? Wie wirkt das Vorgefundene auf den Betrachter? Welche Wirkung ist gewünscht, welche Veränderung in der Wirkung soll durch eine Neu- oder Umgestaltung ausgelöst werden? Welche gesellschaftlichen Erwartungen bestehen? Diese werden durch die Landschaftsarchitekten anhand sehr konkreter, bildhafter Vorstellungen diskutiert. „Der Raum stellt an die Imaginationsfähigkeit ebenso hohe Anforderungen, wie seine Geschichte komplex ist", sagt A.W. Faust. Dabei unterscheiden die Landschaftsarchitekten Ausstellung und Raum, die zwar im Zusammenhang entworfen werden, aber unterschiedliche Aufgaben haben. Der Raum wird vor allem durch Markierungen verdeutlicht, in seinen historischen Bezügen und Funktionen angedeutet. Diese Markierungen können von unterschiedlicher Materialität, Optik und Haptik sein, oder wie in Bergen-Belsen auch durch Weglassungen entstehen. Die Ausstellung dagegen ist der Sache, der Information gewidmet. Dabei ist genau zu unterscheiden zwischen Geschichtsort und Gedenkort. Allein die Aura eines historisch besetzten Ortes ist den Landschaftsarchitekten für diese Differenzierung als Kategorie zu uneindeutig; sie unterstützen und lenken in einem Gedenkort bewusst durch Verstärkungen, Reduktionen und auch Irritationen.

The information system	Das Informationssystem
Marker	Markierung
Main orientation stele	Zentrale Orientierungsstele
Information stele	Informationsstele
Signpost	Wegweiser

15
Assmann, Aleida: Cultural
Memory and Western
Civilization, New York 2011,
p. 314–315
16
Ibid.

15
Assmann, Aleida: Erinne-
rungsräume, München 1999,
5. Aufl. 2010, S. 331
16
Ebda.

In the manner of these insights sinai are sceptical of recent innovations in modern museum education programmes: "What cannot be conveyed through written or visual media should have a strong impact on visitors at the actual historical scene of the events; in other words, they should be struck by the unfathomable aura of the place. This approach corresponds not only to the age-old desire of pilgrims and travellers to see significant places for themselves, but also to a new form of museology that tries to convey history via lived experience."[15] For sinai, such educationally directed, perceptually prescribed and cognitively activated spaces for communicating history as an experience, are precisely not an option for places of remembrance. Such places are also places of memory. They are about setting in motion a "semiotic cycle"[16] in which the place of remembrance, as do other possible exhibits, serves as an expression of and starting point for viewpoints on the past, as a bearer of meaning, but is not portrayed as an authentic message in itself. On no account should the visitor feel transported back into the past.

Entsprechend zurückhaltend reagieren sinai auf die Innovationen der Museumspädagogik. „Was schriftliche oder visuelle Medien nicht vermitteln können, soll den Besucher am historischen Schauplatz unvermittelt anwehen: die in keinem Medium reproduzierbare Aura des Ortes. Diese Einstellung entspricht nicht nur einer uralten inneren Bereitschaft von Wallfahrern und Bildungstouristen, sondern auch einer neuen museumspädagogischen Ausrichtung, die Geschichte als Erlebnis vermittelt."[15] Einen solchen museumspädagogisch erzeugten, sinnlich konkreten und die kognitive Erfahrung affektiv herausfordernden Erfahrungsraum von Geschichte als Erlebnis schließen sinai für Gedenkorte gerade aus. Denn diese sind zugleich Gedächtnisorte. Es geht darum, einen „semiotischen Kreislauf"[16] in Gang zu setzen, in dem der Erinnerungsort, wie auch sonst Sammlungsobjekte, als Ausdruck und Ausgangsort für Haltungen gegenüber der Vergangenheit, als Bedeutungsträger, aber nicht selbst als authentische Botschaft inszeniert wird. Auf keinen Fall soll sich der Besucher in die Geschichte zurückversetzt wähnen.

Plateau with two models
1944/present day
Top view

Plateau mit zwei Modellen
1944/heute
Aufsicht

Bookmarks
Visualisation and description
of individual sections
of the camp
Top view

Lesezeichen
Darstellung und Erläuterung
einzelner Lagerteile
Aufsicht

17
Ebda., S. 332
18
Klüger, Ruth: Still Alive,
New York 2001, p. 64
19
Assmann, Cultural Memory
and Western Civilization,
op. cit., p. 317–318

17
Ibid., p. 316
18
Klüger, Ruth: weiter leben,
Göttingen 1992, S. 70
19
Assmann, Aleida:
Erinnerungsräume, München
1999, S. 333f.

The paradox of authenticity

For such places of remembrance, and for the design of such places, it is important that they are able to reflect the different perspectives and backgrounds that condition this semiotic cycle of the perception of a museum (as opposed to the scene of a crime). Aleida Assmann has vividly described the difference between "memory learned" and "memory experienced", pointing out that it is not possible to reproduce the direct experience of a place of remembrance for a visitor but that at the same time a former concentration camp is always both a place of information and remembrance as well as "a therapeutic aid for the survivors."

Assmann cites Ruth Klüger, who "experienced Auschwitz" and in her autobiographical novel *weiter leben* (Still Alive) weighs up "the pros and cons of transforming concentration camps into memorials"[17]:

"[The untied knot left behind by] violated taboos, such as child murder and mass murder, turn their victims into spirits, whom we offer a kind of home that they may haunt at will."[18]

"Underlying such places of memory that have been turned into memorials and museums is a deep-seated paradox: their conservation, which is meant to serve the purpose of authenticity, in fact leads inevitably to a loss of authenticity. By the very fact of their preservation, they have already been covered up and replaced. There is no other way for them to survive. [...] With the passage of time, authenticity must rely more and more on the simple 'here and now' of location instead of on the actual relics. Anyone who attaches too much importance to the mnemonic powers of the location will therefore run the risk of confusing the refashioned place he is visiting with the historical place where the inmates lived and died. [...] The gap between the place of the crime and the place of the visitor must be made obvious, so that the emotional potential mobilised by the place should not lead to a merging of temporal horizons and an illusion of easy identification."[19] This is the approach that sinai landscape architects have taken for their redesign of the Bergen-Belsen Concentration Camp Memorial.

Das Paradox der Authentizität

Wichtig für einen solchen Gedächtnisort, den gestalterischen Umgang mit solchen Orten, ist es, unterschiedliche Perspektiven und Erfahrungshintergründe zu reflektieren, die diesen semiotischen Kreislauf der Wahrnehmung eines Museums (anstelle eines Tatortes) bedingen. Aleida Assmann erläutert an Beispielen eindringlich den Unterschied von „Lerngedächtnis" und „Erfahrungsgedächtnis" und verweist darauf, dass die Unmittelbarkeit der Erfahrung an einem Gedächtnisort für den informierten Bildungsbesucher nicht reproduzierbar sein kann, dass aber zugleich ein ehemaliges Konzentrationslager immer beides ist, ein Ort der Information und Erinnerung und zugleich „eine therapeutische Stütze für die Überlebenden".

Assmann zitiert Ruth Klüger, der „Auschwitz widerfahren" ist und die in ihrem autobiografischen Roman *weiter leben* Überlegungen anstellt „über den Nutzen und Nachteil von KZ-Gedenkstätten"[17]: „Der ungelöste Knoten, den so ein verletztes Tabu wie Massenmord, Kindermord hinterlässt, verwandelt sich zum unerlösten Gespenst, dem wir eine Art Heimat gewähren, wo es spuken darf."[18]

„Die zu Gedenkstätten und Museen umgestalteten Erinnerungsorte unterliegen einem tiefgreifenden Paradox: Die Konservierung dieser Orte im Interesse der Authentizität bedeutet unweigerlich einen Verlust an Authentizität. Indem der Ort bewahrt wird, wird er bereits verdeckt und ersetzt. Das geht gar nicht anders. [...] Die Authentizität wird sich mit der Zeit von den Relikten immer mehr auf das schiere ‚Hier' der Örtlichkeit zurückziehen. Wer zuviel Gewicht legt auf die Gedächtniskraft des Ortes, läuft Gefahr, den umgestalteten Gedenkort, den Ort der Besucher, mit dem historischen Ort, dem Ort der Häftlinge, zu verwechseln. [...] Der Hiat zwischen dem Ort der Opfer und der Besucher muss sinnfällig gemacht werden, wenn das affektive Potenzial, was der Erinnerungsort mobilisiert, nicht zu einer ‚Horizontverschmelzung' und illusionären Identifikation führen soll."[19] Hier setzt die Idee von sinai Landschaftsarchitekten für die Neugestaltung der KZ-Gedenkstätte Bergen-Belsen an. Der groß dimensionierte Raum wirkte vor seiner Umgestaltung als landschaftlicher Leerraum mit wenigen, kleineren Objekten und damit quasi selbst als Monument des Unbegreiflichen. Die Geschichte des Nationalsozialismus und des Mordens wurde als ein Dimen-

The system of clearings demarcates the axis of the camp as well as its inner and outer perimeters.
Section 1:400

Das System der Rodungen kennzeichnet die Lagerachse sowie innere und äußere Grenzen.
Schnitt 1:400

Green corridor
60 m wide

Rasenkorridor
60 m breit

Prior to the redesign, the large expanse of space looked like an empty stretch of landscape with just a few, smaller objects and was itself so to speak a monument to the incomprehensible. The history of National Socialism and extermination was portrayed as a loss of dimensions of inconceivable proportions and as such refrained from any sense of individual mourning. This incomprehensibility was supposed to reflect the inhumanity – and this message the post-war design was able to convey.

By retracing the extents of the site, revealing its dimensions and measuring out the emptiness using removed sections of vegetation, sinai also reflect the phases of development of the camp in their design. Taking the woodland, now regrown, as their starting point, they have cut channels of cleared vegetation along the lines of the former borders of the camp. The broad strip of the main axis that was added later, when compared with the curving paths of the first camp, illustrates how much energy went into extending the camp during the war years. As ever-new sectors were added, these were connected via the camp road to the crematorium at the end of the route. The camp road is an especially important element for the design as it provides a dimensional reference through which, based on the aerial photograph from 1944, the positions of the info-steles and the concrete-cast models were determined.

sinai landscape architects elected in their design to accept the natural landscape, allowing it to stand in contrast to the documents of death and of survival, to the personal histories told in the information centre, and to the cleared corridors that delineate the extent of the grounds and mark out its history.

The result of the renewal of the memorial is not so much a place of individual mourning as a place of remembrance for a situation that remains incomprehensible. How can a society that has achieved so much, including things of beauty, so radically redefine the order of the civilised world, so immorally abuse it and barbarically violate it, and treat the lives of fellow human beings with such brutality?

Bergen-Belsen is a place of questions – and this is how visitors experience it today.

sionsverlust ohne greifbare Proportionen und damit ohne individuelle Betroffenheit inszeniert. Die Unbegreiflichkeit sollte der Unmenschlichkeit entsprechen – diese Aussage vermochte die Gestaltung der Nachkriegszeit zu treffen.

Wenn nun sinai das Areal wieder nachzeichnen, die Dimensionen zeigen, den Leerraum vermessen durch Rodungen, reflektieren sie im Entwurf auch die Phasen der Entwicklung des Lagers. Der Wald als Ausgangszustand wie als Aufwuchs wird durchschnitten von den gerodeten Schneisen entlang ehemaliger Grenzen der Lager. Die breite Schneise der später angelegten Hauptachse des Lagers zeigt im Vergleich zu den geschwungenen Wegen des ersten Arbeitslagers, mit welcher Dynamik die Lager in den Kriegsjahren erweitert wurden. Die immer neuen Sektoren waren durch diese Lagerstraße mit dem Krematorium am Ende der Trasse verbunden. Im Entwurf ist diese Lagerstraße ein besonders wichtiges, weil dimensionierendes Element, an dem die Informationsstelen sowie die in Beton gegossenen Modelle platziert sind, die nach dem Luftbild aus dem Jahr 1944 geformt wurden.

sinai Landschaftsarchitekten entschieden sich für die Akzeptanz des Landschaftlichen, das nun im Kontrast steht zu den Dokumenten des Todes und des Überlebens, zu den Geschichten, die im Informationszentrum erzählt werden, und zu den Einschnitten, die die Dimension des Ortes und der Geschichte markieren. Entstanden ist in der Überarbeitung der Gedenkstätte weniger ein Ort individuellen Trauerns als vielmehr der Erinnerungsort an eine unbegreifliche Situation. Wie kann eine Gesellschaft, die so vieles, auch Schönes umgibt, die Ordnung der zivilisierten Welt so radikal umdefinieren, Ordnung so unmoralisch missbrauchen und barbarisch durchbrechen, so brutal mit dem Leben, den Mitmenschen umgehen?

Ein Ort der Fragen – so erlebt der Besucher heute Bergen-Belsen.

Boundary between two
internment sections within the camp
7.5 m wide

Lagergrenzen/Sektoren
7,5 m breit

Outer perimeter
of the camp
10 m wide

Äußere Lagergrenze
10 m breit

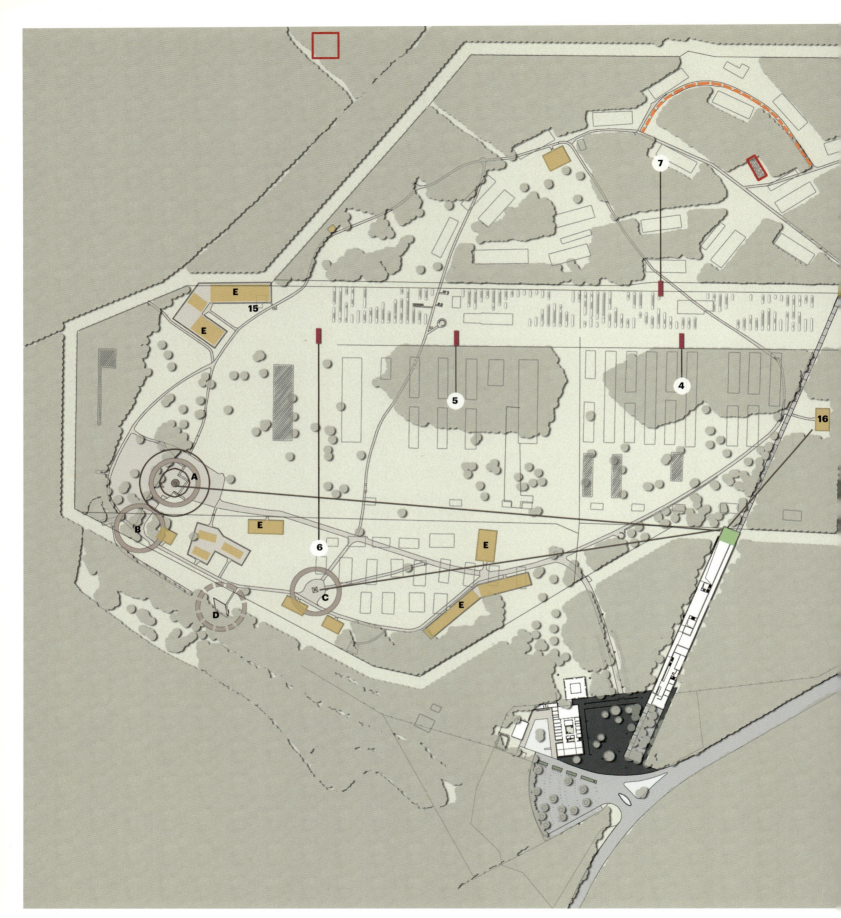

Master plan from 2005: Development aims include maintaining the memorial installations at the west end of the site (memorial area) and the securing of the few remaining built relics in the eastern section (exploration area) of the camp. The marking and didactic presentation of the historic sites has already been undertaken.

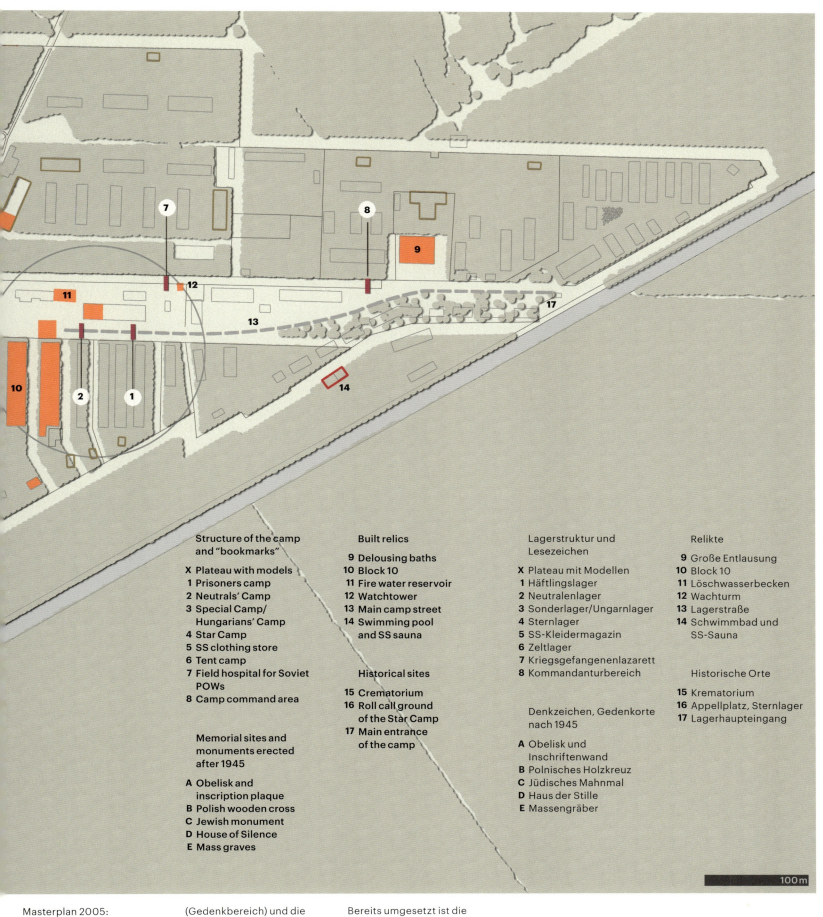

Structure of the camp and "bookmarks"

X Plateau with models
1 Prisoners camp
2 Neutrals' Camp
3 Special Camp/ Hungarians' Camp
4 Star Camp
5 SS clothing store
6 Tent camp
7 Field hospital for Soviet POWs
8 Camp command area

Memorial sites and monuments erected after 1945

A Obelisk and inscription plaque
B Polish wooden cross
C Jewish monument
D House of Silence
E Mass graves

Built relics

9 Delousing baths
10 Block 10
11 Fire water reservoir
12 Watchtower
13 Main camp street
14 Swimming pool and SS sauna

Historical sites

15 Crematorium
16 Roll call ground of the Star Camp
17 Main entrance of the camp

Lagerstruktur und Lesezeichen

X Plateau mit Modellen
1 Häftlingslager
2 Neutralenlager
3 Sonderlager/Ungarnlager
4 Sternlager
5 SS-Kleidermagazin
6 Zeltlager
7 Kriegsgefangenenlazarett
8 Kommandanturbereich

Denkzeichen, Gedenkorte nach 1945

A Obelisk und Inschriftenwand
B Polnisches Holzkreuz
C Jüdisches Mahnmal
D Haus der Stille
E Massengräber

Relikte

9 Große Entlausung
10 Block 10
11 Löschwasserbecken
12 Wachturm
13 Lagerstraße
14 Schwimmbad und SS-Sauna

Historische Orte

15 Krematorium
16 Appellplatz, Sternlager
17 Lagerhaupteingang

100 m

Masterplan 2005: Entwicklungsziele sind der pflegende Erhalt der Gedenkinstallationen im Westen (Gedenkbereich) und die Sicherung der wenigen erhaltenen baulichen Relikte im Osten (Erkundungsbereich). Bereits umgesetzt ist die Markierung und didaktische Aufbereitung historischer Orte.

**Stony path next to the
historic roll call grounds**

Steinerner Weg am
historischen Appellplatz

The twin models in the plateau make it possible to compare the historical and current situation of the site.

Vergleich der historischen mit der heutigen Situation im Doppelmodell am Plateau

Corridor marking the boundary between two internment
sections within the camp

Schneise zur Kennzeichnung
einer Grenze zwischen
Häftlingsbereichen

Fire water basin and vege-
table cellar as topographical
depressions in the mown
corridor

Löschwasserbecken und
Gemüsekeller als topo-
grafische Einschnitte im
Rasenkorridor

Route of the camp road
as a mown strip in the grass
corridor

Verlauf der Lagerstraße
als gemähter Streifen im
Rasenkorridor

End wall of the documen-
tation centre where it meets
the boundary of the former
camp

Gebäudekopf des
Dokumentationszentrums
an der Lagergrenze

Forum Vogelsang, Euskirchen/Eifel
2008–2014

Forum Vogelsang, Euskirchen/Eifel
2008–2014

**vogelsang ip/Eifel
– Ideology, Identity,
Internationalism**

vogelsang ip/Eifel
– Ideologie, Identität,
Internationalität

1
Ley, Robert: Der Weg zur Ordensburg, Special edition by the Reich Organisation Leader of the NSDAP, n.d.

1
Ley, Robert: Der Weg zur Ordensburg, Sonderdruck des Reichsorganisations-leiters der NSDAP

Vogelsang in the Eifel mountains not only has the ring of birdsong to its name but also commands a position in the landscape that could hardly be more perfect. At this exceptional location, a new project is currently under construction: the vogelsang ip – vogelsang international place. This information, conference and recreation centre in the Eifel National Park is being built on the site of an exceptionally complicated property: Vogelsang was originally built as an *Ordensburg* for the National Socialists.

The embedding of this complex of buildings, one of the largest built legacies of the Nazi era, in an impressive natural setting was an explicit aim of the National Socialist German Workers' Party (NSDAP) and the German Labour Front (DAF). The *Ordensburgen* were the brainchild of the Reich Organisation Leader Dr. Robert Ley and were conceived as schools for the "training of political leaders". On the occasion of the presentation of the first *Ordensburg* at Vogelsang to Adolf Hitler in 1936, Ley himself described the *Ordensburg* as being part of a National Socialist education system founded on strict selection, and gave a speech rich in ideological imagery: "Standing alone in the Eifel, not far from Gemünd, lies Burg Vogelsang. From a cleft in the valley, a sliver of the Urftsee glints out of the depths at us like a vast bar of silver. Defiantly, the towers and walls clasp the hills and mountains. Nothing lies between them and the landscape; they are part of the landscape. They are landscape, these walls, these halls, these proud towers, because we were purposefully of a mind not to dispel nature but to place it in the service of the great work. Despite the massive dimensions of the Burg, the essence and fundamental laws of the scenery of the landscape have been observed; their natural elements not only remain visible but heighten the immensity of the overall impression."[1]

Vogelsang in der Eifel ist nicht nur ein wohlklingender Name, sondern auch ein Ort, der wie nur wenige landschaftlich perfekt gewählt ist. An diesem herausgehobenen Ort entsteht derzeit vogelsang ip – vogelsang international place. Dieses Informations-, Tagungs- und Freizeitzentrum im Nationalpark Eifel nutzt eine äußerst komplizierte Immobilie. Denn erbaut wurde Vogelsang als „Ordensburg" der Nationalsozialisten.

Die beeindruckende landschaftliche Einbettung dieses Baukomplexes, der zu den größten baulichen Hinterlassenschaften des NS-Regimes gehört, war explizites Planungsziel der Nationalsozialistischen Deutschen Arbeiterpartei NSDAP und der Deutschen Arbeitsfront DAF. Auf deren Reichsorganisationsleiter Dr. Robert Ley gehen die Ordensburgen als Einrichtungen zur „Erziehung der politischen Leiter" zurück. Ley selbst hat diese Ordensburg als Teil eines auf strikte Selektion gegründeten nationalsozialistischen Bildungssystems anlässlich der Übergabe der ersten Ordensburg Vogelsang an Adolf Hitler im Jahr 1936 wortreich und voller ideologischer Bilder beschrieben: „Einsam in der Eifel, unweit von Gemünd, liegt die Burg Vogelsang. Aus einem Taleinschnitt blinkt in der Tiefe, wie ein großer Silberbarren, ein Stück des Urftsees zu uns herauf. Trutzig greifen Turm und Mauern über die Hügel und Berge. Nichts Trennendes legen sie zwischen sich und die Landschaft, sie sind Landschaft. Sie sind Landschaft, diese Mauern, diese Hallen, dieser stolze Turm, weil man zielbewusst darauf bedacht war, die Natur nicht zu verdrängen, sondern sie dem großen Werk dienstbar zu machen. Trotz der gewaltigen Dimensionen der Burg sind Wesen und Lebensgesetze der landschaftlichen Szenerie gewahrt worden, ihre natürlichen Elemente bleiben nicht nur sichtbar, sondern steigern das Gesamtbild ins Gigantische."[1]

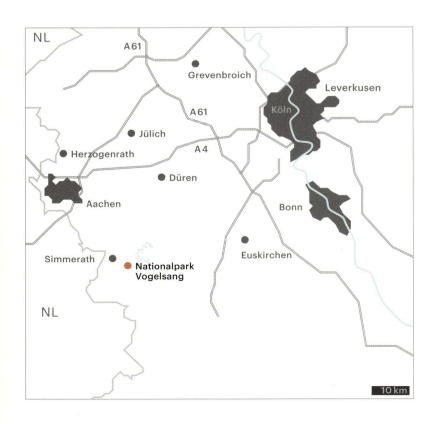

2
Ritter, Joachim: "Landschaft"
(1963), in: Ritter, Joachim:
Subjektivität, Frankfurt a. M.
1974, p. 141
3
Ibid., p. 146

2
Ritter, Joachim: Landschaft
(1963), in: Ritter, Joachim:
Subjektivität, Frankfurt a. M.
1974, S. 141
3
Ebda., S. 146

Today, the view over the landscape from this elevated position at Vogelsang still conveys a sense of what Petrarca must have felt, as one of "the first of the moderns", on ascending Mont Ventoux in Provence in 1335 where he recounts that he "had seen and appreciated the shape of the landscape as something more or less beautiful".[2] Petrarca's mountain climb was a reflection on the aesthetic enjoyment of nature as landscape: "Nature as landscape is the result and product of theoretical thought."[3] Immanuel Kant comprehensively examines the basis of this deliberation in his philosophy of aesthetics, *The Critique of Judgement*, defining the appreciation of "beauty" as that of being in a state of "disinterested pleasure", whereby he differentiates between the aesthetic judgement of the beautiful and the sublime from that of teleological judgement concerned with purpose.

In Ley's description of the *Ordensburg* as landscape, however, aesthetic judgement, and with it the idea of scenic landscape, is exploited for personal aims and the interests of his party. Instead of disinterested pleasure, Kant's basis for the judgement of beauty, the National Socialists used the idea of the beautiful landscape as an ideological motif. Landscape becomes an argument, as does the attraction of beauty, in a fanatical speech on the principles of selection, leadership and racial ideology. This fascist biologism of aesthetics in the landscape ideology of National Socialism continues to weigh on our understanding of landscape to the present day.

Der erhöhte Blick über die Landschaft von diesem Ort Vogelsang aus vermittelt heute noch, was Petrarca 1335 bei der Besteigung des Mont Ventoux in der Provence als einer der „frühesten unter den Modernen" empfand, die „die Gestalt der Landschaft als etwas mehr oder weniger Schönes wahrgenommen und genossen haben".[2] Petrarca begründete mit dieser Bergbesteigung das ästhetische Verhältnis zur Natur als Landschaft. „Natur als Landschaft ist Frucht und Erzeugnis des theoretischen Geistes."[3] Immanuel Kant hat die Grundlagen dieser Überlegungen in seiner Philosophie der Ästhetik, der *Kritik der Urteilskraft*, maßgeblich untersucht und das Empfinden von „Schönheit" als „interesseloses Wohlgefallen" definiert, womit er das ästhetische, auf Schönheit und Erhabenheit orientierte Urteil vom teleologischen, auf Zweckmäßigkeit bezogenen Urteil unterscheidet. Ley allerdings instrumentalisiert in seiner Beschreibung der Ordensburgen als Landschaft das ästhetische Urteil, und damit die Idee des Landschaftsbildes schlechthin, für seine Interessen und die Interessen seiner Partei. Statt interesselosem Wohlgefallen, für Immanuel Kant die Grundlage für ein Urteil über das Schöne, nutzen die Nationalsozialisten diese Idee der schönen Landschaft als ideologisches Motiv. Landschaft wird als Argument und Anreiz der Schönheit eingebunden in eine fanatische Betonung von Prinzipien der Auslese, Führungsstärke und Rassenideologie. Dieser faschistische Biologismus des Ästhetischen in der Landschaftsideologie des Nationalsozialismus belastet unser Verständnis von Landschaft bis heute.

Vogelsang 1940
View of the complex from
the Kermeter hills

Vogelsang 1940
Blick auf die Gesamtanlage
vom Kermeter

Scenic beauty – ideological purpose

Today and in the future, a place like Vogelsang is both a logical as well as a problematic place from which to communicate the qualities of a national park. On the one hand, the location itself needs careful explanation, and on the other, the landscape speaks for itself and is beguiling in its beauty. Can one use landscape architecture to negate the ideological exploitation of the effect of landscape? Then again, is this even desirable given that the beauty of the Eifel region is what attracts people to visit and find out about this place and its history?

For sinai, these questions present themselves directly in their work on the Vogelsang project. Together with vogelsang ip and the Berlin-based architecture office Mola+Winkelmüller, the landscape architects are responsible for designing and making this place accessible. Unlike many of sinai's other projects, this place is not about the victims of National Socialism but about the perpetrators themselves, who came here to receive comprehensive and cultural training in inhumanity. Alongside training in physical fitness, racial doctrine, resolute leadership and self-control, the future leaders of the NS-regime were also expected to learn diplomatic skills, an interest in culture, and to experience the most beautiful landscapes in Germany and their people. The landscape itself was therefore a part of this monstrous ideal of a culture of domination.

In cases like Vogelsang, where nature conservation aspects are to be communicated in a national park information centre on the site of a former NSDAP *Ordensburg*, it is important to clearly differentiate between the National Socialist idea of landscape and a conservation-oriented idea of the landscape that is rooted in nature protection and cultural heritage. Any restoration or development of both the built and the natural heritage must avoid repeating the problematic ideological attribution of landscape.

Landschaftliche Schönheit – ideologische Wirkung

An einem Ort wie Vogelsang heute und in Zukunft über einen Naturpark zu informieren, ist einerseits schlüssig, andererseits aber ein heikles Unterfangen. Der Ort benötigt sehr viel Erklärung, die Landschaft spricht andererseits unmittelbar für sich selbst und blendet mit ihrer Schönheit. Kann man mit Mitteln der Landschaftsarchitektur diese ideologisch ausgenutzte Wirkung von Landschaft brechen? Will man dies überhaupt, wo doch die Schönheit der Eifel gerade Anreiz ist für die Neugierde der Besucher auf diesen Ort und seine Geschichte?

Für sinai stellen sich diese Fragen ganz unmittelbar in der Arbeit am Projekt Vogelsang. Gemeinsam mit vogelsang ip und den Berliner Architekten Mola+Winkelmüller sind die Landschaftsarchitekten verantwortlich für die Gestaltung und Erschließung dieses Ortes. Dieser Ort ist, anders als bei anderen Projekten von sinai, nicht auf die Opfer des Nationalsozialismus zu beziehen, sondern auf die Täter selbst, die hier eine umfassende, auch kulturelle Bildung zur Unmenschlichkeit erhielten. Diplomatisches Geschick, kulturelles Interesse, ein Erleben der schönsten Landschaften Deutschlands und ihrer Bewohner sollten die NS-Führungskräfte ebenso erfahren und erproben wie körperliche Leistungsfähigkeit, Rassenlehre, Entschluss- und Führungskraft und Selbstbeherrschung. Die Landschaft selbst war Teil dieses monströsen Ideals einer Herrschaftskultur.

Gerade wenn es im Projekt Vogelsang heute darum geht, Inhalte des Naturschutzes in einem Nationalparkzentrum am Ort der ehemaligen Ordensburg der NSDAP zu vermitteln, muss die NS-Landschaftsidee genau von der konservativen Idee der Landschaft, auf die Natur- und Heimatschutz zurückgehen, unterschieden werden. Denn eine Pflege und Entwicklung dieses baulichen und landschaftlichen Erbes darf nicht in der Wiederholung einer fragwürdigen Ideologisierung von Landschaft münden.

The monumental west wing of the Adlerhof with the panorama of the Eifel National Park behind
—
Roll call ground enclosed by the solid stone wall of the north facade of the Adlerhof

Der monumentale Westflügel des Adlerhofs vor dem landschaftlichen Panorama des Nationalparks Eifel
—
Appellplatz vor der mächtigen Nordfassade des Adlerhofs

4
Trepl, Ludwig: Die Idee der
Landschaft, Bielefeld 2012,
p.190ff.

4
Trepl, Ludwig: Die Idee der
Landschaft, Bielefeld 2012,
S.190 f.

Ludwig Trepl, in his investigation into the cultural history of the idea of landscape from the age of Enlightenment to the ecological movement, undertakes an attempt at differentiation: "The idea of the landscape was of great ideological relevance for National Socialism. [...] In the ideas of liberalism (by contrast) landscape is of little relevance. But in the other influential and progressive worldview, democratic Enlightenment, the landscape [...] is indeed accorded a role. The idea of virtue in a democratic sense was, after all, a key idea in the origin of the landscaped garden. Kant's notion of the sublime, which can be ascribed to the same tradition, also accords a high status to the sight of particular landscape phenomena: through it one is made conscious of the highest significance of mankind. But here too, the importance of the idea of landscape remains comparatively modest compared with the importance it is accorded in worldviews that are generally regarded as being non-progressive: the romantic, the conservative, and also that of national socialism.

In the conservative worldview, landscape was of similarly outstanding significance as in National Socialism. But the significance was another. This is often, or perhaps even most of the time, wrongly understood: the ideology of National Socialism is imagined to be a radicalisation of the conservative, i.e. that it is in essence similar; the differentiation is not qualitative but quantitative. "[4]

Eine solche Differenzierung leistet beispielsweise Ludwig Trepl, der die Idee der Landschaft als Kulturgeschichte von der Aufklärung bis zur Ökologiebewegung untersucht hat. „Die Idee der Landschaft war für den Nationalsozialismus von größter ideologischer Relevanz. [...] In der Gedankenwelt des Liberalismus ist die Landschaft (dagegen) kaum relevant. In der anderen einflussreichen progressiven Weltanschauung, der demokratischen Aufklärung, kommt der Landschaft [...] zwar durchaus eine Rolle zu. Immerhin war der Gedanke der Tugend im demokratischen Sinn ein wesentliches Motiv bei der Entstehung des Landschaftsgartens. Auch gab die kantische Deutung des Erhabenen, die man dieser Traditionslinie zuordnen kann, dem Anblick bestimmter landschaftlicher Phänomene einen hohen Rang: Man wurde sich anhand ihrer der höchsten Bestimmung des Menschen bewusst. Aber auch hier nimmt sich die Bedeutung der Landschaftsidee eher bescheiden aus, vergleicht man sie mit dem, was man mit ihr in den Weltanschauungen verbindet, die man gewöhnlich als nicht-progressiv einordnet: der romantischen, der konservativen und eben auch der nationalsozialistischen.

In der konservativen Weltanschauung hatte Landschaft eine ähnlich überragende Bedeutung wie im Nationalsozialismus. Aber es war eine ganz andere. Das wird oft, vielleicht sogar meist, falsch gesehen: Man hält die nationalsozialistische Ideologie für eine Radikalisierung der konservativen, also für im Wesen gleich, für nicht qualitativ unterschieden, sondern nur quantitativ."[4]

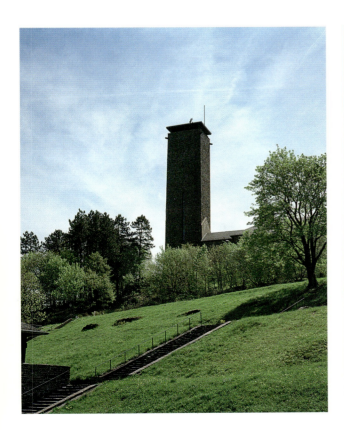

The "keep" of the Adlerhof:
a landmark in the landscape

Bergfried des Adlerhofs als
landschaftliche Dominante

Can current landscape architecture respond adequately to such an ideologically amplified idea of landscape? Should not a landscape like that in the Eifel, which has served so directly as a testimony of the greatness of an ideology and a race, be removed from view, obscured or altered in some way? Can a landscape be laid to blame simply because it is beautiful?

According to Trepl, it is both possible and instructive to differentiate between conservative and National Socialist ideals of the landscape even when "prominent conservatives such as Martin Heidegger or Carl Schmitt" or other "important people in this context" such as the "architect [...] and preservationist Paul Schultze-Naumburg", the "Reichlandschaftsanwalt [Landscape Counsel of the Reich] Alwin Seifert" or the "nature conservationist Walther Schoenichen initially welcomed National Socialism with open arms." Furthermore, it appears that "at least at first glance the radicalisation hypothesis would seem to be plausible for some aspects [...] such as for authority, nationalism and militarism. Nevertheless, this hypothesis is wrong. There is a qualitative difference and the structure of both ideologies differs fundamentally. This can be seen

Kann aktuelle Landschaftsarchitektur auf eine derartige ideologische Überhöhung der Landschaft angemessen reagieren? Muss die Landschaft selbst, die dort in der Eifel so unmittelbar als Zeugnis der Bedeutung einer Ideologie, einer Rasse genutzt wurde, nicht eigentlich von der Bildfläche verschwinden, verhängt und verstellt werden? Kann Landschaft aufgrund ihrer Schönheit Schuld auf sich laden?

Folgt man Trepl, ist eine Unterscheidung von konservativen und nationalsozialistischen Landschaftsidealen möglich und sinnvoll, auch wenn "prominente Konservative wie Martin Heidegger oder Carl Schmitt" oder die "für unsere Fragen wichtige[n] Personen" wie der "Architekt [...] und Heimatschützer Paul Schultze-Naumburg", der "Reichslandschaftsanwalt Alwin Seifert" oder der "Naturschützer Walther Schoenichen den Nationalsozialismus zumindest zunächst begeistert begrüßten". Zudem scheint "zumindest bei flüchtiger Betrachtung die Radikalisierungsthese für bestimmte Themen eine gewisse Plausibilität zu haben [...], etwa für Autorität, Nationalismus und Militarismus. Dennoch ist diese These falsch. Der Unterschied ist qualitativ, die Struktur beider Ideologien unterscheidet sich grundlegend. Das erkennt man an der jeweiligen Idee der Landschaft besonders deutlich.

View overlooking the Urftsee, a local attraction in the Eifel even before its appropriation by the National Socialists

Blick auf den Urftsees: Bereits vor der Inbesitznahme durch die Nationalsozialisten ein Anziehungspunkt in der Eiffel

5
Ibid., p.191 ff.

5
Ebda., S.191 f.

clearly in their respective ideas of landscape. A first clue in this respect can be found by comparing their respective relationships to technical progress. For the conservative critique of civilisation, this represents the destruction of the landscape, of the organic unity of land and people." By contrast, "the relationship of National Socialism not only to the (traditional German) landscape, but also to technical and industrial progress was euphoric. [...] How was National Socialist ideology able to unite what for conservatism was held to be irreconcilable? This was made possible by finding a racist reinterpretation for the idea of the unity of land and people. This reinterpretation was a product of the Blood-and-Soil theory. It was racism that made possible the combination of homeland cult and technological euphoria, and it also made possible the combination of territorial expansionism in a form that would have been unthinkable in the conservative idea of landscape."[5]
The objective of the project is therefore to intelligently combine a National Park Centre dedicated to conserving the scenic beauty of the landscape and the natural habitat with an explicitly anti-fascist and anti-racist approach to the redevelopment of the form and content of the site. The fact that the declared educational focus of the Ordensburg Vogelsang was to educate its cadets in the racial ideology of National Socialism makes this all the more important. At Vogelsang, an appropriate response to this problem has been found with the creation of the international place.

Um einen ersten Hinweis zu erhalten, muss man sich nur das Verhältnis beider zum technischen Fortschritt vor Augen führen. Für die konservative Zivilisationskritik bedeutet dieser eine Zerstörung von Landschaft, also von organischen Land-und-Leute-Einheiten." Dagegen war „das Verhältnis des Nationalsozialismus nicht nur zur (traditionellen deutschen) Landschaft, sondern auch zum technisch-industriellen Fortschritt euphorisch. [...] Wie ließ sich in der NS-Ideologie vereinen, was für den Konservatismus unversöhnliche Gegensätze waren? Sie zu vereinen wurde möglich durch eine rassistische Umdeutung der Idee der Land-und-Leute-Einheit. Eben diese Umdeutung nahm die Blut-und-Boden-Theorie vor. Es war der Rassismus, der die Verbindung von Heimatkult und Technikeuphorie ermöglichte, und er ermöglichte auch die Verbindung mit einem territorialen Expansionismus, wie er in der konservativen Landschaftsvorstellung unmöglich war."[5]
Es gilt also ein Nationalparkzentrum, das sich der Bewahrung der landschaftlichen Schönheit und des Naturraumes verpflichtet sieht, hier am Standort Vogelsang intelligent zu verknüpfen mit einer explizit antifaschistischen, antirassistischen Haltung in Inhalt und Form der Weiterentwicklung dieses Ortes. Dies ist um so wichtiger, weil der Ausbildungsschwerpunkt auf der Ordensburg Vogelsang explizit die NS-Rassenideologie sein sollte. Mit dem international place ist für Vogelsang eine solche Antwort gefunden worden.

Covered walkway of the Adlerhof framing an iconic vista of the Urftsee

Wandelhalle des Adlerhofs als Rahmung des „Urftseeblicks"

6
Ley, op. cit.

6
Ley, a.a.O.

What was an *Ordensburg*?

Reich Organisation Leader Ley described the concept behind the *Ordensburgen* in the following words: "The [...] three *Ordensburgen* are totally new constructions [in addition to Vogelsang in the Eifel region, two further *Ordensburgen* were built between 1934 and 1936 in Krössinsee in Pomerania and Sonthofen in Allgäu, Bavaria]. Where they now stand, was nothing previously. It was my opinion that the National Socialist idea cannot be proclaimed and preached from within old walls. As new and revolutionary these ideas are, as great and worthy the German people are, so must the buildings be in which our leaders will be trained."[6]

Nearly 2,000 aspiring leaders of National Socialism received training in Vogelsang before the site was needed for military purposes at the beginning of the Second World War. After its capture by the Allied Forces, Vogelsang was used as a military barracks until 2005. Today, wars are waged in other ways, tanks are used less often, and the training grounds used to practice with these weapons have not been used since the end of the Cold War. Planners have since been entrusted with the conversion of these military land holdings.

The Vogelsang Development Company steers the conversion process of some 100 hectares of land on behalf of the Institute of Federal Real Estate (BImA) with the aim of lending the development of the location an integrated and clear profile. The first project to be undertaken is the Forum Vogelsang. This project paves the way for the development of this special site and for dealing with this difficult historic monument.

Was war eine Ordensburg?

Über die Idee der NS-Ordensburg ließ sich Reichsorganisationsleiter Ley mit den folgenden Worten aus: „Die [...] drei Ordensburgen [neben Vogelsang in der Eifel wurden zwischen 1934 und 1936 noch die Ordensburgen Krössinsee in Pommern sowie Sonthofen im Allgäu gebaut] sind vollkommen neu erbaut. Wo sie heute stehen, war vorher nichts. Ich war der Meinung, dass man die nationalsozialistische Idee nicht in alten Gemäuern verkünden und predigen kann. Genauso, wie diese Idee neu und revolutionär, groß und würdig des deutschen Volkes ist, mussten auch die Gebäude sein, in denen unsere Führer herangebildet werden."[6]

Ca. 2.000 Führungskräfte des Nationalsozialismus wurden in Vogelsang ausgebildet, bevor der Ort im Zweiten Weltkrieg für militärische Aufgaben benötigt wurde. Nach dem Sieg der Alliierten blieb Vogelsang bis 2005 Kaserne. Heute jedoch werden Kriege auf andere Art geführt, Panzer immer weniger benötigt, die Flächen für die Übung mit diesen Waffen fielen mit dem Ende der Frontstellung der Blöcke des Kalten Krieges brach. Konversion militärischer Liegenschaften wurde zur Aufgabe der Planer.

Die Standortentwicklungsgesellschaft Vogelsang steuert diesen Konversionsprozess für die rund 100 ha große Liegenschaft der Bundesanstalt für Immobilienaufgaben im Sinne einer integrierenden Standortentwicklung mit klarem Profil. Das Initialprojekt stellt das Forum Vogelsang dar. Es soll wegweisend sein für die Entwicklung dieses besonderen Ortes und den Umgang mit diesem schwierigen Baudenkmal.

Accommodation for the *Ordensjunker*: barracks for the cadets below the Adlerhof

Unterkunft für die Ordensjunker: Kameradschaftshäuser unter dem Adlerhof

A park plateau

A key role in the development of Vogelsang to vogelsang ip is the park plateau. At a central position on the extensive site, originally intended for the building of a vast "House of Knowledge" housing a library and classrooms, of which by 1945 only the foundations had been completed, an international meeting place is being created. At this pivotal location for the site and for the concept, sinai landscape architects have designed the Vogelsang Open Air Theater. A sunken area with stage, theatre balcony and a secondary stage and a forum are embedded like a clearing in a stretch of woodland. The plateau is defined by the space enclosed by the foundation walls of the originally planned „House of Knowledge". The design needed to respond sensitively to a range of aspects as well as avoid establishing any unintentional, problematic references. The selection of tree species, for example, can be seen as both a sign and a statement: the plan envisages a free arrangement of Scots pine (an indigenous species) and a native variant of Norway maple along with Japanese pagoda trees. sinai note that they were only permitted to use these trees under certain conditions: "The use of tree species that do not conform to those found in the National Park requires that measures be taken to prevent their seed from spreading into the National Park." In this context, any choice of wording, however sensible it may be, should prompt us to consider the origins of our ideas of landscape and nature.

A new orientation system and a network of paths connect the park plateau with the other elements at Vogelsang. A conference centre, youth hostel, forest guesthouse for young people and hotel augment the functions on the plateau and are housed in new buildings. The new functions of the "Forum" on the Adlerhof, designed by Mola + Winkelmüller architects, have for the most part been integrated into the existing pattern of trees. The "Burgschänke", the former tavern, has been retained as a legacy of the National Socialist history of the site as has the historically listed bowling alley. The other exhibition areas, i.e. the documentation of the site's National Socialist past, the so-called "Schaufenster Eifel-Ardennes" describing the region and the National Park Centre will be integrated into the existing buildings.

Das Parkplateau

Eine Schlüsselbedeutung für die Entwicklung von Vogelsang zum vogelsang ip hat das Parkplateau. Am zentralen Standort des weitläufigen Geländes, der ehemals vorgesehen war für ein riesiges „Haus des Wissens" mit Bibliothek und Schulungsräumen, von denen bis 1945 nur die Grundmauern fertig gestellt waren, entsteht ein internationaler Ort der Begegnung. sinai Landschaftsarchitekten entwarfen für diesen ideellen und räumlichen Gravitationsort des Areals das Vogelsang Open Air Theater. Ein abgesenkter Platz mit Bühne und Theaterbalkon mit einer Nebenbühne und einem Forum werden lichtungsartig in einen Waldsaum eingebettet. Das Plateau ergibt sich aus den Grundmauern des ehemals geplanten „Hauses des Wissens". Die Planung war sensibel auf viele Bezüge und auch auf ungewollte problematische Bezugnahmen hin zu überprüfen. Die Auswahl der Bäume beispielsweise für diesen Ort ist auch als Zeichen und Statement zu verstehen: In freier Baumstellung finden wir die Wald-Kiefer (einheimische Art) und den heimischen Spitz-Ahorn gemeinsam mit dem Japanischen Schnurbaum. sinai weisen bewusst darauf hin, dass die Verwendung dieser Baumart zu Auflagen führte: „Bei der Verwendung von nicht-nationalparkkonformen Gehölzen ist darauf zu achten, dass diese sich nicht in den National-park aussamen können." Hier ist jede Formulierung, sinnvoll oder nicht, immer auch ein Anlass, sich über die Herkunft unserer Vorstellungen von Landschaft und Natur Gedanken zu machen.

Das Parkplateau ist durch ein neues Wege- und Orientierungssystem mit weiteren Angeboten am Standort Vogelsang verbunden. Ein Tagungszentrum, Jugendherberge, Jugendwaldheim und Hotel ergänzen die Nutzungen am Plateau in neuen Gebäuden. Die neuen Funktionen des „Forums" am Adlerhof werden durch Mola + Winkelmüller Architekten vor allem in den vorhandenen Baubestand integriert. Erhalten bleiben die „Burgschänke" und die denkmalgeschützte Kegelbahn als Exponate der NS-Geschichte. Die weiteren Ausstellungsbereiche, d.h. die NS-Dokumentation, das Schaufenster – Eifel-Ardennen – als Regionalschau sowie das Nationalparkzentrum werden in die Bauten integriert.

The surviving buildings of the Ordensburg are kept and their ideological meaning explained. For the east wing near the tower, an exhibition on the National Park is planned, the architecural design of which takes its cue from the topography. One further but conspicuous intervention by the architects signals that this place goes further than conserving a National Socialist site, creating instead a new place in the context of its history. The "Schaufenster Eifel" is a new visitor and service centre that is immediately visible on reaching the site as its contemporary architecture subverts the pre-existing hierarchy of spaces and axes. This window onto the landscape is the most important of the new building structures for the site which Mola + Winkelmüller have described as "inlays". Situated in amidst the existing buildings, the new building is the centre of attention, drawing visitors in and then – by physically breaking through the existing structure – towards a large newly-created window opening offering a panoramic view over the landscape of the Eifel. This new view of the Eifel is also symbolically important in that it emphasises the outlook and the situation while disengaging the view of the landscape from the ideology of the builders of the *Ordensburg*.

Die baulichen Zeugnisse werden in ihrer ideologischen Bedeutung erläutert. Im Ostflügel nahe dem Turm wird eine Ausstellung zum Natonalpark zu sehen sein, gezeigt in einer topografisch bewegten Ausstellungsarchitektur. Mit einem einzigen deutlich sichtbaren Eingriff zeigen die Architekten allerdings, dass hier nicht ein Ort der Nationalsozialisten konserviert, sondern ein neuer Ort in Kenntnis dieser Geschichte geschaffen wird. Mit dem Schaufenster Eifel, dem neuen Besucher- und Servicezentrum, das als bauliche Hinzufügung sofort zu erkennen ist, durchbricht die heutige Architektur die ehemalige Hierarchie der Räume und Blicke. Dieser Durchblick auf die Landschaft ist das wichtigste der neuen baulichen Strukturen, die Mola + Winkelmüller als „Inlays" bezeichnen. Inmitten der Bauten lenkt dieses Zentrum den Blick auf sich und dann – aufgrund des physischen Aufbrechens der Strukturen – durch einen großen Fensterdurchbruch auf die Eifellandschaft. Dieser neue Blick auf die Eifel ist auch symbolisch von Bedeutung, unterstreicht er doch die Position, diesen Ort und diese Landschaft nicht der Ideologie der Erbauer der Ordensburgen zu überlassen.

Mastering the terrain: monumental topographic structures are a part of the architecture

Beherrschung des Reliefs: monumentale topografische Bauwerke als Teil der Architektur

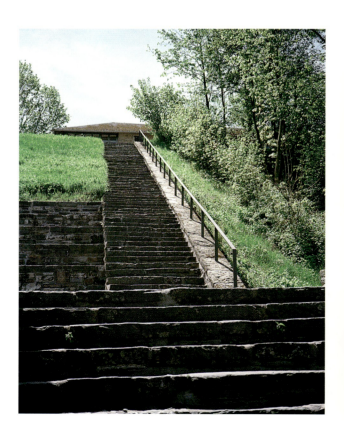

Heritage protection and extermination

As in the past, future visitors to Vogelsang will remember it in connection with an incomparable view of the outstanding beauty of the Eifel landscape and the Urftsee lake. This view can be seen from the windows and the terrace of Vogelsang. For the new National Park Information and Service Centre, this view – now re-framed – is just as iconic as it was for the National Socialist "elite" that were selected to be sent to the Ordensburg. These so-called *Ordensjunker* (literally "Young Lords of the Order") or *Stammesführer* (racial leaders) were later deployed in leading positions in Eastern Europe in particular, for example as District Commissioners in the Reich Commissariats of the Ukraine and of the "Eastern Land" (Baltic countries and Belarussia), and played an instrumental role in the extermination of the Jewish population and other Nazi crimes against civilians. This contradiction between the stimulating aesthetic impression of the landscape and ideologically motivated totalitarian subjugation and extermination is immanent in Vogelsang.

The impressive view from this point, that would later become the location of an *Ordensburg*, was discovered by the architect Clemens Klotz from Cologne, who was also responsible for designing another *Ordensburg* in Pomerania as well as the vast "*Kraft durch Freude*" (Strength through Joy) beach resort in Prora on the Baltic Coast. Klotz carefully incorporated the view over the landscape into the design of the buildings. At the same time the buildings, which mark the landscape and adhere to the *Heimatschutz* (homeland protection) style, are modern in their structure. The Ordensburg was hailed as a "triumph of technology" (Ley).

Heimatschutz und Vernichtung

In Erinnerung an den Ort Vogelsang bleibt auch zukünftig ein unvergleichlich schöner Blick über die außergewöhnliche Eifellandschaft mit dem Urftsee im Kopf. Dieser Blick bietet sich aus den Fenstern und von den Terrassen von Vogelsang. Für das heutige Naturpark-Informations- und Freizeitzentrum ist dieser – hier neu inszenierte – Blick ebenso prägend, wie er es für die auf die Ordensburg entsandte „Auslese" der NS-Faschisten war. Diese „Ordensjunker" oder „Stammesführer" waren gerade im Osten in führenden Stellungen etwa als Gebietskommissare in den Reichskommissariaten Ukraine und Ostland maßgeblich an der planmäßigen Ermordung der jüdischen Bevölkerung und weiterer NS-Verbrechen gegen die Zivilgesellschaft beteiligt. Dieser Widerspruch aus anregender Landschaftsästhetik und ideologisch motivierter, totalitärer Eroberung und Vernichtung bleibt diesem Ort Vogelsang immanent.

Entdeckt wurde der beeindruckende Blick, der dann zum Ort einer Ordensburg wurde, vom Kölner Architekten Clemens Klotz, der auch für den Entwurf einer weiteren Ordensburg in Pommern sowie für das KdF-Seebad Prora auf Rügen verantwortlich war. Dem Blick über die Landschaft sind die Bauten von Klotz in besonderer Weise angepasst. Zugleich sind diese das Landschaftsbild prägenden, im Heimatschutzstil gehaltenen Gebäude der Ordensburg Vogelsang durchaus modern strukturiert. Die Ordensburgen galten als „Triumph der Technik" (Ley).

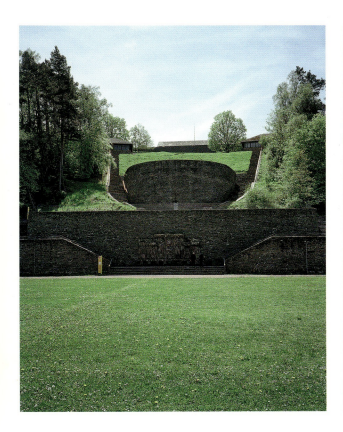

Ideological recreation: the "Thingplatz", an assembly or meeting place, overlooking the sports ground

Ideologisches Freiraumprogramm: Der „Thingplatz" über den Sportanlagen

Today, one might respectfully speak of these buildings, which display a mixture of homeland protection style and modernism, as a rural style of building. An architectural style that blends into its surroundings and at the same time makes a demonstrative statement that pays tribute to the landscape in which it sits, presents an ideological image of extraordinary coherence. For today's architects and landscape architects, this degree of coherence must be approached with care: the landscape here is quite obviously not the antecedent, original, pure imagery, the other of culture, the image of freedom which we attribute to the idea of nature, especially for the purposes of tourism or in the design of gardens. Landscape in its beauty, can also be used to lend expression to ideologies that are inhuman. How then can this landscape be communicated in the present day?

Heute würde man angesichts dieser Bauten in ihrer Mischung aus Heimatschutzstil und Moderne respektvoll von landschaftlichem Bauen sprechen. Eine Architektur, die sich derart zurücknimmt und zugleich so deutliche Zeichen setzt, indem sie dem Landschaftsraum huldigt, ist eine ideologische Inszenierung von hoher Stimmigkeit. Den Landschaftsarchitekten und Architekten der Gegenwart muss diese Stimmigkeit zu denken geben: Ist doch Landschaft hier ganz offensichtlich nicht die vorgängige, ursprüngliche, reine Bilderwelt, das Andere der Kultur, die Freiheit, als die wir Landschaft als Abbild unserer Idee von Natur auch heute häufig verherrlichen, gerade im Tourismus und in der Gartenkunst. Landschaft kommt in ihrer Schönheit auch zum Nutzen menschenverachtender Ideologien zum Ausdruck. Wie ist diese Landschaft heute zu inszenieren?

Military pragmatism: a further layer of built remains left over from the Belgian Army's use of the site as a military training ground.

Militärischer Pragmatismus: Die Jahre als Truppenübungsplatz der belgischen Armee haben eine eigene bauliche Schicht hinterlassen.

Everyday activities but not trivialised

Today, the buildings are to be re-used for tourism purposes, with multi-functional facilities including National Park exhibitions and administration, an astronomy workshop (the Eifel is to be a so-called dark-sky preserve), a centre for events in the former cinema of the Belgian Army, and a museum on the work of the Red Cross. An existing swimming pool will be renovated and a youth hostel will provide a place to stay on site. The everyday reality of each of these current and future uses cannot help but stand in some way in relation to the idea of an educational landscape as the Nazis saw it.

Locally, the argument is that this place should be reclaimed from the Nazis, that Vogelsang should be recast as a place of outstanding natural beauty, and that it cannot be left solely as a testimony to the ideology of National Socialism. But after the cessation of military activities, there was a need to find a new use for the site. As a product of both these considerations, a concept for a mix of uses resulted – that would also conserve the historic building substance.

Alltag ohne Banalisierung

Es ist eine tourismuswirtschaftliche Nachnutzung der Gebäude geplant, eine multifunktionale Nutzung durch den Naturpark für Ausstellungen und Verwaltung, eine Werkstatt der Astronomie (die Eifel soll ein sogenanntes Dark-Sky-Reservat werden), ein Veranstaltungszentrum im ehemaligen Kino der belgischen Armee, ein Museum zur Arbeit des Roten Kreuzes. Ein Schwimmbad wird wieder genutzt, eine Jugendherberge lädt heute zum Aufenthalt auf Vogelsang ein. Jede dieser heutigen und zukünftigen Nutzungen steht in ihrem Alltag im Verhältnis zur Idee einer Bildungslandschaft, wie sie die Nationalsozialisten erfanden.

Vor Ort argumentiert man, man wolle sich diesen Ort von den Nazis zurückholen, Vogelsang solle als besonderer landschaftlicher Ort wiedergewonnen werden, man dürfe diesen Ort nicht der Ideologie des Nationalsozialismus überlassen. Aber selbstverständlich gab es auch einen Verwertungsdruck nach der Aufgabe der militärischen Nutzung; die Liegenschaft musste einer neuen Nutzung zugeführt werden. Aus beiden Überlegungen entstand das Konzept einer gemischten Nutzung – auch um die historische Bausubstanz zu bewahren.

Not a place of commemoration

In their proposal for the "framework concept for the landscaping, access and lighting" of Vogelsang, sinai landscape architects argued strongly that Vogelsang should not be perceived as a place of remembrance. Each new design gesture, each material used, each piece of furniture and equipment, from the wastepaper basket to the wayfinding and information system should avoid glorifying the location any further. The site should be interpreted as an everyday place, as it already was to a certain extent during its military use after the Second World War – except that now this place caters to the public, that there are visitors to welcome, guests to feed and hikers to inform. At the same time, the everyday facilities on the site should not render it banal; even when it is not a place of remembrance, it is still a place with history, a place of education and a place with a complex historical legacy.

Kein Gedenkort

sinai Landschaftsarchitekten legten in ihrer Konzeptentwicklung für die „Rahmenplanung Freiraum, Erschließung, Beleuchtung" großen Wert darauf, diesen Ort nicht als Gedenkort zu verstehen. Jede weitere gestalterische Geste, jedes verwendete Material, jedes Möbelstück und Ausstattungselement vom Papierkorb bis zum Informationssystem soll nicht einer neuen Heroisierung Vorschub leisten. Der Ort ist so alltäglich zu interpretieren, wie er es auch während der militärischen Nutzung nach dem Zweiten Weltkrieg in gewisser Hinsicht schon war – nur dass dieser Ort nun der Öffentlichkeit gewidmet ist, dass Besucher empfangen, Gäste bewirtet und Wanderer informiert werden wollen. Zugleich darf der Ort in seiner Alltags-Ausstattung nicht banalisiert werden, denn er bleibt auch als Nicht-Gedenkort ein Ort der Geschichte, der Bildung und ein Ort mit einem komplexen historischen Erbe.

An international architecture competition for the Forum Vogelsang was held in 2008 to establish a starting point for the framework plan, which was then developed by consensus principle, and now serves as the basis for all further development. The competition aimed to find a conservation concept for the site as a whole and included the design of the external areas of the "international place" and a landscape concept to support the vision of an open, international place. The jury unanimously recommended the project by sinai landscape architects together with Mola + Winkelmüller architects. Their design served as the basis for the framework plan, which incorporates and elaborates on the specific requirements and visions of the client.

Today, unlike during the period of National Socialism, we can consider landscape, buildings and spirit separately, making it possible to re-use such places for recreational purposes. In a democratic civil society, this kind of historically informed use is conceivable, and that is what characterises our social system.

Grundlagen für die in einem Konsensverfahren erarbeitete Rahmenplanung, die Basis für alle weiteren Entwicklungen, erbrachte ein internationaler Architekturwettbewerb Forum Vogelsang im Jahr 2008, der auf Aussagen zum Denkmalbereich als Ganzes zielte. Aufgabenstellung war die freiräumliche Gestaltung des „Internationalen Platzes" und die Entwicklung eines landschaftsgestalterischen Ausdrucks für die Vision eines offenen, internationalen Ortes. Das Preisgericht empfahl die Arbeit von sinai Landschaftsarchitekten mit Mola + Winkelmüller Architekten einstimmig zur Umsetzung. Auf dieser Grundlage wurde die Rahmenplanung mit den Anforderungen und Visionen des Auftraggebers abgestimmt und konkretisiert.

Anders als zur Zeit des Nationalsozialismus ist es heute möglich, Landschaft, Gebäude und Geist soweit zu trennen, dass eine Nachnutzung für Freizeitzwecke möglich ist. Einer demokratisch verfassten Zivilgesellschaft ist eine solche geschichtsbewusste Nutzung angemessen, das zeichnet unsere Gesellschaftsordnung aus.

A place with several characters: the hillside view is more reminiscent of a homeland scene than of monumentalism.

Zwitterwesen: Ansichten der Bergseite, eher heimelig als monumental

7
Christmann, Gabriela P.
2008: Was Identität ist – und
was Identität heißt, wenn wir
sie auf Räume beziehen,
Statement des IRS Leibniz-
Institut für Regionalentwick-
lung und Strukturplanung
zum 26. Brandenburger
Regionalgespräch „Die
kreativen Spielräume der
Peripherie" on 12 November
2008
8
Hard 1995, p. 63

7
Christmann, Gabriela P.
2008: Was Identität ist – und
was Identität heißt, wenn wir
sie auf Räume beziehen,
Statement des IRS Leibniz-
Institut für Regionalentwick-
lung und Strukturplanung
zum 26. Brandenburger
Regionalgespräch „Die
kreativen Spielräume der
Peripherie" am 12.11.2008
8
Hard 1995, S. 63

Identity as construction

The history of this place is something that "the Germans" cannot liberate themselves from. We can, however, secure traces and learn to read them, with a view to clarifying the relationship between place and identity and identity and landscape. We can question the image that the landscape communicates. And we can use the means of landscape architecture to strengthen the identity of a place while simultaneously calling this identity into question.

For this, we must realise that space does not have an intrinsic identity that is permanently bound to it. Identity as a sociological as well as a philosophical category is a product of negotiation with others through communicative processes. That means that landscape architecture and planning always represent an opportunity for communication. Design creates an instance and at the same time reflects the communicative processes of identity formation. "Only through communication and interaction with others can collective attributions of the meaning of a place be established and consolidated. [...] In the process of place-related discourse in particular, [...] typical, regularly recurring attributions of meaning, or topics, crystallise over the course of history and in turn reflect back on the people. The citizens can examine these topics and see how they relate to them personally.

Against this background, the development of identity should also always be seen in the context of the shared history of a society or group. It rests on the historical legacy of a society or group, is embedded in collective memory, and draws on traditional knowledge. As such, place-related collective identities are always highly complex cultural constructs, something that is often underestimated in political and planning practice."[7] In order to understand space and landscape as just such a cultural construct and to design for it, sinai employ a technique of reading the traces of a site to identify and reveal objects in the landscape and their layers of meaning. The German geographer Gerhard Hard describes this and proposes the reading of landscape and its vegetation as artefacts, as the traces of human interventions. "Nothing is in itself an indication or a trace, but almost anything can become one: simply because there is very little that does not interact with something else and could therefore be its trace or indication. Reading traces means to employ one's knowledge of causes and other correlations."[8] sinai understand landscape architecture in this sense as a semiotic system, and this search for traces, their reading and interpretation are carried over into the design itself, and not just in the analysis of the space.

Identität als Konstruktion

Befreien können sich „die Deutschen" aus dieser Geschichte nicht. Wir können aber Spuren sichern und lesen lernen und damit das Verhältnis von Identität und Ort, von Identität und Landschaft aufklären helfen. Wir können Landschaft im Sinne ihrer Bildwirkung hinterfragen. Und wir können mit den Mitteln der Landschaftsarchitektur die Identität eines Ortes stärken, indem wir diese Identität zugleich in Frage stellen. Voraussetzung ist, dass wir nicht dem Missverständnis unterliegen, ein Raum habe per se eine Identität, die ihm quasi anhaftet. Identität als sozialwissenschaftliche wie als philosophische Kategorie entsteht in Auseinandersetzung mit anderen, in kommunikativen Prozessen. Das macht die Landschaftsarchitektur, macht Planung generell immer auch zu einem Kommunikationsanbieter. Gestaltung schafft Anlass und reflektiert zugleich kommunikative Prozesse der Identitätsbildung. „Erst im kommunikativen Austausch können gemeinsame Bedeutungszuschreibungen auf einen Raum entwickelt und gefestigt werden. [...] Insbesondere im Rahmen raumbezogener Diskurse [...] bilden sich im historischen Verlauf typische, regelmäßig wiederkehrende Bedeutungszuschreibungen bzw. Themen heraus, die wiederum auf die Bürger zurückwirken. Die Bürger können die Themen aufgreifen und sich dazu persönlich in Bezug setzen. Vor diesem Hintergrund ist Identitätsentwicklung auch immer im Zusammenhang mit der gemeinsamen Geschichte einer Gesellschaft oder Gruppe zu sehen. Sie ruht auf dem historischen Erbe der Gesellschaft bzw. Gruppe, ist eingebettet in kollektives Erinnern, bezieht sich auf tradiertes Wissen. Damit sind raumbezogene kollektive Identitäten immer hochgradig komplexe kulturelle Konstrukte, was oft in der politisch-planerischen Praxis unterschätzt wird."[7] Um Raum und Landschaft als ein solches kulturelles Konstrukt verstehen und gestalten zu können, nutzen sinai zur Erfassung landschaftsräumlicher Gegenstände und ihrer Bedeutungsschichten das Konzept des Spurenlesens. Gerhard Hard hat dieses beschrieben und schlägt vor, Landschaften inklusive ihrer Vegetation als Artefakte zu lesen, als Handlungsspuren menschlicher Eingriffe. „Nichts ist an sich ein Anzeichen oder eine Spur, aber fast alles kann es werden: einfach weil es fast nichts gibt, was nicht mit anderem interagiert und dessen Anzeichen oder Spur sein könnte. Spurensichern ist Ausnutzen eines Wissens über Verursachungen und andere Korrelationen."[8] sinai verstehen Landschaftsarchitektur in diesem Sinne als Zeichenlehre, und dieses Suchen, Lesen und Interpretieren von Spuren wird auf die Gestaltung selbst, nicht allein auf die Analyse des Raumes, übertragen.

Framework plan detailing the strategy of discreet built insertions and landscape design of the 100-hectare grounds of vogelsang ip

1 Forum Vogelsang with National Park visitor centre, National Socialism documentation centre, Eifel-Ardennes panorama window
2 Youth hostel and international youth meeting centre
3 Forest youth centre
4 Cinema
5 National Park administration

Rahmenplan mit den räumlichen Setzungen für eine zurückhaltende bauliche und freiräumliche Entwicklung der 100-Hektar-Liegenschaft vogelsang ip

1 Forum Vogelsang/ Besucherzentrum, NS-Dokumentationszentrum, Schaufenster Eifel/ Ardennen
2 DJH/Internationale Begegnungsstätte
3 Jugendwaldheim
4 Kino
5 Nationalparkverwaltung

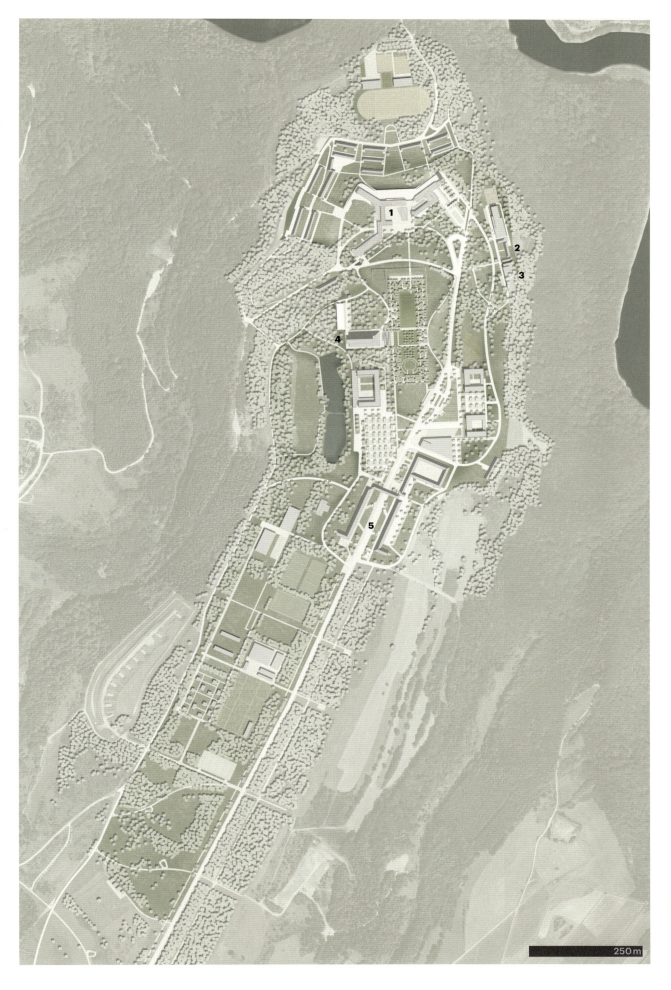

250 m

Pointing the way

Existing and newly inserted signs not only communicate information about the present of a place, i.e. offer orientation in its present state; they can also act as traces and contribute to an understanding of uses, events and conditions from the past. In this respect, it is logical that the landscape architects have left the material substance of Vogelsang largely untouched, instead choosing to introduce a new system of signs that lends the space a new sense of identity while simultaneously communicating the role of Vogelsang as the site of a former *Ordensburg*.

Of special relevance here is the orientation and way-finding system. This is essential for the perception of Vogelsang as a tourist site and for its future development in this respect. The orientation system has to fulfil various functions:
– Provide directions to specific sites
– Provide information
– Advertise (by presenting the uses
   to the visitor at the relevant location)

Zeichen setzen

Vorhandene und neu hinzugefügte Zeichen vermitteln nicht nur Informationen zur Gegenwart eines Ortes, bieten also Orientierung im Jetzt des Raumes. Sondern Zeichen können zugleich Spuren sein und somit auch zum Verstehen früherer Nutzungen, Ereignisse und Zustände beitragen. In diesem Sinne ist es konsequent, dass die Landschaftsarchitekten die vorgefundene materielle Substanz des Ortes Vogelsang weitgehend belassen, diesen Raum aber mit einem neuen Zeichensystem seiner neuen Identität entsprechend interpretieren helfen und vermitteln, was den Ort Vogelsang als ehemalige Ordensburg ausmachte.

Eine besondere Bedeutung kommt dabei dem Leit- und Orientierungssystem zu. Dieses ist Grundvoraussetzung dafür, dass Vogelsang als touristischer Ort wahrgenommen wird und sich als solcher weiterentwickeln kann. Das Orientierungssystem muss unterschiedliche Anforderungen erfüllen:
– Auffinden von Orten
– Informieren
– Werben (durch Präsentation der Nutzungen/
   Nutzer am Standort)

Forum Vogelsang: the Adlerhof ensemble serves as the basis for the development of the site.
 1 Adlerhof
 2 Covered walkway with vista of the Urftsee
 3 Entrance building
 4 "Keep"

Forum Vogelsang: Das Ensemble Adlerhof als Ausgangspunkt der Entwicklung
 1 Adlerhof
 2 Wandelhalle/Urftseeblick
 3 Eingangsgebäude
 4 Bergfried

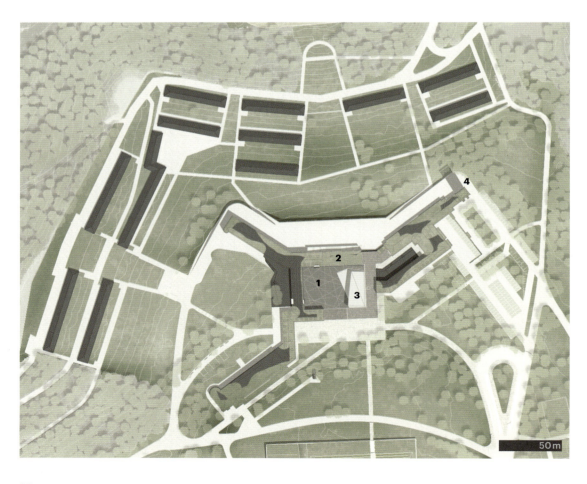

50 m

The orientation system of vogelsang ip includes different kinds of information bearers – focus points, pylons, freestanding steles – all in a distinctive amber colour. These bearers are employed extensively as opposed to intensively: the number of elements is kept to the minimum necessary to provide sufficient orientation. The framework also stipulates that signage elements and additional fittings for the new uses should be discreet, uniform and employ simple materials. Despite the different types of information and information bearers, Vogelsang should be presented as a whole, and fences, hedges or other dividing elements are not envisaged. The work of sinai landscape architects and Mola + Winkelmüller architects at Vogelsang makes a contemporary and independent contribution through its landscape architecture and reveals the revitalisation potential of the site through the incorporation of new uses in an urban masterplan rather than by proposing a design for a new image of the landscape. sinai describes this as introducing "new cells with new uses" that take root in the place, relate the history of the region and help one to see the Eifel and the Ardennes in their natural and socio-historical context. The National Park emphasises the region – as opposed to the nation – as the frame of reference for the visitors' experience as well as its own sphere of responsibility. At the same time, vogelsang ip is a European project, and thus international in its outlook and its message.

The landscape architecture cannot counteract the impression of the landscape, nor can it negate it given the sheer scale of the landscape. But it can clarify and make clear that this very landscape was exploited to serve the interests of a destructive ideology and a fascist social system. While the landscape here has not been abused, it is also not innocent.

Das Orientierungssystem des vogelsang ip umfasst verschiedene Informationsträger (Focus, Pylon, Stele) in der Leitfarbe sonnengelb. Es wird auf die zur Orientierung unbedingt notwendige Anzahl an Elementen beschränkt. Zurückhaltung, Einheitlichkeit und Schlichtheit in der Materialwahl sind auch die Maßgaben für die im Rahmenplan vorgegebenen Hinzufügungen einer Ausstattung für die neuen Nutzungen. Trotz unterschiedlicher Angebote und Träger ist Vogelsang als Einheit zu zeigen; Zäune, Hecken oder andere trennende Elemente sind nicht vorgesehen. Die Arbeit von sinai Landschaftsarchitekten und Mola + Winkelmüller Architekten zu Vogelsang leistet einen zeitgemäßen und eigenständigen Beitrag der Landschaftsarchitektur, indem die Möglichkeiten einer Revitalisierung durch neue Nutzungen in Form eines städtebaulichen Masterplans – statt als Entwurf eines neuen Landschaftsbildes – aufgezeigt werden. „Neue Nutzungszellen", so nennen es sinai, sollen den Ort neu besetzen, sollen die Geschichte der Region erzählen, also die Eifel und die Ardennen im landschafts- wie sozialgeschichtlichen Kontext erkennen helfen. Dieser Nationalpark betont die Dimension der Region statt der Nation als Erfahrungs- und Verantwortungsraum. vogelsang ip ist angelegt als europäisches Projekt, grenzüberschreitend in seiner Aussage und Wirkung. Die Landschaftsarchitektur kann die Wirkung der Landschaft nicht konterkarieren, negieren kann sie dieses Übermaß an Landschaft schon gar nicht. Aber sie muss aufklären, muss deutlich machen, dass Landschaft auch gebraucht wurde, um eine zerstörerische Ideologie, ein faschistisches Gesellschaftssystem zu überhöhen. Landschaft ist hier nicht missbraucht worden, aber unschuldig ist sie eben auch nicht.

Entrance courtyard and new entrance building that punctures and passes beneath the existing buildings (design: Mola + Winkelmüller architects)

Zugangsebene und Eingangsgebäude unter dem Adlerhof als Durchdringung des Bestandes (Architektur: Mola + Winkelmüller Architekten)

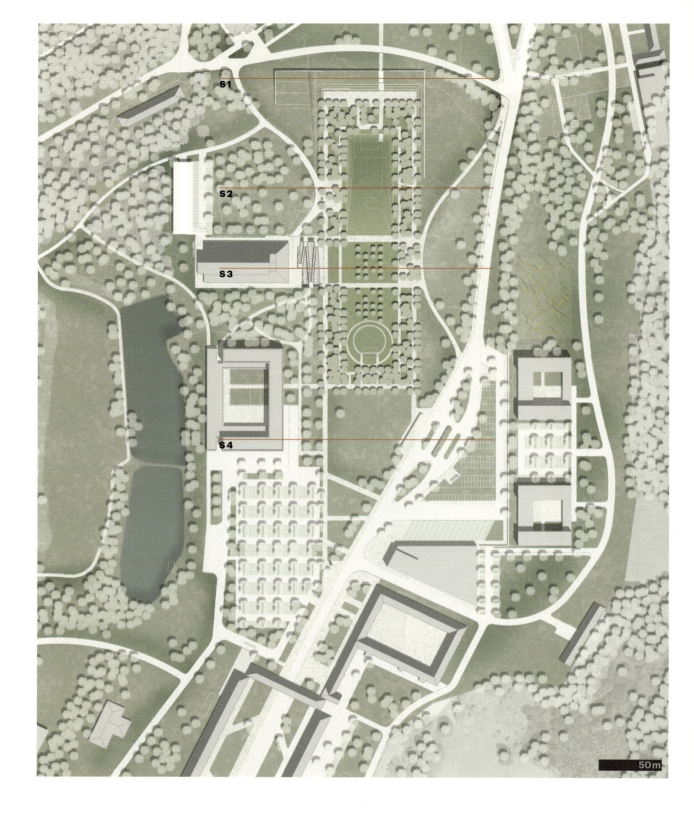

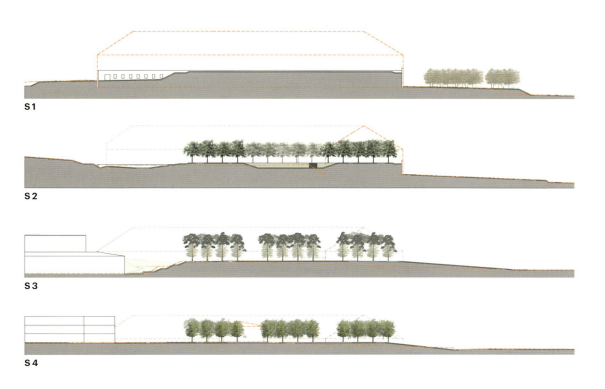

S 1

S 2

S 3

S 4

Sequence of sections
through the park plateau on
the site of the planned but
unbuilt "House of Know-
ledge", showing the clearing
for the open-air theatre set
into the slanting plane of
the site.

Schnittsequenz:
Parkplateau auf der Grund-
fläche des ehemals geplanten „Hauses des Wissens"
mit eingesenkten Theater-
lichtungen in der schiefen
Ebene

**View from the park plateau
looking towards the "keep"
of the Adlerhof**

Blick vom Parkplateau
zum Bergfried am Adlerhof

**Mühldorfer Hart Concentration Camp Memorial,
Waldkraiburg near Mühldorf am Inn,
competition, 2012**

KZ-Gedenkstätte Mühldorfer Hart,
Waldkraiburg bei Mühldorf am Inn,
Wettbewerb, 2012

**Mühldorfer Hart
– The Fascination
of Failure**

Mühldorfer Hart
– Faszination
des Scheiterns

Several concentration camps and labour camps in what is now the Mühldorfer Hart Woodland and Landscape Conservation Area between Waldkraiburg and Mühldorf am Inn in Upper Bavaria served between 1944 and 1945 as subcamps of Dachau concentration camp for the manufacture of armaments. The site was to produce the Messerschmidt ME 262 jet-powered aircraft in a bunker complex partially submerged in the ground. The abundant supply of gravel, its good rail connections, proximity to the Inn River and the natural camouflage offered by a densely wooded site not far from Munich made Mühldorf an ideal location for a "secret project" of this kind. To this end a supporting infrastructure of railway lines, an airfield, forced labour and concentration camps and other facilities were constructed for Organisation Todt, the Nazi's civil and military engineering group responsible for building the vast production facilities. In the neighbouring camp at Waldkraiburg, explosives were made for the production of munitions. From the very beginning, the site of the secret arms production facilities near the railway junction at Mühldorf has been shrouded in rumours, legend and repressed memories. This was due not least to the fact that the ME 262 was reportedly "a weapon that will decide the outcome of the war", although production never actually began at the site. Today, the remnants of the manufacturing site and the legends surrounding the aircraft continue to attract visitors to the site. That this place is not just a feat of technical and engineering prowess but also a place in which some 4,000 inmates died as a result of the harsh working conditions is what visitors need to be made aware of.

Mehrere Konzentrations- und Arbeitslager im heutigen Wald- und Landschaftsschutzgebiet Mühldorfer Hart, gelegen zwischen Waldkraiburg und Mühldorf am Inn im östlichen Bayern, dienten zwischen 1944 und 1945 als Außenlager des KZ Dachau der Rüstungsproduktion. In einem halb unter der Erde versteckten Bunkergelände sollte das Strahltriebwerksflugzeug Messerschmidt ME 262 gebaut werden. Umfangreiche Kiesvorkommen, gute Eisenbahnanschlüsse, die Lage am Inn und die zugleich versteckte Waldlage in der Nähe Münchens ließen diesen Ort prädestiniert erscheinen für ein solches „Geheimprojekt". Rund um das Rüstungsareal war eine regelrechte Infrastruktur aus Bahntrassen, Fliegerhorst, Zwangsarbeiterlagern, Konzentrationslagern und Einrichtungen der Organisation Todt geschaffen worden. Diese verantwortete den Bau der riesigen Produktionsstätte. Im benachbarten Waldkraiburg wurde zudem Sprengstoff für die Munitionsproduktion hergestellt.
Der Ort ist als geheimer Rüstungsort nahe des Eisenbahnknotens Mühldorf von Anfang an ein Ort der Gerüchte, Legenden und versteckten Erinnerungen gewesen. Dazu trug der Ruf der ME 262 als „kriegsentscheidende Waffe" wesentlich bei, deren Produktion an diesem Ort jedoch nie aufgenommen wurde. Baustellenrelikt und Flugzeuglegende sorgen auch heute für eine Neugierde auf den Ort. Dass hier jedoch nicht nur Technikgeschichte geschrieben und Ingenieurarbeit geleistet wurde, sondern ungefähr 4.000 Häftlinge aufgrund der Arbeitsbelastungen auf der Baustelle zu Tode kamen, ist Gegenstand des zu weckenden Interesses.

Landshut

Erding

Dachau

Mühldorf am Inn
Mühldorfer Hart
Waldkraiburg

München

Starnberg

10 km

The memory of the structures of the camp, including mass graves, hut camps and production facilities, has been mostly lost. Sections of the massive concrete construction of the bunker were to be demolished by explosion, and most of the vaults were indeed destroyed. One, however, withstood the blasting and now stands like a monument in the middle of the now re-grown woodlands. A somewhat bizarre attraction, this arch now tells of a mysterious-looking construction from the past.

The subcamp at Mühldorf, also known as the Mühldorf concentration camp complex, was one of 169 satellites of the concentration camp at Dachau. That this particular site still offers a glimpse of the atrocious history of arms production in Germany during the period of National Socialism can be attributed to this indestructible concrete relic.

Seven teams of landscape architects were invited in 2012 to submit design proposals for developing this space to better communicate its history. The participants were asked to develop "appropriate design responses", as Walter Irlinger from the Bavarian Conservation Department called it, for three sites of remembrance in the Mühldorfer Hart: the camp in the woods, a mass grave and the site of the former bunker complex.

Early on in the design process, sinai landscape architects realised that the concept could be given greater depth and intensity with the help of scenographers. To this end, sinai enlisted the help of chezweitz & partner office for scenography.

Die Erinnerung an die Lagerstrukturen mit Massengräbern, Barackenlagern und Produktionsstätten ging weitgehend verloren. Teile der massiven Betonkonstruktion der Bunker sollten durch Sprengungen beseitigt werden. Ein Großteil der Betonbögen wurde dabei zerstört, einer hielt jedoch stand und wirkt nun wie ein Monument im wieder aufgewachsenen Wald. Als skurrile Attraktion kündet dieser Bogen seitdem von einer seltsam anmutenden Bautätigkeit der Vergangenheit.

Das KZ-Außenkommando Mühldorf, auch KZ-Lagergruppe Mühldorf genannt, war eines von 169 Außenlagern des KZ Dachau. Dass an diesem Ort heute besondere Aufmerksamkeit für die unmenschliche Geschichte der Aufrüstung Deutschlands im Nationalsozialismus möglich ist, ist diesem nicht zu beseitigenden Beton-Relikt geschuldet.

Sieben Arbeitsgruppen aus Landschaftsarchitekten wurden 2012 aufgefordert, Vorschläge zur Entwicklung dieses Raumes im Sinne der Vermittlung seiner Geschichte zu entwerfen. Für drei Erinnerungsstätten im Mühldorfer Hart – das Waldlager, ein Massengrab und das ehemalige Bunkergelände – galt es eine „würdige Gestaltung" zu finden, wie Walter Irlinger vom Bayerischen Landesamt für Denkmalpflege es formulierte. Frühzeitig wurde von sinai Landschaftsarchitekten erkannt, dass in der Zusammenarbeit mit Szenografen eine besondere Tiefe und Intensität des Konzepts erreicht werden könnte. Somit wandten sich sinai an die Szenografen chezweitz & partner.

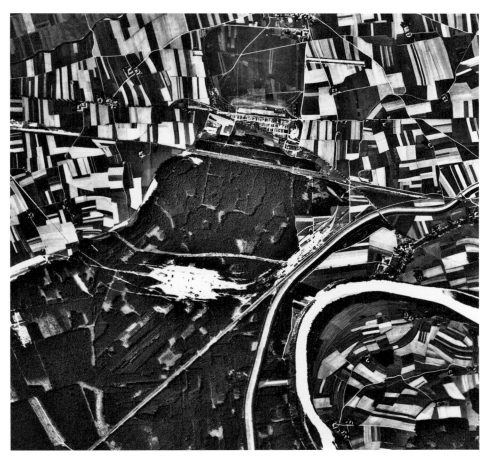

Aerial photograph
from 27 August 1945

Luftbild vom
27. August 1945

1
Nasser, Stephen: My Brother's Voice. How a Young Hungarian Boy Survived the Holocaust: A True Story, Las Vegas 2003, p. 87

1
Nasser, Stephen: Die Stimme meines Bruders, Aspach (Österreich) 2011, S. 89

A giant and a wonder-weapon

Visitors to the woodland and nature conservation areas are often astonished by the sheer size of the remaining segment of the bunker and the now moss-covered ventilation shaft to one side of the remaining arch. However, these concrete structures, each several metres thick, only hint at the actual dimensions of the site at Mühldorfer Hart shortly before the end of the Second World War. The recollections of Stephen Nasser, a former camp inmate, provide an impression of the scale of the complex: "A new project – From today's vantage point at the opposite end of the big clearing, we've a bird's eye view of the colossal scope of the project on which we're being forced to work. Below us yawns a man-made canyon of gigantic proportions, at least two hundred feet deep [60 m] and half a mile wide [800 m]. I can't estimate its length, since it's already solidly built in, with only the roof still under construction. From here, what's already been built resembles a giant web of steel. The unfinished section of the roof alone is five hundred feet long [150 m]. As for the rest of it, who knows? It stretches 'way under the forest. Trains already run into the structure on two different elevations. It looks like the entrance itself is three stories high, and the roof easily adds another fifty feet [15 m]. Over this steel maze bridges span across, wide enough to carry narrow gauge industrial trains with a cargo of ready-mixed cement."[1]

Stephen Nasser describes not only the scale of the project but also recounts the hardship suffered by the inmates who were forced to work on the construction site. He himself narrowly escaped death on several occasions and was repeatedly beaten and threatened with death by SS overseers. Towards the end of the war, the hygienic conditions, malnutrition and treatment by the guards in the camps were catastrophic in all of the camps in the complex.

Today, the woodland and nature conservation area offers no indication of the brutality of life and death in the camps that had been set up under the cynical codename Weingut I (Vineyard I) solely for the construction of aircraft. The large nature conservation area is now a recreation area for walkers and hikers. On the local Mühldorf am Inn tourism homepage, the metre-thick concrete arch standing in the middle of the woodlands is described as part of a "gigantic project" for "the production of a wonder-weapon": "In the six-storey underground structure, forced labourers would have bolted, welded and assembled armaments. Thousands of inmates – most of whom had come from the concentration camp at Dachau or the camps that had been vacated in Poland – were held captive in so-called

Gigant und Wunderwaffe

Die Besucher des Wald- und Wandergebietes sind vor allem von der Dimension des erhaltenen Bunkersegments sowie den inzwischen bemoosten Lüftungsbauwerken seitlich des erhaltenen Bunkerbogens beeindruckt. Diese meterdicken Betonkonstruktionen deuten jedoch nur noch ansatzweise an, welche Dimension die Baustelle im Mühldorfer Hart kurz vor Ende des Zweiten Weltkrieges hatte. Die Erinnerungen von Stephen Nasser, einem der Lagerhäftlinge, geben ein Bild davon: „Ein neues Projekt – Von dem heutigen Aussichtspunkt am gegenüberliegenden Ende der großen Lichtung haben wir einen Blick aus der Vogelperspektive auf die kolossalen Ausmaße des Projektes, an dem wir zu arbeiten gezwungen sind. Unter uns gähnt eine von Menschen gemachte Schlucht mit riesigen Ausmaßen, mindestens 60 Meter tief und 800 Meter breit. Die Länge kann ich nicht abschätzen, weil sie schon fest bebaut ist und nur noch am Dach gearbeitet wird. Von unserem Standpunkt aus ähnelt das bereits Erbaute einem riesigen Netz aus Stahl. Der unvollendete Teil des Daches ist allein um die 150 Meter lang. Und was den Rest betrifft, wer weiß das schon? Er erstreckt sich weit in den Wald hinein. Das Gebäude wird schon von Zügen auf zwei verschiedenen Ebenen befahren. Es sieht so aus, dass allein der Eingang drei Stockwerke hoch ist, und bis zum Dach schließen sich leicht weitere 15 Meter an. Über dieses Stahllabyrinth spannen sich Brücken, die breit genug sind, um schmalspurige Transportzüge mit ihrer Ladung aus Fertigbeton zu tragen."[1]

Stephen Nasser schildert aber nicht allein die Dimension des Baus, sondern vor allem die Leiden der Häftlinge, die auf dieser Baustelle zur Zwangsarbeit eingesetzt waren. Er selbst wäre mehrfach fast gestorben und wurde von SS-Aufsehern immer wieder gequält und mit dem Tod bedroht. Hygienische Verhältnisse, Ernährung, Bewachung, in diesen Lagern war zum Ende des Krieges hin alles katastrophal.

Die Brutalität des Lebens und Sterbens an diesen Orten, die unter dem zynischen Decknamen „Weingut I" für den Bau der Flugzeuge eingerichtet wurden, ist im heutigen Waldgebiet und Ausflugsort Mühldorfer Hart nicht mehr zu erahnen. Das großflächige Landschaftsschutzgebiet lädt zu Wanderungen ein, der Segmentbogen aus meterdickem Beton mitten im Wald gilt auf der Werbewebseite des Landkreises Mühldorf am Inn als „gigantisches Projekt" für „die Produktion der Wunderwaffe": „In sechs unterirdischen Stockwerken hätten die Zwangsarbeiter schrauben, schweißen und armieren sollen.

Waldlager (woodland camps). Large numbers died of starvation, illness or collapsed as a result of the brutal working conditions. [...] What remains of the mass graves can still be seen as depressions in the landscape."

The design by sinai landscape architects takes this perception of the place – one that fluctuates between a sense of wonderment and moral responsibility – as its starting point. Their intention is not primarily to develop a memorial site but rather to build on the interest in the "tourist attractions" to establish a connection between the fascination of the place and the history of the construction relics. "An invitation to engage" is how A. W. Faust describes this approach. The scenography that sinai developed together with chezweitz & partner therefore allows the woodland to continue to be actively used as a recreational area. At the same time the project reveals the spatial as well as contextual dimension of this infrastructure of extermination, in the process making the visitor aware of its meaning.

Die Häftlinge selbst – zumeist kamen sie aus dem KZ Dachau oder aus bis dahin schon aufgelösten polnischen Konzentrationslagern – wurden zu Tausenden im sogenannten Waldlager gefangen gehalten. Dort verhungerten sie, starben an Krankheiten oder brachen an der Last der schweren Arbeit zusammen. [...] Bis heute sind die Überreste der Massengräber in der Landschaft als Vertiefungen sichtbar."

Der Entwurf von sinai Landschaftsarchitekten greift diese Wahrnehmung des Ortes aktiv auf, die zwischen Staunen und moralischer Verantwortung changiert. Es geht den Landschaftsarchitekten nicht vordringlich darum, eine Gedenkstätte zu entwickeln, sondern das Interesse an der ‚Sehenswürdigkeit' zu nutzen, um die Faszination dieses Ortes mit dem Wissen um die Geschichte der baulichen Relikte zu verbinden. „Zur Vermittlung einladen", nennt A.W. Faust diese Haltung. Daher ermöglicht die Szenografie, die sinai gemeinsam mit chezweitz & partner entwickelte, weiterhin eine aktive Freizeitnutzung des Waldes. Dabei wird aber zugleich die räumliche wie die inhaltliche Dimension dieser Vernichtungsinfrastruktur vor Augen geführt und damit der Blick auf ihre Bedeutung geöffnet.

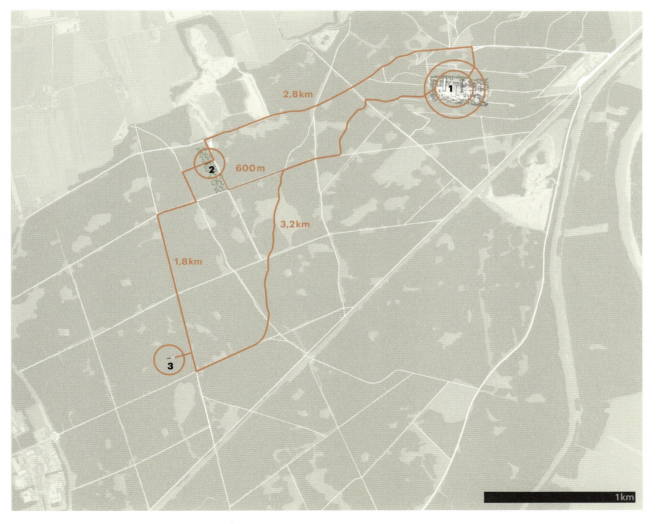

Overview of the memorial site
1 Relic of the bunker
  (main information)
2 Woodland camp
3 Mass grave

Übersichtsplan Gedenkort
1 Bunkerrelikt
  (Hauptinformation)
2 Waldlager
3 Massengrab

Double exposure

The vast scale of the bunker structure, the technological feat of its construction and not least the romantic aura of a mysterious ruin in the midst of the woods elicit a compelling fascination that all too easily obscures the murderous conditions under which it was created. As the scale of the space and the relic is impressive enough in its own right for it to have become a tourist attraction and destination for outings, the scenery presenting itself to today's visitors represents a suitable starting point on which to base an exploration of the origins of this relic. This is the design approach that sinai and chezweitz follow.

At present, the relics in the Mühldorfer Hart are perceived without any clear context. One sees objects that appear to be indestructible, but have quite obviously been heavily damaged. This ambivalence is probably part of their attraction: visitors stand in wonderment in front of them and attempt to unravel the mystery behind them. Rather than stifling this sense of curiosity through the provision of explanatory information panels and signs, the landscape architects looked for other ways in which they could cultivate this curiosity and connect these massive relics with the fractured history of their development, and more importantly with the moral debt owed to those who died working on the construction site and in captivity.

Doppelbelichtung

Die gewaltigen Ausmaße, die ausgefeilte Bautechnologie, nicht zuletzt die romantische Aura einer rätselhaften Ruine in der Waldwildnis: Allzu leicht verdeckt die Faszination für die Reste des Bunkers im Mühldorfer Hart die mörderischen Umstände seiner Entstehung. Wenn allein die Dimension des Raumes und der Relikte so beeindruckt, dass diese zur Sehenswürdigkeit taugen und als Ausflugsziel besucht werden, bietet eine solche Szenerie in der Landschaft einen geeigneten Anlass, einen Ausgangspunkt, um sich auf die Suche nach der Herkunft dieser Relikte zu begeben – so der Entwurfsansatz von sinai und chezweitz.

Die im Mühldorfer Hart stehenden Relikte werden bisher in einem nur undeutlichen Kontext wahrgenommen. Sie scheinen unzerstörbar und sind doch so deutlich sichtbar zerstört worden. Diese Ambivalenz macht wohl die Anziehungskraft dieser Objekte aus, denen die Besucher rätselnd und erstaunt gegenübertreten. Diese rätselnde Neugierde nun durch Erklärungen, durch Infotafeln und Schilder abzuwürgen, schien den Landschaftsarchitekten als falscher Ansatz. Daher wurde im Entwurf geprüft, ob die vorhandene Neugierde noch stärker herauszufordern ist, indem die massiven Relikte mit der Brüchigkeit ihrer Entwicklungsgeschichte und vor allem mit der Schuld gegenüber den Opfern der Baustelle und der Lagerhaft in Verbindung gebracht werden können.

In many parts of the camp and the bunker construction site, as well as in the woodland camp, there are scant remains that can be used to reveal the history of the site. In addition to the woodland camp directly next to the bunker, there were further camps in the immediate vicinity, such as the camp at Mettenheim. No traces remain of these smaller and quite primitively equipped camps, that typically consisted of little more than a couple of dozen huts usually without any sanitary facilities or permanent buildings. The site of the former camp at Mettenheim, for example, was cleared after the war and is now occupied by a housing estate.

Interviews with survivors of the camp, as well as with residents and relatives, conducted by the Concentration Camp Memorial Association (Verein für das Erinnern – KZ-Gedenkstätte Mühldorfer Hart e. V.), revealed that local residents were well aware of the camps at the time when they were in operation. The prisoners of the Mühldorf camp complex were not only put to work on building the secret armaments factory but also forced to work on other building projects and in agriculture. The camp at Mühldorf was not a totally separate, cordoned-off area but a large-scale building site with many sections and connections. It is the task of the landscape architecture to chart these various dimensions and communicate them to the visitors.

In vielen Bereichen der Lager und der Baustelle des Rüstungsbunkers, so im Bereich des Waldlagers, ist die Geschichte des Ortes nur noch anhand weniger Bodenrelikte zu erahnen. Neben dem Waldlager direkt am Rüstungsbunker befanden sich weitere Lager, wie das Lager Mettenheim, in unmittelbarer Umgebung. Von diesen kleineren, äußerst primitiv ausgestatteten Lagern aus einigen Dutzend Baracken, meist ohne sanitäre Anlagen oder sonstige feste bauliche Infrastrukturen, sind heute keine Spuren mehr erhalten. Auf dem Areal des nach dem Krieg komplett beseitigten Lagers Mettenheim beispielsweise steht heute eine Neubausiedlung.

In Zeitzeugengesprächen mit ehemaligen Lagerinsassen wie auch mit Anwohnern und Angehörigen, die der Verein Für das Erinnern – KZ-Gedenkstätte Mühldorfer Hart e.V. führte, bestätigte sich, dass es schon damals Kenntnis von den Lagern gab. Denn die Häftlinge der Lagergruppe Mühldorf wurden nicht nur zum Bau der geheimen Rüstungsfabrik eingesetzt, sondern auch zu Arbeiten an anderen Bauprojekten und in der Landwirtschaft gezwungen. Es handelte sich beim Lager Mühldorf also nicht um einen abgeschotteten Bereich, sondern um eine Großbaustelle mit vielen Arealen und Bezügen. Diese Dimensionen zu kartieren und den Besuchern zu vermitteln, ist Aufgabe der Landschaftsarchitektur.

The relic of the bunker: the central place of information and remembrance
1 Car parking
   with initial information
2 Exploratory gangway
3 Information platform
4 Area for events

Das Bunkerrelikt als zentraler Ort der Information und des Gedenkens
1 Parkplatz mit
   Vorinformation
2 Erkundungssteg
3 Ausstellungssteg
4 Veranstaltungsplatz

Shelter and information point at the car park near the relic of the bunker
Ground plan and view

Unterstand am Parkplatz
Bunkerrelikt
Grundriss und Ansicht

**Dr. Gabriele Hammermann,
Director of Dachau Concentration Camp Memorial
Site**

2
Dr. Gabriele Hammermann,
Leiterin der KZ-Gedenkstätte
Dachau

Three locations that form an ensemble …

Both the spatial distribution of the camp complex at Mühldorf as well as the functional processes in the camp's operation can be made clear through the consideration of three separate spaces: the historical location of the ruin, the woodland camp and the former mass grave. sinai landscape architects propose "investing these places with meaning", accentuating in each a different aspect: the structure and the building of the bunker, the living conditions of the inmates, the fates that befell them and the numerous victims. The site of the bunker in Mühldorfer Hart "is one of the last remaining sites of the Holocaust in which 'extermination through labour' is so patently visible." [2]

A two-hour-long circular path totalling a length of eight kilometres connects the different parts of the former camp with one another. This path can also be used as a regular woodland trail and is equipped with the usual system of signs, distance markers and orientation maps.

Drei Orte als Ensemble …

Sowohl die räumliche Ausdehnung als auch die funktionalen Abläufe im Außenlagerkomplex Mühldorf werden mittels der Wahrnehmung dreier räumlich getrennter historischer Bereiche – Ruine, Waldlager, ehemaliges Massengrab – deutlich. sinai Landschaftsarchitekten schlagen vor, die Orte zu „verinhaltlichen" und dabei unterschiedlich zu akzentuieren: Das Bauwerk und der Bau des Bunkers, die Lebensbedingungen der Häftlinge, ihre Schicksale und die zahlreichen Opfer. Denn das Bunkergelände im Mühldorfer Hart „ist einer der letzten Schauplätze des Holocaust, an dem die ,Vernichtung durch Arbeit' derart sichtbar ist". [2]
Ein zweistündiger Rundweg von acht Kilometer Länge soll die Bereiche der ehemaligen Lager untereinander verbinden. Diesen Rundweg kann man als Wanderweg nutzen, alle typischen Informationen wie Leitmarkierungen mit Entfernungsangaben oder Lagepläne sind vorhanden.

**Shrine holding the
name-stencils**

Schrein mit Namensschablonen

**Waymarkers and display
tables with site maps on
the information platform**

Wegemarken und
Kartentische am
Ausstellungssteg

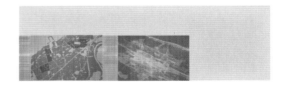

**Active remembrance: the
trees around the ruins of the
bunker are stencilled with
the names of the victims.**

Aktives Gedenken: Die
Bäume um das Bunkerrelikt
werden mit den Namen der
Opfer beschriftet.

... and the ruin as the central location

It is to be expected that the majority of visitors will come to visit the bunker and will not see any more of the site. This central location will therefore have the task of relating the dual layers of the historical narrative: that of the structure and the building of the bunker on the one hand and of the living conditions of the prisoners and their fate on the other. The built relic of the bunker, which dominates everything else on the site, has to become a central place of information as well as of commemoration in the Mühldorfer Hart.

For this, the first step is to make visible the full dimensions of the bunker site. The project proposes thinning out tree growth in a strip that runs around the perimeter of the ruin and the earth embankments over the tunnels. The area occupied by the ruin itself in the centre of this area is largely free of trees and shrubs. This results in a clearing around this area with an indistinct shape. The soft transitions at its edges are a reminder that the site is more than just the ruin itself but also the vast expanse of the construction site.

... und die Ruine als Zentralort

Es ist davon auszugehen, dass ein großer Teil der Besucher wegen des Bunkers kommt und sich mit dem Besuch dieses Ortes begnügen wird. Dem zentralen Ort kommt daher die Aufgabe zu, vollständig die doppelschichtige historische Erzählung zum Bauwerk und dem Bau des Bunkers einerseits und zu den Lebensbedingungen und Schicksalen der Häftlinge anderseits zu liefern. Das alles dominierende bauliche Relikt des Bunkers muss zum zentralen Ort der Information und auch zum Gedenkort im Mühldorfer Hart werden.

Dafür muss in einem ersten Schritt die Dimension des Bunkerareals wieder erkennbar werden. In einem Saumstreifen um das Ruinenfeld und die Erdwälle über den Tunneln wird der Baumbewuchs aufgelockert. Die Bunkerruine im Zentrum dieses Bereichs ist von Gehölzbewuchs weitgehend frei. Um diesen Bereich herum entsteht eine scheinbar formlose Lichtung. Die weichen Übergänge machen deutlich, dass nicht allein der Bau des Bunkers zu beachten, sondern die gewaltig ausgreifende Baustelle insgesamt Thema des Erinnerns ist.

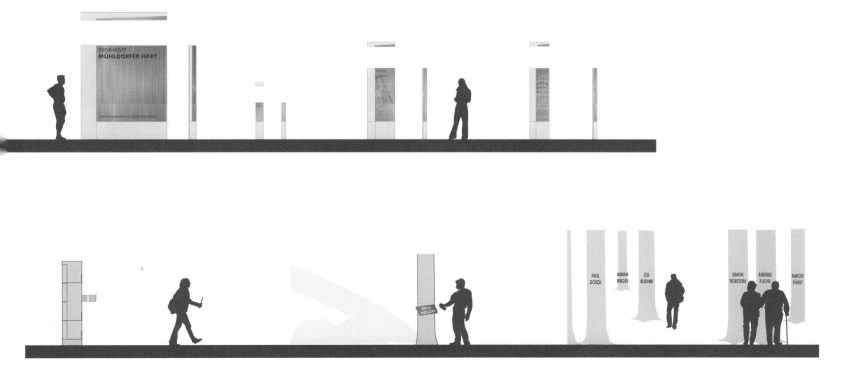

Mown every year, the border strip around the ruin will gradually develop into a meadow and the paths and open areas of gravel surfacing will over time become as visible as the distinctive technical contours of the building site. Related to but separate from the historical figure on the ground are a few discreet insertions that are immediately recognisable as conveyors of information. Folded and floating planes made of steel are superimposed over the "horizon of evidence" without impacting on it.

The site can be explored in the region of the sixth arch. A simple gangway with balustrade leads out over the rubble of the demolished bunker segment, making it possible to experience this otherwise inaccessible area. A central exhibition and visitor area with two levels serves as a lookout point from which visitors can examine the former construction site and retrace its former processes of operation. The main part of the open-air exhibition is displayed on two long table-height cabinets showing the site maps. The information presented here concentrates on the parallel presentation of the historical and current situation of the entire camp complex. The second raised plateau overlooking the arch is the principal place of remembrance on the site of the bunker. Learning about the history of the site and remembering come together at this point. The landscape architects' intention is to shift the current meeting point beneath the bunker arch to this elevated position on the lookout platform, in the process inviting visitors to consider the situation as a whole rather than to gaze in wonderment at only one aspect of it.

Jährlich gemäht, entwickelt sich der Saumstreifen um die Ruine als Wiese. Wege und offene Kiesfelder werden als Teile eines Bodenbildes ebenso sichtbar wie das markante technische Relief der Baustelle. In Abgrenzung zum historisch definierten Bodenbild gibt es einige wenige Hinzufügungen, die eine sofort erkennbare Informationsebene bilden. Gefaltete und leicht schwebende Stahlplateaus überlagern den Zeugnis-Horizont, ohne ihn zu zerstören.

Im Bereich des Bogens 6 kann das Bauwerk erkundet werden. Ein einfacher Stichsteg, mit Geländern markiert, führt auf das Trümmerfeld der gesprengten Bunkersegmente. Er macht damit den ansonsten unzugänglichen Bereich erfahrbar.

Ein zentraler Ausstellungs- und Versammlungsort auf zwei Ebenen dient der Erkundung der ehemaligen Baustelle und ihrer Abläufe. Zwei langgestreckte „Kartentische" bilden den Kern der Freiluftausstellung. Die Information beschränkt sich hier auf eine Doppeldarstellung der historischen wie der heutigen Situation des gesamten Außenlagers.

Das erhöhte zweite Plateau über dem Bogen ist der zentrale Erinnerungsort am Bunker. Historisches Lernen und Gedenken berühren sich an dieser Stelle. Die Idee der Landschaftsarchitekten ist es, den bisherigen Treffpunkt unter dem Bunkerbogen auf diese höhere Warte zu verlagern, den Besucher also einzuladen, sich einen Überblick zu verschaffen, statt allein das Detail zu bestaunen.

Active remembrance

The method of deriving a design from "charting" the space is a design approach that sinai has also used in other projects. In this project, the landscape architects go a step further: visitors to the site are invited to actively participate in this charting of the infrastructure of extermination, making the process of remembrance a personal experience in which the visitor is made aware of the fate of the individuals behind the planned underground armaments factory.

At first sight, the cleared strip of land around the bunker looks like idyllic woodland, however on closer inspection one sees the names of victims of the camp displayed at eye level on the dark trunks of the spruce trees. This ring around the bunker therefore serves as place of remembrance for the victims of the camp. It is not possible to approach the relic without becoming aware of the victims. The stencilling of the names of the victims in white paint on the tree trunks is a joint initiative undertaken by youth groups, school classes and associations. This process extends its function as a place of remembrance into a place of action.

This process is also linked to the location of the former mass grave, the "Shrine of Names". In a clearing in the woods, a depression in the ground is uncovered and made visible. In itself, the actual relic of the empty grave is unspectacular, and yet a nameless mass grave is a powerful image for the total loss of individual identity. Between the path and the grave, the landscape architects have placed a box-like container, in which the stencils used for applying the names to the trunks are stored. Every year some of the stencils are taken out and the weathered names on the trunks are refreshed. On this simple shrine, the names of the victims are displayed in alphabetical order. The archive can be extended to correspond to new research findings. With this insertion, the landscape architects aim to respond to the extermination of people that took place here not with a neutral portrayal of the number of victims of the camp, but with an approach that explicitly reverses this anonymity so that the people are remembered not solely as victims.

Aktives Gedenken

Die Methode, das Gestalten aus dem „Kartieren" des Raumes abzuleiten, wird als Entwurfsansatz auch in anderen Projekten von sinai verwendet. Hier jedoch gehen die Landschaftsarchitekten einen Schritt weiter: Die Besucher des Ortes werden in diese Kartierung der Vernichtungsinfrastruktur aktiv einbezogen, um die Erinnerung zu personalisieren, die Schicksale Einzelner hinter der geplanten unterirdischen Rüstungsfabrik sichtbar zu machen.

Nur auf den ersten Blick stellt sich der Lichtungssaum um den Bunker als Waldidyll dar. In Augenhöhe sind auf den dunklen Fichtenstämmen die Namen der Opfer angebracht. Der Saumbereich wird damit als Ganzes zum Gedenkort für die Opfer, eine Annäherung an das Relikt ohne Wahrnehmung der Opfer ist nicht möglich. Das Aufbringen der Namen auf die Stämme mit weißer Farbe ist Gegenstand eines gemeinsamen Handelns von Jugendgruppen, Schulklassen, Vereinen. Es erweitert die Funktionsweise des Gedenkortes hin zu einem Ort der Tätigkeit.

Mit diesem gemeinsamen Handeln ist auch der Ort des ehemaligen Massengrabes, der Schrein der Namen, verknüpft. Auf einer gerodeten Lichtung wird eine Mulde wieder sichtbar. Das eigentliche Relikt des leeren Grabes ist nicht spektakulär, und dennoch ist dieses namenlose Massengrab Sinnbild für den Totalverlust individueller Identität. Zwischen Weg und Grab platzieren die Landschaftsarchitekten ein kastenförmiges Behältnis. In diesem werden die Schablonen für die Beschriftung der Stämme aufbewahrt. Einmal jährlich wird ein Teil der Schablonen herausgenommen und die verwitterten Schriften am Bunker werden erneuert. Auf diesem einfachen Schrein sind die Namen der Opfer in alphabetischer Folge aufgebracht. Je nach Forschungsstand kann das Archiv erweitert werden. Es geht den Landschaftsarchitekten darum, auf die Vernichtung der Menschen nicht mit einer neutralen Inszenierung der Zahl der Opfer zu reagieren, sondern die Anonymität aufzuheben, die Menschen nicht allein als Opfer in Erinnerung zu bringen.

Viewing platform
overlooking
the bunker arch

Aussichtspunkt
am Bunkerbogen

sinai's design for the memorial site at Mühldorfer Hart is also a statement about ways of remembrance. For a site that has been largely banished from memory for 70 years and yet continues to exert a fascination despite the lack of actual built remains, aside from one segment of the bunker, this response along with a proposal for a means of active remembrance seems most plausible. In the landscape architecture competition, sinai's concept was awarded second prize. The first prize was awarded to a concept by the landscape architects Latz + Partner from Kranzberg near Freising. According to the head of the district administration, Georg Huber, their winning design intervenes least in the existing context. Latz + Partner explicitly wanted to avoid glorifying the site. The guiding principle of their design is "understanding the political and historical context – against falling into oblivion" and proposes, in addition to stones of remembrance and three open areas with information, a walkway made of rusted steel that affords visitors a view of the full extent of the bunker complex.

Mit dem Entwurf für den Gedenkort Mühldorfer Hart nehmen sinai Landschaftsarchitekten auch zur Art des Gedenkens Stellung. 70 Jahre der Verdrängung und zugleich der Neugierde auf diesen Ort, der außer dem Bunkersegment kaum bauliche Spuren hinterließ, lassen eine solche Antwort und das Angebot einer aktiven Erinnerungsarbeit plausibel erscheinen. Im landschaftsarchitektonischen Wettbewerb erhielt dieses Konzept den 2. Preis.
Mit dem 1. Preis ausgezeichnet wurde das Konzept der Landschaftsarchitekten Latz + Partner, Kranzberg bei Freising. Dies sei der Plan, der am wenigsten stark in die Umgebung eingreife, erläuterte Landrat Georg Huber. Latz + Partner geht es insbesondere darum, keine Verherrlichung des Geländes zu erzeugen. „Zusammenhänge verstehen – gegen das Vergessen" heißt die Leitidee dieses Entwurfs, der neben Erinnerungssteinen und drei offenen Räumen der Information einen Steg aus rostendem Stahl vorschlägt, um Besuchern einen Überblick über das Ausmaß der Anlage zu ermöglichen.

Shrine holding the name-stencils at the site of the mass grave

Schrein mit Namensschablonen am Massengrab

Flossenbürg
– Finding a New Approach

Flossenbürg
– Den Zugang finden

Flossenbürg is a memorial site that also addresses – indeed must address – the way National Socialism was dealt with in German post-war history. Flossenbürg's role as the site of a former concentration camp was only more widely perceived comparatively late after the war. After 1945, parts of the site were converted back to everyday use as housing, an act that required supressing the memory of what had taken place during the Nazi period. This too was a reason for establishing a new, more conscious appreciation of the history of this place, through a design for the Concentration Camp Memorial. sinai's concept was selected as the winner of an invited competition. For sinai, the task of designing a "means of accessing" the site of the former concentration camp – now a memorial – can be interpreted in several senses. Their approach to the Flossenbürg project shows that the landscape architects have over time developed their own experience of working on "difficult places". Their principle is to always start out from what exists, i.e. from the situation they find on site at the moment in which they undertake the respective design task. "Using a discreet system of marks, we make the historical site legible by tracing its lost structures. These marks or signs we use in a slightly abstract form to stimulate the viewers' imagination."

Flossenbürg ist ein Gedenkort, der auch den Umgang mit dem Nationalsozialismus in der deutschen Nachkriegsgeschichte thematisiert, thematisieren muss. Denn Flossenbürg wird erst relativ spät als ehemaliges Konzentrationslager wahrgenommen. Im Alltag wurden Teile des Ortes nach 1945 als Wohngebiete überformt. Voraussetzung dafür war die Verdrängung des vorherigen nationalsozialistischen Alltags. Auch deshalb gilt es, mittels der Gestaltung der KZ-Gedenkstätte einen neuen, einen bewussten Zugang zur Geschichte dieses Ortes zu ermöglichen.
Der Entwurf konnte sich in einem eingeladenen Wettbewerb durchsetzen. Die Aufgabenstellung, einen „Zugang" zu dem Gelände des ehemaligen Konzentrationslagers – nun Gedenkstätte – zu entwerfen, wurde von sinai durchaus doppelsinnig interpretiert. Der Zugang zur Aufgabe Flossenbürg zeigt, dass sich im Laufe der Arbeit an „schwierigen Orten" eine eigenständige Erfahrung der Landschaftsarchitekten herausgebildet hat. Ihr Prinzip ist, konsequent vom Vorgefundenen auszugehen, also von dem Zustand, der zur Zeit der jeweiligen Aufgabenstellung besteht. „Mit einem gestalterisch zurückhaltenden System von Nachzeichnungen wird der historische Ort anhand seiner verlorenen Strukturen lesbar gemacht. Die Zeichen weisen dabei einen gewissen Abstraktionsgrad auf, um die Imagination des Betrachters herauszufordern."

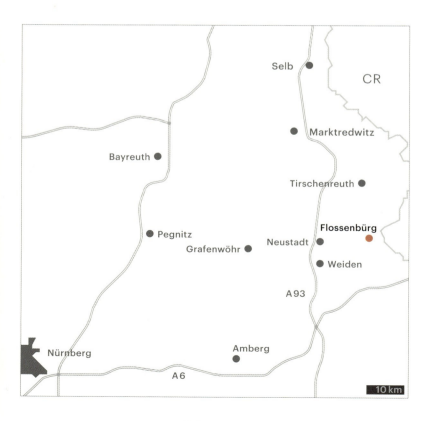

What remains of Flossenbürg is a cemetery of honour created for the victims of the concentration camp in 1957 and the crematorium. In 1946, a first memorial, the "Valley of Death", was constructed by survivors of the camp and leads from the former camp gate along the camp fence to the crematorium, execution area and the pyramid of ashes. As a work created by the camp survivors, this path of suffering must remain untouched. Any new design for remembering the concentration camp must therefore differentiate itself clearly from this historical memorial while respecting the "Valley of Death" as an authentic symbol of mourning and a memorial to those who died.

The greater part of the former concentration camp was, however, cleared for the building of housing in 1958. The arrangement and terrain of the post-war housing still indicate where the prisoners' barracks once stood on the sloping site. Storage buildings in the surrounding areas as well as the stone quarry itself were also used after the war. The quarry had been the original reason for building a camp at Flossenbürg in 1938. Initially, criminals and then later ever larger numbers of prisoners of war were interned in the camp and forced to work in the quarry. The site was leased by the DEST (German Earth and Stone Works) from the State of Bavaria for mining the granite deposits of the Wurmstein. The DEST was a company founded by the SS specifically for exploiting forced labour for the sourcing of building materials for the expansion of the so-called "Führer cities" in Berlin, Nuremberg and Munich, as well as for building motorways.

In Flossenbürg ist neben einem Ehrenfriedhof, der 1957 für Opfer des Arbeitslagers angelegt wurde, noch das Krematorium erhalten. Bereits 1946 gestalteten Überlebende das „Tal des Todes" als Weg entlang von Lagerportal, Lagerzaun, Krematorium, Hinrichtungsstätte und einer Aschepyramide. Dieser Leidensweg ist ein unantastbares Werk der Überlebenden. Eine ergänzende Gestaltung der Erinnerung an das Lager Flossenbürg musste sich von diesem Zeitzeugnis deutlich unterscheiden und zugleich das „Tal des Todes" als eingängiges Zeichen der Trauer und des Gedächtnisses an die Toten respektieren.

Die weitaus größten Bereiche des ehemaligen Lagers wurden 1958 durch eine Wohnsiedlung überbaut. Anordnung und Unterbau der Gebäude lassen die vorherige Struktur der Gefangenenunterkünfte, die dort am Hang lagen, noch erkennen. In benachbarten Arealen blieben Lagerhallen erhalten und wurden weiter genutzt, auch der Steinbruch wurde nach dem Krieg weiterhin betrieben. Dieser Steinbruch war der Anlass für den Bau des Lagers Flossenbürg gewesen, das im Jahr 1938 angelegt wurde. Gefangene Kriminelle und dann immer mehr Kriegsgefangene waren in diesem Lager interniert und wurden zur Arbeit im Steinbruch gezwungen. Das Granitvorkommen am Wurmstein veranlasste die Deutschen Erd- und Steinwerke, das Gelände vom Land Bayern zu pachten. Dieses Unternehmen war eigens von der SS gegründet worden, um entrechtete Zwangsarbeiter auszubeuten und Baumaterialien für die 1938 geplanten Ausbauten der „Führerstädte" Berlin, Nürnberg und München sowie den Bau der Autobahnen zu produzieren.

Flossenbürg Concentration Camp, 1940

KZ Flossenbürg, 1940

As such, Flossenbürg was a kind of concentration camp that on the one hand furthered the economic aims of the SS, and on the other served the purpose of what has been termed "extermination through labour". These camps were production facilities in their respective regions and the local populations were involved in equipping the camps and supplying them with food. Flossenbürg was an integral part of local economic activities in the region – and consequently continued to be used after the liberation of the camp in 1945. 100,000 prisoners were exploited as forced labour in the permanently overcrowded camp at Flossenbürg, and 30,000 died as a result of the inhuman work conditions and inadequate provisions. From 1943 onwards, Flossenbürg concentration camp also became the centre of a network of subcamps that made their prisoners work in armaments factories and elsewhere. Flossenbürg is also known to have been the site of inhuman medical experiments. In April 1945, members of the German resistance including Dietrich Bonhoeffer, Wilhelm Canaris, Ludwig Gehre, Hans Oster, Theodor Strünck and Friedrich von Rabenau were hanged on the orders of Adolf Hitler.

Flossenbürg gehörte damit zu einer Art von Konzentrationslagern, die einerseits wirtschaftlichen Zielen der SS dienten und deren Zweck andererseits mit „Vernichtung durch Arbeit" bezeichnet wurde. Diese Lager waren als Wirtschaftsbetriebe in ihrer Umgebung bekannt, die Bevölkerung war an der Ausstattung dieser Lager beteiligt, ebenso an der Lebensmittelversorgung. Flossenbürg war eingebunden in die wirtschaftliche Tätigkeit in der Region – und so wurde auch nach der Befreiung des Lagers 1945 die Nutzung dieses Ortes fortgesetzt.
100.000 Gefangene waren im stets überfüllten Lager Flossenbürg zur Arbeit gezwungen worden, 30.000 starben aufgrund der unmenschlichen Arbeitsbedingungen und der schlechten Versorgung. Zudem war das KZ Flossenbürg ab 1943 zu einem Netz von Außenlagern ausgebaut worden, deren Gefangene unter anderem in der Rüstungsindustrie eingesetzt wurden. Bekannt war Flossenbürg für menschenverachtende medizinische Versuche. Und in Flossenbürg wurden im April 1945 die Widerstandskämpfer Dietrich Bonhoeffer, Wilhelm Canaris, Ludwig Gehre, Hans Oster, Theodor Strünck und Friedrich von Rabenau auf Befehl Adolf Hitlers erhängt.

Areal photograph from 23 March 1945: The camp fence between the prisoners' and guards' areas is clearly visible as well as the roll call ground between the kitchen and wash house.

Luftbild vom 23. März 1945: Gut erkennbar sind der Lagerzaun zwischen Häftlings- und Mannschaftsbereich sowie der Appellplatz zwischen Küche und Wäscherei.

Texture of the camp: traces mark the long sides of the barracks and a switch in the colour of the surfacing differentiates the guards' area from that of the prisoners.
Site plan 1: 2,500

1 Roll call ground with pair of models
2 Kitchen (exhibition)
3 Wash house (exhibition)
4 Camp gate/camp fence
5 Commandant's office (administration)
6 Casino (seminar rooms)
7 Transformer station building

Textur des Lagers: Die Nachzeichnung der Langseiten der Baracken und ein inverser Farbwechsel der Bodenbeläge kennzeichnet den Unterschied zwischen Mannschafts- und Häftlingsbereichen.
Lageplan 1: 2.500

1 Appellplatz mit Doppelmodell
2 Küche (Ausstellung)
3 Wäscherei (Ausstellung)
4 Lagertor/Lagerzaun
5 Kommandantur (Verwaltung)
6 Casino (Seminar)
7 Trafogebäude

Investigations on the site

Despite its significance in German history, Flossenbürg concentration camp first became the subject of detailed investigations decades after the end of the war and the liberation of the camp. The site of the former camp, including the surviving buildings from the Nazi period, the SS housing area and the quarry, was only declared a national monument in 2006. The design by sinai landscape architects also responds to this long period of historical amnesia.

In their work, sinai aim not to pass judgement but rather to install a rational instance. The given formulation of a design task reflects the specific level of awareness in society, a readiness to confront the history of a particular place. Once a sufficient level of social awareness of the history of National Socialism has been attained, and then backed with political resolution, this starting point is then recorded in the design. What exists on the site at this moment in time – the material remnants and traces – needs to be revealed, and what no longer exists needs to be discovered.

The design for the former concentration camp at Flossenbürg uses marks – insertions that delineate, trace and supplement what exists – as a means of both spatial and historical orientation. Wherever visitors to the site happen to be, it must be immediately apparent that these marks and information systems are later additions. All these additions have been realised using concrete in a variety of different forms. While in the SS areas the markings are flush with the terrain, raised sections mark the location of the former barracks within the bounda-

Ermittlungen zum Ort

Die Auseinandersetzung mit dem KZ Flossenbürg setzte trotz der Bedeutung dieses Ortes für die deutsche Geschichte erst Jahrzehnte nach Kriegsende und Befreiung ein. Erst 2006 wurde das ehemalige Lager mit den Bauten der NS-Zeit, der SS-Siedlung und dem Steinbruch zum Denkmal erklärt. Auch auf diese Geschichtsvergessenheit reagiert der Entwurf von sinai Landschaftsarchitekten.

Es ist die Haltung von sinai, dass sie mit ihren Arbeiten nicht urteilen, sondern einen rationalen Moment installieren möchten. Die jeweilige Formulierung einer Aufgabenstellung spiegelt einen bestimmten zivilgesellschaftlichen Grad an Bewusstheit, eine Bereitschaft zur Auseinandersetzung mit der Geschichte des jeweiligen Ortes wider. Ist eine Stufe des gesellschaftlichen Bewusstseins der NS-Geschichte erst einmal erreicht und in politische Beschlussfassungen gemündet, ist diese im Entwurf als Ausgangssituation festzuhalten. Das zu diesem Zeitpunkt Vorgefundene, das materiell Vorgefundene, die Spuren, gilt es aufzuschließen, das nicht mehr Vorgefundene zu entdecken. Der Entwurf für das ehemalige Konzentrationslager Flossenbürg sieht zum Zweck der überlagerten räumlichen und historischen Orientierung Nachzeichnungen, also Ergänzungen im Raum vor. Die Nachträglichkeit der Nachzeichnungen und Infosysteme soll für den Besucher an jedem Ort sofort erkennbar sein. Das Material für diese Nachzeichnungen ist durchgängig Beton in unterschiedlichen Ausführungen. Während die Nachzeichnungen im SS-Bereich bündig mit dem vorhandenen Terrain abschließen, kennzeichnen erhabene Nachzeichnungen die Standorte der verloren gegangenen Baracken im Lagerinnern. Der Beton erhält als Zuschlagsstoff einen gelblichen Granit, der auf die Arbeit der Häftlinge im benachbarten Steinbruch verweist. Für die Markierung des Lagerzauns

Insertions made of concrete
with a granite aggregate:

Nachzeichnungen aus Beton
mit Zuschlägen aus Granit:

Camp gate

Portal

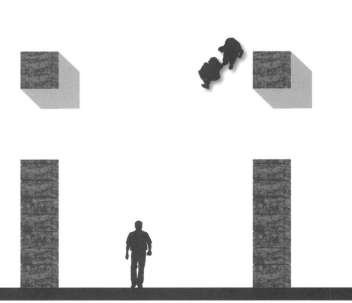

ries of the camp. The concrete mixture contains a granite aggregate with a yellowish colour, a reference to the work of the inmates in the neighbouring quarry. The camp fence is delineated by a row of freestanding slender concrete steles that are as high as the former camp fence once was. The intervals of these steles correspond with the placement of the original fence posts. A mown strip in the grass runs parallel to the fence, marking the separation between the former camp and the former surroundings.

"Parts of the site of the former concentration camp at Flossenbürg were returned to everyday use in post-Nazi society." This diplomatically worded statement in the competition submission reveals sinai's amazement at the sheer ignorance and repression of local Nazi history which prevailed for many years. "The aim is to establish a cognitive as well as emotional connection to a site that has remained concealed and obscured by new constructions for many years. The concept traces the structures that have been lost and creates a logical succession of didactic stations."

A central aspect of the design is therefore the area of the former barracks. On the site of the memorial these are marked by shallow concrete sills. Rather than delineating the perimeter of each building, the placement of the sills emphasises the character of the overall structure (the "battery of barracks") as opposed to conveying the presence and meaning of each individual building. Archaeological excavations conducted on site will be left open for longer periods and explained to the visitors. The opportunities for intervention in the housing area to the north are more limited. To better comprehend the structure of the original camp, the landscape architects

werden schlanke Betonstelen in der Höhe des ehemaligen Lagerzauns verwendet. Die Taktung entspricht dem Abstand der Zaunpfähle. Ein gemähter Rasenweg begleitet die Zaunanlage und trennt ehemaliges Lager und ehemalige Nachbarschaft.

„Teile des Areals des ehemaligen Konzentrationslagers Flossenbürg waren in den Alltag einer postnationalsozialistischen Gesellschaft überführt worden." So brachten sinai Landschaftsarchitekten im Wettbewerbsbeitrag diplomatisch ihr Erstaunen zum Ausdruck über die schlichte Ignoranz und die Verdrängung der NS-Geschichte, die vor Ort lange Jahre vorherrschten. „Ziel ist die kognitive und emotionale Erschließung eines Geländes, das lange verborgen und verstellt war. Im Mittelpunkt stehen die Nachzeichnung verlorener Strukturen und eine schlüssige Folge didaktischer Stationen."

Ein Schwerpunkt des Entwurfs sind daher die Barackenfelder. Sie werden auf dem Gedenkstättengelände mit flachen Betonschwellen nachgezeichnet. Auf ein Schließen der Gebäudekonturen wird bewusst verzichtet: Der Charakter der zusammenhängenden Struktur („Barackenfeld") wird damit gestärkt, die gegenständliche Bedeutung des einzelnen Gebäudes zurückgenommen. Archäologische Grabungsbereiche werden zeitweise offengehalten und den Besuchern erläutert. Für den Siedlungsbereich im Norden bestehen dagegen nur sehr eingeschränkt Handlungsmöglichkeiten. Zum Verständnis der Lagerstruktur wären übergreifende Elemente wünschenswert, um die Barackenfelder auch hangwärts erkennbar werden zu lassen. Konzeptionelle Idee der Landschaftsarchitekten ist es, in einer Nachbarschaftsinitiative mit öffentlicher Unterstützung die jeweiligen Grundstücksgrenzen in den Baufluchten mit vereinheitlichten Heckenstrukturen zu bepflanzen. Die allzu große Dominanz der baulichen Details am Hang würde damit ebenfalls gemildert.

Camp fence

Lagerzaun

Barracks (long sides)

Baracken (Langseiten)

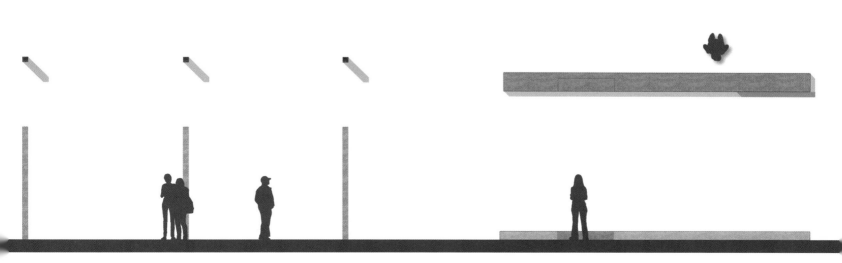

looked for elements that can be used to mark the former barracks both inside as well as outside the memorial site on the incline. Their conceptual idea involves working with the neighbourhood in a public initiative to plant strips of hedges along the plot boundaries in line with the buildings, creating a unifying pattern of hedges. This would also mitigate the rather dominant presence of the respective buildings on the slope.

There are three constituent elements to the design by sinai for Flossenbürg Concentration Camp Memorial: the *windows of exploration* embedded in the visible post-war history and design of the site; the accentuation of the *atmospheric field* of Flossenbürg, which is primarily a product of the expectations and knowledge of the history of the concentration camp and only secondarily a product of its design; and the *memorial as a space of movement*, in which the focus of design lies not on the consideration of the historical situation but rather on how one experiences it in the present day.

All three elements are used in similar constellations in sinai's other work, for example in the Berlin Wall Memorial or in the design for Bergen-Belsen. Similarly, the method of visibly "charting" a site, of marking previous structures, is a recurring motif in their design approach. These markings invite the visitor to compare their expectations and knowledge of the history of the site, the images they have in their minds, with the reality of the situation – and ultimately, according to sinai, to engage personally with the history of the place.

Es sind drei Elemente, die den Entwurf von sinai für die Gedenkstätte Flossenbürg ausmachen: die *Erkundungsfenster*, eingebettet in eine sichtbare Nachkriegsgeschichte und -gestaltung des Ortes; die Betonung des *atmosphärischen Feldes* Flossenbürg, das sich aus der Erwartung, dem Wissen um die Geschichte des Konzentrationslagers speist und erst in zweiter Linie aus seiner Gestaltung; und die *Gedenkstätte als Bewegungsraum*, also die Betrachtung nicht der historischen Situation, sondern ihrer heutigen Aneignung im Mittelpunkt des Entwurfs.

Alle drei Elemente finden sich in ähnlicher Weise auch in anderen Arbeiten von sinai wieder, so in der Gedenkstätte Berliner Mauer oder im Entwurf für Bergen-Belsen. Auch die in der Gestaltung sichtbare „Kartierung" eines Geländes, die Markierung vorheriger Strukturen, ist ein wiederkehrendes Motiv. Diese Markierungen regen an, die Erwartungen der Besucher, das Wissen um die Geschichte, das als Bild im Kopf gespeichert ist, mit der vorgefundenen Realität abzugleichen – und letztlich, so ist es von sinai kalkuliert, zu einer Auseinandersetzung mit Geschichte zu gelangen.

Information system

Informationssystem

Signs

Wegweiser

Information steles

Informationsträger

Pair of models showing the site in 1945 and today

Doppelmodell zum Gelände 1945 und heute

The site of the former concentration camp at Flossenbürg is conceived as a circuit consisting of didactic stations that serve as anchors for remembering or imagining. On arriving at the site, visitors are directed to a converted former electricity substation, in which they receive information on the facilities and activities provided by the present-day memorial. By way of a prologue, they receive a basic introduction to the camp and site plan. In the area of the roll call ground, two 1:250 scale models show the historical and current situation, making it possible to compare in detail the remaining structures and the traces of the previous camp situation as marked by the new insertions. The intention is not primarily to communicate facts and knowledge but to awaken associations in the visitor through the markings and traces.

In addition to these three elements, the memorial area with the crematorium, known as the "Valley of Death", remains the principle area of remembrance, as it has been since the 1950s. This area, with its elements of burial culture such as the "Pyramid of Ashes", the crematorium and the "Square of Nations" and its memorial at the execution area, has deliberately been left untouched and exists alongside the new markings made throughout the rest of the site.

Der Raum des ehemaligen Konzentrationslagers Flossenbürg wird als Rundgang gedacht, in dem didaktische Stationen Anker des Erinnerns oder Vorstellens bieten. Am Ankunftsort für den Besucher, einer umgebauten ehemaligen Trafostation, erhält der Besucher alle Informationen zu den Einrichtungen und Angeboten der heutigen Gedenkstätte. Mit Grundwissen zum Lager, einschließlich der Lagepläne, wird der Besucher also bereits zum Prolog vertraut gemacht. Im Bereich des Appellplatzes zeigt ein Doppelmodell im Maßstab 1:250 den historischen und den heutigen Zustand und ermöglicht einen detaillierten Abgleich der erhaltenen Strukturen und Nachzeichnungen mit dem lagerzeitlichen Zustand. Es kommt dabei nicht vordringlich darauf an, den Besucher zur Aufnahme von Wissen und Fakten zu animieren, sondern ihn mittels Spuren und Markierungen zu Assoziationen anzuregen.

Neben diesen drei Elementen bleibt das als „Tal des Todes" bezeichnete Areal am Krematorium erhalten, seit den 1950er Jahren der Schwerpunkt des Gedenkens. Diesen Bereich mit den Elementen einer Grabkultur wie der Aschepyramide, dem Krematorium selbst, dem Platz der Nationen und der Erinnerung an die Hinrichtungsstätte lässt der Entwurf zur Weiterentwicklung der Gedenkstätte bewusst unberührt neben den auf dem gesamten Areal hinzugefügten neuen Nachzeichnungen bestehen.

Place for individual remembrance: freestanding wall with names between the roll call ground and the "Valley of Death"

Ort des individuellen Gedenkens: Wandscheibe mit Namen zwischen Appellplatz und „Tal des Todes"

Bracketing the space and linking the historical remains of the camp with the memorial site to the east is a "mineral band". On arriving in the grounds of the memorial, visitors are immediately confronted by this open space. As wide as the former roll call ground and devoid of all vegetation, this plain surface extends as a wide band across the entire historical camp. The atmospheric impression of entering a space not overgrown and dominated by plants that conceal the presence of the former camp, is extraordinary and immediately palpable as soon as one arrives. The buildings stand alone and isolated within this space. A sudden change in the surfacing material from light-coloured gravel to a dark water-bound gritted surface marks the boundary between the former guards' area and the former prisoners' barracks. This band starts at one end with the introductory prologue and ends at the "Archive of Names" between the cemetery and the roll call ground. Visitors can choose whether or not to follow the path across the band or to pursue a path of their own. Freed of all superfluous structures, this area serves as a space of movement, an open window of exploration and an atmospheric field.

Räumlich verklammert ein „mineralisches Band" die historischen Lagerteile mit der Gedenklandschaft im Osten. Mit diesem offenen Raum ist der Besucher unmittelbar mit Betreten des Gedenkstättengeländes konfrontiert. In der Breite des ehemaligen Appellplatzes durchzieht das vegetationslose, spröde Feld die historische Lagerstruktur. Dieser atmosphärisch außergewöhnliche Raumeindruck einer nicht durch Pflanzen, durch ein Überwuchern kaschierten Präsenz des historischen Lagers wird sofort am Ankunftsort spürbar. Die Gebäude stehen ohne jede Einbindung auf der Platzfläche. Durch einen markanten Belagswechsel von heller Schotterdecke zu dunkler wassergebundener Wegedecke wird der Unterschied zwischen Mannschafts- und Häftlingsbereich markiert. Das Feld wird durch diesen einführenden Prolog eröffnet und mit dem Archiv der Namen zwischen Friedhof und Appellplatz abgeschlossen. Es bleibt dem Besucher überlassen, ob er den Erzählspuren über den Platz folgt oder sich seine Wege selbst wählt. Der von allen überflüssigen Strukturen befreite Raum dient als Bewegungsraum, offenes Erkundungsfenster und atmosphärisches Feld.

New entrance to the camp: survivors of the camp took down the original columns of the gate and relocated them to the "Valley of Death" memorial.

Markierung des Lagereingangs: Überlebende versetzten die Portalsäulen in den Gedenkbereich am „Tal des Todes".

**Roll call ground between
the exhibitions in the former
kitchen and wash house**

Appellplatz zwischen den
Ausstellungsgebäuden in
Küche und Wäscherei

Outdoor areas of the Federal Foundation Flight, Expulsion, Reconciliation, Berlin-Kreuzberg, invited competition, 2013

Außenanlagen Bundesstiftung Flucht, Vertreibung, Versöhnung, Berlin-Kreuzberg, beschränkter Wettbewerb, 2013

**Flight, Expulsion,
Reconciliation
– Cumulus and Fraxinus**

Flucht, Vertreibung,
Versöhnung
– Cumulus und Fraxinus

Flight, expulsion, reconciliation – three words that represent the complexity of the long-term consequences of German history, and three words for which the foundation stands. The intention of the landscape architecture competition was to capture the complexity of this relationship in the design of two small outdoor areas on the forecourt area of the Deutschlandhaus in Berlin-Kreuzberg. sinai landscape architects along with the Berlin-based artist duo stoebo – Oliver Störmer & Cisca Bogman – were awarded second prize for their provocative sculptural and garden design proposal for the competition site.

The competition called for a design that symbolically marks an outdoor area in front of the Deutschlandhaus, incorporating the existing pavement with cobblestones and concrete paving, an underground railway station entrance, a café garden, a sweeping cycle path and a triangular forecourt. From 2016, the Deutschlandhaus will house the foundation's exhibition, documentation and information centre on flight and expulsion. Until 1999, the building housed the headquarters of the representatives of the politically controversial Federation of Expellees.

Flucht, Vertreibung, Versöhnung – die gleichnamige Stiftung steht für die komplizierte Wirkungsfolge deutscher Geschichte. Dieses spannungsreiche Verhältnis in die Gestaltung zweier kleiner Freiräume eines Trottoirs vor dem Deutschlandhaus in Berlin-Kreuzberg zu fassen, war die Aufgabe eines Landschaftsarchitekturwettbewerbs. Für ihre bildhauerische und gartenkünstlerische Provokation wurden sinai Landschaftsarchitekten in diesem Wettbewerb 2013 gemeinsam mit den Künstlern stoebo – Oliver Störmer & Cisca Bogman, beide Berlin, mit einem zweiten Preis ausgezeichnet.

Wo heute ein Gehweg mit Kleinstein- und Betonpflaster, S-Bahn-Abgang, Café-Garten und verschwenktem Radweg sich vor dem Deutschlandhaus zu einem Dreieck aufweitet, wird ein Zeichen erwartet, ein besonders markierter Freiraum. Denn das Deutschlandhaus soll ab 2016 der Stiftung als Ausstellungs-, Dokumentations- und Informationszentrum zu Flucht und Vertreibung dienen. Bis 1999 hatten die Landsmannschaften des politisch umstrittenen Bundes der Vertriebenen dort ihren Sitz.

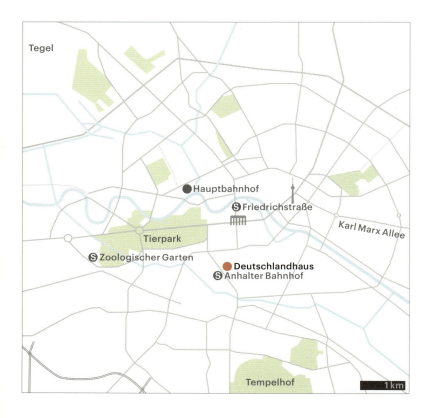

At the beginning of the 1930s, the corner of Stresemann-strasse and Anhalter Strasse opposite the square at Askanischer Platz and the Anhalter Bahnhof was one of the most vibrant places in Berlin. Today, all that remains of the former railway terminal are the ruins of the portal arches of the end wall. In front of the railway station an ornate constellation of trees and flowerbeds marked the location as one of the most important railway stations in the city. Opposite this vibrant station, an office building, now known as the Deutschlandhaus, was built from 1926–31 according to a design by Richard Bielenberg and Josef Moser in a transitional style between expressionism and modernism. In 1935, a second building, the Europahaus, was built next door and was at the time the tallest building in Berlin. The twelve-storey high-rise complex contained a cinema and music hall, a beer hall, shops, cafés and offices, and its new illuminated signage made it one of the most photographed buildings in the city.

The rise of National Socialism put an abrupt end to the burgeoning modernism. The Stresemannstrasse was renamed the Saarlandstrasse and Berlin became "Capital of the German Reich" and the centre from which the Germans planned the Second World War. Towards the end of the war, the Europahaus complex was partially destroyed and its reconstruction did not happen until 1960. The lower wing to the east was initially called the Haus der ostdeutschen Heimat (House of the East German Homeland) and in 1974 was renamed the Deutschlandhaus. During this period, the Stresemannstrasse and Anhalter Strasse lay not far from the Berlin Wall in the West German district of Kreuzberg.

After the reunification of Berlin, the new urban quarter of the Potsdamer Platz was erected a short way away from the site; the Berlin House of Representatives moved into the former Prussian Parliament Building, also nearby; the Topography of Terror memorial was built a few hundred meters away; the Federal Ministry for Economic Cooperation and Development moved into the Europahaus; and the Tempodrom, a concrete tent, was built on the site of the former Anhalter Bahnhof as a venue for concerts, followed some years after by the creation of a park for sport and recreation at Gleisdreieck, the former triangular rail junction.

The site of the future home of the Federal Foundation Flight, Expulsion, Reconciliation is today once again a key spot in the inner city of Berlin.

Zu Beginn der 1930er Jahre war die Kreuzung Stresemannstraße Ecke Anhalter Straße am Askanischen Platz gegenüber dem Anhalter Bahnhof einer der lebendigsten Orte Berlins. Von diesem Kopfbahnhof zeugt bis heute die bogenförmige Ruine der Bahnhofsfront. Vor dem Bahnhof betonte eine gartenkünstlerisch aufwändige Gestaltung mit Baumgruppen und Blumeninseln die Bedeutung dieses Ortes als eines der wichtigsten Bahnhöfe der Stadt. Gegenüber dem belebten Anhalter Bahnhof wurde 1926 – 31 das heutige Deutschlandhaus nach dem Entwurf von Richard Bielenberg und Josef Moser errichtet, ein Bürobau aus der Übergangszeit des Expressionismus zur Moderne. 1935 kam Berlins höchstes Haus, das Europahaus, hinzu. Der bis zu zwölfgeschossige Hochhauskomplex beherbergte einen Kino- und Varietésaal, ein Hofbräuhaus, Läden, Cafés und Büros. Mit seiner damals neuartigen Leuchtreklame war dieses Gebäude eines der meistfotografierten Motive der Stadt.

Diese Modernität nahm ein jähes Ende. Die Nationalsozialisten benannten die Stresemannstraße in Saarlandstraße um. Berlin wurde zur „Reichshauptstadt", von hier aus planten und organisierten die Deutschen den Zweiten Weltkrieg. Der Gebäudekomplex des Europahauses wurde am Ende dieses Krieges teilweise zerstört. Nach seinem Wiederaufbau 1960 wurde der flachere Ostflügel zum Haus der ostdeutschen Heimat und 1974 in Deutschlandhaus umbenannt. Stresemann- und Anhalter Straße lagen in diesen Jahrzehnten im Schatten der Berliner Mauer im westlichen Bezirk Kreuzberg.

Nach der Vereinigung der Stadt wurde nahe dieser Kreuzung der Potsdamer Platz neu errichtet, bezog das Berliner Abgeordnetenhaus den ebenfalls benachbarten ehemaligen Preußischen Landtag als neues gesamtstädtisches Quartier, entstand die Gedenkstätte Topographie des Terrors einige hundert Meter entfernt, nutzt das Bundesministerium für wirtschaftliche Zusammenarbeit und Entwicklung das Europahaus und wurden auf dem Gelände des ehemaligen Anhalter Bahnhofs das Betonzelt des Tempodrom für Konzerte sowie im Anschluss der Park auf dem Gleisdreieck für Sport und Spiel neu angelegt.

Der Ort, an dem die Stiftung Flucht, Vertreibung, Versöhnung ihren zukünftigen Sitz hat, ist heute einer der Knotenpunkte der Berliner Innenstadt.

The Europahaus c. 1936

Das Europahaus um 1936

Not a place of commemoration

From the pavement in front of the Deutschlandhaus, however, this potential is not immediately apparent. This was the motivation behind the idea of representing the work of the foundation in the design of a public space in front of the foundation's headquarters. The building is set back slightly from the building line along the Stresemannstrasse and a further step back from the diagonally intersecting Anhalter Strasse, which results in two outdoor spaces. Spatial interventions in these two forecourt areas should transport the themes of flight, expulsion and reconciliation into the public realm in front of the Deutschlandhaus.

The two interventions that the design proposes – supplemented by an otherwise restrained surfacing of small grey cobblestones – are not consistent with one another: after flight and expulsion, reconciliation does not necessarily follow. The aggressor cannot simultaneously be a victim. But this is precisely the historical experience of hundreds of thousands who died fleeing East Prussia, Silesia, Pomerania and the Sudetenland, or were expelled from their homeland. The German attacks on its neighbouring countries set in motion a chain of extermination and expulsion, and yet it took decades for Germany to agree to relate the history of expulsion in this context. The mission of the Foundation Flight, Expulsion, Reconciliation is "to preserve, in the spirit of reconciliation, the memory and commemoration of flight and expulsion in the twentieth century against the historical background of World War Two and the National Socialist policies of expansionism and extermination and their consequences." A central focus of the foundation's work is to present "the flight and expulsion of Germans, which will be embedded in the context of expulsions in twentieth-century Europe." The complicated formulation of the purpose of the foundation, itself the result of years of social and political debate, shows how necessary the work of the foundation is, but also how it borders on the impossible. How can, through the work of a foundation in Germany, an adequate means of expression be found for both the guilt the nation heaped upon itself as well as for the innocence of many individuals who lost their homeland, died while trying to flee or had to resettle in a new place to live and integrate into new post-war societies? The foundation's concrete tasks include research and evaluation along with the documentation of flight and expulsion in permanent and temporary exhibitions. For the space in front of this research and exhibition centre, a means of articulation needs to be found that captures this field of tension as eloquently as possible. The space in front of the Deutschlandhaus is not about commemorating, but it is about remembering. And all of this needs to be achieved within a confined space – next to a café – using the means of art and landscape architecture.

Kein Gedenkort

Dem Ort selbst, den Gehsteigen vor dem Deutschlandhaus, sieht man diese potenzielle Bedeutung allerdings derzeit nicht an. Das erklärt die Idee, vor dem Stiftungssitz die Themen der Stiftungsarbeit zum Gegenstand der Gestaltung dieses öffentlichen Raumes zu machen. Das Gebäude verspringt gegenüber der Bauflucht des Berliner Blockrandes um etwa fünf Meter. Dieser Rücksprung entlang der Stresemannstraße sowie ein weiterer Versprung zur über Eck liegenden Anhalter Straße bilden zwei Teilräume. Diese beiden Vorplätze sollen nun mittels einer Raumintervention die Themen Flucht, Vertreibung, Versöhnung vor das Deutschlandhaus in den öffentlichen Raum tragen. Die beiden Setzungen, die der Entwurf vorsieht und die er sehr zurückhaltend mit einer Pflasterfläche aus grauem Kleinsteinmosaik ergänzt, sind beide in sich inkonsistent. Auf Flucht und Vertreibung folgte nicht zwingend Versöhnung. Der Angreifer kann nicht gleichzeitig Opfer sein. Und dennoch haben Hunderttausende die Geschichte so erlebt, sie starben auf der Flucht aus Ostpreußen, Schlesien, Pommern und dem Sudetenland, wurden vertrieben aus ihren Heimatorten. Die Angriffe Deutschlands auf die Nachbarstaaten hatten diese Kette aus Vernichtung und Vertreibung ausgelöst, und doch hat es Jahrzehnte gebraucht, um sich in Deutschland zu einigen, die Geschichte der Vertreibung in diesem Kontext zu erzählen. „Zweck der Stiftung Flucht, Vertreibung, Versöhnung ist es, im Geiste der Versöhnung die Erinnerung und das Gedenken an Flucht und Vertreibung im 20. Jahrhundert im historischen Kontext des Zweiten Weltkrieges und der nationalsozialistischen Expansions- und Vernichtungspolitik und ihren Folgen wachzuhalten", lautet die Mission der Stiftung. „Flucht und Vertreibung der Deutschen bilden einen Hauptakzent der Stiftungsarbeit und werden im Zusammenhang europäischer Vertreibungen im 20. Jahrhundert dargestellt." Schon diese komplexe Formulierung des Stiftungszwecks als Ergebnis langjähriger gesellschaftlicher und politischer Auseinandersetzungen zeigt, dass die Arbeit der Stiftung ebenso notwendig wie fast unmöglich ist. Wie kann durch die Arbeit einer Stiftung in Deutschland der Schuld ebenso Ausdruck verliehen werden wie der Unschuld Einzelner, die ihre Heimat verloren, auf der Flucht getötet wurden oder sich an neuen Orten in neue Nachkriegsgesellschaften eingliedern mussten? Forschung und Aufarbeitung sowie die Dokumentation von Flucht und Vertreibung in einer Dauer- und in Wechselausstellungen sind die konkreten Aufgaben der Stiftung. Für den Raum vor diesem Ausstellungs- und Arbeitsort musste ein Ausdruck gefunden werden, der dieses Spannungsfeld möglichst eindeutig zeigt. Es geht vor dem Deutschlandhaus nicht um einen Ort des Gedenkens, wohl aber um einen Ort der Erinnerung. Und dies auf knappstem Raum, neben der Außengastronomie, mit den Mitteln der Kunst am Bau wie der Landschaftsarchitektur.

The artists and landscape architects faced the challenge of investing a location with a "new" history (or way of looking at history), of creating a location that does not derive its future identity from its specific past, but at the same time to design a space for everyday use in Berlin, which this junction used to be in the past and will continue to be in future. Many of the project submissions therefore employ the semiotic character of advertising billboards, formulating historical insights in the manner of brand claims.

sinai and stoebo instead remain ambiguous. Two interventions, one sculptural, the other horticultural, lend each of the two parts of the space a different expression, the simple, cobbled surfacing serving as a frame uniting the entire space. The meaning of the objects, both of the sculpture as well as of the tree sculpture, depends on the viewer's own interpretation.

Die Künstler und Landschaftsarchitekten standen vor der Herausforderung, einen Ort mit einer „neuen" Geschichte (Geschichtsbetrachtung) zu besetzen, seine zukünftige Identität nicht aus seiner konkreten Vergangenheit abzuleiten, zugleich aber einen Ort des Alltags in Berlin zu gestalten, der diese Kreuzung in der Vergangenheit war und weiterhin sein wird. Viele der eingereichten Arbeiten setzten daher an der Zeichenhaftigkeit von Reklametafeln an und formulierten Geschichtserkenntnis als Markenbotschaft.

sinai und stoebo blieben uneindeutig. Zwei Setzungen, eine bildhauerische und eine gartenkünstlerische, geben den beiden Teilräumen jeweils einen anderen Ausdruck. Über die einfache Pflasterdecke wird der Raum zu einem einheitlichen Rahmen zusammengefasst. Die Bedeutung der Objekte, sowohl der Skulptur wie der Baumskulptur, bleibt abhängig von den Interpretationen der Betrachter.

Two sides, two insertions: a sculpture at the main entrance and a cluster of trees along Anhalter Strasse

Zwei Seiten, zwei Setzungen: Skulptur am Haupteingang und Baumgruppe an der Anhalter Straße

25 m

Cumulus

The sculpture developed by stoebo – Oliver Störmer & Cisca Bogman – is a sculptural insertion that emphasises the imaginary. Designed using a computer, the three-dimensional model expresses Germany's development over the course of the 20th century as a kind of sculptural puzzle. An issue that has repeatedly been the subject of discussion in the history of the foundation and its predecessors is the question of the borders of Germany – and the borders at which time in history? stoebo and sinai phrase this question in the form of a sculpture: "The three historical borders of Germany in the 20th century, that is the outlines of the border from the years 1918, 1937 and 1990 are extruded out of the cartographic plane into physical bodies. The three situations are arranged at angles to one another so that all three intersect at an imaginary point in the centre. The respective angles of the three extruded objects are arranged around a notional circle so that the respective year corresponds to the minute hand of a clock (15 min = 1925, 30 min = 1950, 45 min = 1975, 0 min = 1900 or 2000). All physical space that is not contained within the intersection of all three of the volumetric instances is removed. What remains is a new, sculptural volume that represents the intersection space of all three forms." The competition jury was at first not sure how to read this sculptural interpretation. Taken at face value as a piece of sculpture in space, one might freely associate it with a bronze piece of rock, a meteorite or perhaps a solidified cloud.

Cumulus: national borders in the form of a historical figure in space

Cumulus: Grenzen als geschichtliches Raummodell

Cumulus

Die von stoebo – Oliver Stoermer & Cisca Bogman – durchentwickelte Skulptur als bildhauerische Setzung betont das Imaginäre. Ein am Computer entworfenes Raummodell bringt in plastischer Form zum Ausdruck, dass Deutschland im Verlauf des 20. Jahrhunderts eine Art Vexierbild eines Staates bildete. Die Frage, die auch in der Geschichte der Stiftung und ihrer Vorläufer immer wieder zu Auseinandersetzungen führte, ist diese Frage nach den Grenzen Deutschlands – Grenzen zu welcher Zeit? stoebo und sinai formulieren diese Frage als Skulptur:
„Die drei historischen Grenzen Deutschlands im 20. Jahrhundert, die Grenzverläufe der Jahre 1918, 1937 und 1990, werden gedanklich aus der kartografischen Fläche zu Raumkörpern extrudiert. Sie werden winkelig zueinander positioniert, so dass alle drei Raumkörper sich in einer imaginären Mitte durchkreuzen. Die jeweiligen Positionswinkel der drei Extrusionsobjekte werden auf einem gedachten Kreis so angeordnet, dass die korrespondierenden Jahreszahlen des Jahrhunderts der Minutenanzeige eines Uhrenziffernblatts entsprechen: 15 min = 1925, 30 min = 1950, 45 min = 1975, 0 min = 1900/2000. Alle Volumina, die nicht Teil der gemeinsamen, räumlichen Schnittmenge aller drei Körper sind, werden verworfen und entfernt. Das verbleibende Restvolumen ergibt einen neuartigen, plastischen Geometriekörper, der die gemeinsame Schnittmenge aller drei Formen repräsentiert."
Diese bildhauerische Setzung überforderte vorübergehend die Wettbewerbsjury. Im Raum sichtbar wäre ein Raumkörper, in dem man ebenso frei und unverfänglich einen bronzenen Fels, einen Meteoriten, vielleicht eine Wolke erkennen könnte.

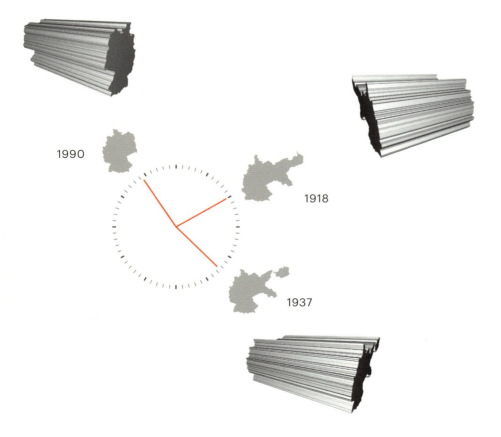

1990

1918

1937

Only on closer inspection do the issues of boundaries, of space and the German nation become apparent. And this is where it becomes contentious, a response that the designers find appropriate. Germany represented as a cloud? Or Germany represented by its past borders? sinai and stoebo describe the sculpture as an "object of speculation with ambiguous meaning": "The initial idea, which is derived from the shape of the territorial boundaries, is more or less discernible depending on one's angle of view. As one moves around in relation to the object, one begins to lose one's concrete image of Germany, setting in motion an associative chain of speculation on its shape and form." This space-border sculpture, made as a bronze cast of a CNC-milled solid, could be placed near the entrance to the foundation where it can, according to the authors, "stimulate people to reflect on the transitory nature of territorial boundaries, on the principles and mutable nature of nationality and on its tragic consequences." Such considerations could, however, also be read as a statement placed in a public space in Berlin on the changeability of boundaries – i.e. as a revisionist idea. Would this artistic reference to the changing borders of Germany support the aim of reconciliation? Or could it also harm it? This ambivalence resulted in the design being awarded second place. The jury wanted to avoid any suggestion of a debate on the borders of the nation at the entrance to this newly established foundation.

Auf den zweiten Blick aber wäre das Thema der Grenzen, des Raumes, der Nation Deutschland wohl erkennbar. Und dies führte zu Irritationen, durchaus im Sinne der Entwurfsverfasser. Deutschland als Wolke? Oder Deutschland in den Grenzen der Vergangenheit? sinai und stoebo argumentieren mit einem „mehrdeutigen Spekulationsobjekt": „Der Ausgangsgedanke, der sich aus der Gestalt territorialer Grenzen ableiten lässt, bleibt je nach Betrachtungswinkel mehr oder weniger zu erahnen, jedoch verliert sich das konkrete Deutschlandbild bei wechselnden Standpunkten (zum Objekt) und gibt Anlass zu assoziativen Spekulationsketten über Form und Gestalt." Diese Raum-Grenz-Skulptur, die aus CNC-gefrästen Raummodellen als Bronzeguss gefügt wird, könnte im Eingangsbereich zur Stiftung, so die Erwartung der Verfasser, „Reflexionen anstoßen über die Flüchtigkeit territorialer Grenzen, über die Prinzipien und Veränderlichkeit von Nationalstaatlichkeit und über ihre tragischen Folgen". Diese Reflexionen hätten jedoch ebenso als ein im öffentlichen Raum Berlins platziertes Statement zur Veränderlichkeit von Grenzen gelesen werden können – also auch als revisionistische Idee. Hätte die künstlerische Bezugnahme auf veränderliche Grenzen Deutschlands das Ziel der Versöhnung gestärkt? Oder schwächen können? Den Entwurf hat diese Mehrdeutigkeit auf den zweiten Platz geführt. Die Jury wollte jeglichen Anschein einer Grenzdebatte vor dem Eingang dieser neu gefügten Stiftung vermeiden.

The main entrance to the exhibition centre on the Stresemannstrasse

Haupteingang zur Ausstellung an der Stresemannstraße

1

2

3

4

From the tree nursery
to a bizarre tree sculpture:
negative geotropism
 1 Tree nursery
 2 Planting
 3 Year 20
 4 Year 50

Vom Baumschulbaum
zur bizarren Baumskulptur:
negativer Geotropismus
 1 Baumschule
 2 Pflanzung
 3 Jahr 20
 4 Jahr 50

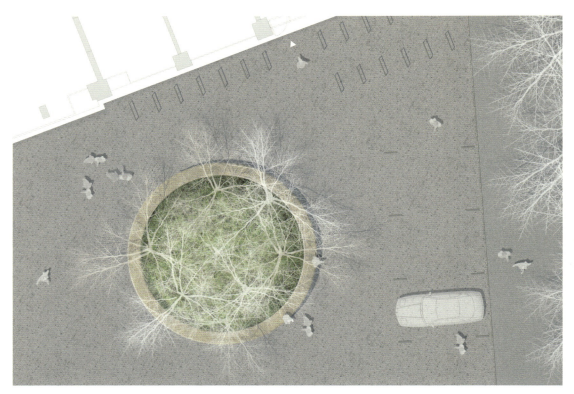

Fraxinus: the cluster of ash trees becomes a focal point in the streetspace.

Fraxinus: Die Eschengruppe entwickelt sich zum räumlichen Schwerpunkt.

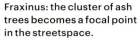

Fraxinus

The horticultural intervention that sinai landscape architects proposed for the space on the Anhalter Strasse is likewise a sculptural intervention and draws on the techniques of arboriculture from the era of the landscape garden. It refers to an epoch that more than any other in the history of horticulture stood for the idea of freedom. sinai combine this with the motif of change and adaption – referring in turn to the possibility of reconciliation after the experience of expulsion.

In the urban realm, a cluster of trees of this kind looks like an artful network of trunks and branches, and deliberately out of place as a tree sculpture. Its placement on the section that extends along the Anhalter Strasse and widens to become a triangle with an edge length of 25 metres, is an expression of a position that both attracts attention and unsettles using the means of landscape architecture.

Fraxinus

Die gartenkünstlerische, ebenfalls skulpturale Setzung, die sinai Landschaftsarchitekten im Bereich der Anhalter Straße vorsehen, geht zurück auf Baumschul-Techniken aus der Zeit des Landschaftsgartens. Zitiert wird damit eine Epoche, die wie keine andere in der Geschichte der Gartenkunst für die Idee der Freiheit steht. sinai verbinden diese mit dem Motiv der Veränderung, der Anpassung – und verweisen damit auf die Versöhnung, die auf Vertreibung folgen kann.

Im städtischen Raum wirkt eine solche Baumgruppe als künstlerisches Geflecht aus Stämmen und Ästen, als Baum-Skulptur absichtsvoll fremd. Ihre Platzierung auf der Erweiterung entlang der Anhalter Straße, die ein Dreieck mit bis zu 25 Meter Seitenlänge bildet, ist Ausdruck einer Haltung, die Irritation und Aufmerksamkeit mit den Mitteln der Landschaftsarchitektur erzeugt.

**Forecourt
on Anhalter Strasse**

Vorplatz an der
Anhalter Straße

The landscape architects frame the tree sculpture with a bench made of anodised expanded mesh that appears to float over the ground's surface and encircles the cluster of ash trees, marking it out as a place to meet in the city. As a horticultural work of art, its figurative quality is a product of the growth of the tree: "In the tree nursery, seven single and twin trunk bushes of *Fraxinus americana* (American ash) are selected. These are then planted in a circular bed ten metres in diameter with a shallow domed profile. The straight trunks of the ash trees are planted at an incline so that they point outwards at an angle of up to 60 degrees. From this moment on, the plants' natural negative geotropism causes the branches of the tree crown to grow upwards in a direction diametrically opposed to the gravitational axis of the centre of the earth. As they become taller and branch out, the trees adapt to their new location, their inclined trunks developing an upright crown, growing together over the years to form a single constellation. The history of their development is, however, always legible in their constitution. The process of their adaptation is part of the design."

The mosaic-like expanse of small cobblestone paving that surrounds the project reuses the existing material and maintains the typical vocabulary of Berlin pavements.

Change is made visible as a break in development, but not as the termination of development. Change leads in a new direction. The design is a powerful symbol that for many people flight and expulsion was also – and continues to be – connected with arrival, was about striking new roots and achieving re-orientation. The strength of this message, at a place where people meet, shows once again how landscape architects know how to translate the figurative potential of history into space.

Die Landschaftsarchitekten haben die Baum-Skulptur mit einer schwebend wirkenden Bank aus eloxiertem Streckmetall umrahmt und diesen Ort damit als Treffpunkt unter Eschen in der Stadt markiert. Wie es einem Gartenkunstwerk eigen ist, wird das Wachstum der Bäume zum gestalterischen Moment. „In der Baumschule werden sieben ein- und doppelstämmige Stammbüsche von *Fraxinus americana* (Amerikanische Esche) ausgesucht. Sie werden in eine kreisförmige, schildartig überwölbte Fläche mit einem Durchmesser von zehn Metern gepflanzt. Die geradegezogenen Stämme werden ‚schief' mit Außenneigungen bis zu 60 Grad gepflanzt. Durch den pflanzentypischen negativen Geotropismus entwickeln sich die Äste der Kronen von diesem Moment an wieder bevorzugt entgegen der Achse zum Erdmittelpunkt. Die Bäume richten sich in ihrem Wuchs auf den neuen Standort ein, entwickeln auf den schief stehenden Stämmen aufrechte Kronen und verwachsen im Lauf der Jahre zu einer gemeinsamen Gestalt. Ihre Entwicklungsgeschichte wird in ihrem Habitus aber immer ablesbar bleiben. Der Prozess der Veränderung wird Teil der Gestaltung."

Für die umgebende Decke aus Mosaikpflaster wird das vorhandene Material wiederverwendet und der tradierte Duktus des Berliner Gehweges aufgegriffen. Veränderung wird als Entwicklungsbruch, aber nicht als Abbruch von Entwicklungen sichtbar. Veränderung führt zu einer Neuausrichtung. Symbolstark zeigt diese Idee, dass Flucht und Vertreibung für viele auch ein Ankommen, ein neues Verankern und eine neue Ausrichtung bedeuteten und bis heute bedeuten. Eine solche Botschaft an einem Ort des Zusammentreffens zeigt einmal mehr, wie die Landschaftsarchitekten mit der räumlichen Bildhaftigkeit von Geschichte umzugehen wissen.

Cemetery of the March Revolution Memorial,
Berlin-Friedrichshain,
Competition (Invited Selection Process) 2010, Completion 2011

Gedenkstätte Friedhof der Märzgefallenen,
Berlin-Friedrichshain,
Wettbewerb (Gutachterverfahren) 2010,
Bau 2011

**Cemetery of the March
Revolution Memorial
– Discovering Democratic
History**

Gedenkstätte Friedhof
der Märzgefallenen
– Entdeckungen demokra-
tischer Geschichte

The year 1848 left its mark on Berlin. While the 20th century – with two world wars, the rise of National Socialism, the downfall of Prussia and the division and later reunification of the city – is a more prominent chapter in the history of Berlin, these developments can be traced back to the preceding revolution in the 19th century. With the suppression of the March Revolution in 1848, the process of democratisation in Germany foundered due to a lack of national unity. While in England and in France, the formation of the nation and the rise of democracy were born out of the same movement, the Prussian and Austrian superpowers stifled democratic reforms in the territories of the German Confederation following the Congress of Vienna in 1814–15. The period that followed, which came to be known as the Vormärz period, was instead characterised by a return to the domestic concerns and provincial comforts synonymous with the Biedermeier period. Like in France and other parts of Europe, the political unrest that arose in 1848 culminated in the revolutions of the night of the 18 March 1848 where the citizens of Berlin erected barricades against the Prussian soldiers. Following the deaths of more than 200 revolutionaries and 200 soldiers and policemen in a single night in Berlin alone, King Friedrich Wilhelm IV relented, promising elections that would lead to the formation of a national assembly. The March uprisings also led to freedom of the press and the introduction of trial by jury. On the 19 March, the King paid his respects to the revolutionaries who died – the Märzgefallenen – in the courtyard of the Berlin City Palace prior to their burial on the 22 March in the Cemetery of the March Revolution. A few months later, however, the old powers were reinstated, the Prussian National Assembly was dissolved and the liberal "March Ministers" were dismissed. The citizens had failed to

Das Jahr 1848 hat Spuren in Berlin hinterlassen. Zwar steht das 20. Jahrhundert mit zwei Weltkriegen, der Herrschaft des Nationalsozialismus und mit der letzten Stufe des Endes von Preußen sowie mit der Teilung und Vereinigung der Stadt im Mittelpunkt der Berliner Geschichte. Doch diese Entwicklungen des 20. Jahrhunderts gehen auf die 48er-Revolution des 19. Jahrhunderts zurück.

Mit der Niederschlagung der Märzrevolution von 1848 scheiterte die Demokratisierung in Deutschland vorerst an fehlender nationalstaatlicher Einheit. Während in England und in Frankreich Nationalstaat und Demokratie aus ein und derselben Bewegung hervorgingen, blockierten nach dem Wiener Kongress 1814–15 die Großmächte Preußen und Österreich demokratische Reformen im Gebiet des Deutschen Bundes. Im sogenannten Vormärz herrschte die Zeit des Biedermeier, in der deutsche Innigkeit und provinzielle Gemütlichkeit gepflegt wurden. Die 1848 ähnlich wie in Frankreich und anderen Teilen Europas ausbrechende Revolution hatte ihren Höhepunkt in der Nacht vom 18. auf den 19. März, als die Bürger in Berlin Barrikaden gegen die preußische Armee errichteten. Über 200 Tote auf Seiten der Revolutionäre und 200 tote Soldaten und Polizisten in einer Nacht allein in Berlin brachten Friedrich Wilhelm IV. zu einem ersten Einlenken. Er versprach, Wahlen zu einem deutschen Nationalparlament zu erlauben. Zu den „Märzerrungenschaften" gehörten auch die Pressefreiheit und die Einsetzung von Schwurgerichten. Den gefallenen Märzrevolutionären bezeugte der König am 19. März im Hof des Berliner Stadtschlosses seine Achtung, bevor die Toten am 22. März auf dem Friedhof der Märzgefallenen bestattet wurden. Doch einige Monate später war die alte Macht wiederhergestellt, das preußische Parlament aufgelöst und das liberale „Märzministerium" entlassen. Das Bürgertum hatte sich gegen Adel und

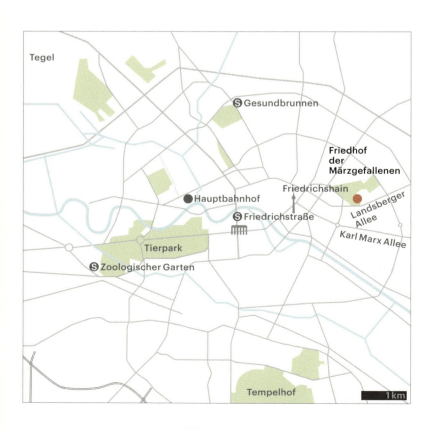

prevail against the nobility and military. The counterrevolution continued into 1849, also in the provinces, in part through the help of Otto von Bismarck, who later became Chancellor under King Wilhelm I. The national unity that Bismarck was able to forge some years later was not, however, the product of civil democracy but rather of Prussian expansionism, and this separation of nation state and democratic movement would later have consequences for Germany (and the world) in the 20th century. Germany's so-called *Sonderweg* – its independent, undemocratic path to the belated formation of a nation state – is regarded as having prepared the ground for the later authoritarian excesses of National Socialism and militarism and the simultaneous discrediting of democratic ideas, in turn laying a foundation for anti-Semitic sentiments and racist and nationalistic ideologies.

What consequences does this first failed attempt at a democratic revolution in March 1848 have for us in the present day? This is the question that sinai and their project partners Weidner Händle Atelier, ON architektur and Mola + Winkelmüller architects faced when they were invited in 2010 to submit a proposal for an exhibition concept for the Cemetery of the March Revolution. The organisers, the Paul Singer Association, proposed converting the already much altered site into a place for learning from history.

Militär nicht durchsetzen können. Die Konterrevolution gelang bis 1849 auch in den Provinzen, unter anderem mit Hilfe Otto von Bismarcks, des späteren Reichskanzlers unter Wilhelm I. Dessen nationale Einigung war dann keine bürgerschaftlich-demokratische, sondern eine preußisch-staatliche Errungenschaft, mit allen Folgen, die aufgrund dieser Trennung von Nationalstaat und Demokratiebewegung im 20. Jahrhundert in Deutschland (und weltweit) hervorgerufen wurden. Erst der undemokratische „Deutsche Sonderweg" zur „verspäteten Nation" ermöglichte die autoritär gelenkte Überhöhung von Nationalismus und Militarismus bei gleichzeitiger Diskreditierung demokratischer Ideen – und legte so den Grundstein für antisemitische Ressentiments und völkisch-nationalistische Ideologien. Welches sind also die Impulse, die von dieser ersten, gescheiterten demokratischen Revolution im März 1848 ausgehen? sinai wurden gemeinsam mit ihren Projektpartnern Weidner Händle Atelier, ON architektur sowie Mola + Winkelmüller Architekten vor diese Frage gestellt, als sie 2010 in einem eingeladenen Gutachterverfahren aufgefordert waren, ein Ausstellungskonzept für den Friedhof der Märzgefallenen zu entwerfen. Dieser mehrfach umgestaltete Ort wird, dafür tritt vor allem der Paul Singer Verein e.V. ein, zu einem Lernort der Geschichte weiterentwickelt.

The graves of the revolutionaries of the March uprising in 1848 in Friedrichshain, Berlin

Gräber der Märzkämpfer 1848 im Berliner Friedrichshain

1
Dr. Susanne Kitschun,
Director of the Cemetery of
the March Revolution project
at the Paul Singer Association

1
Dr. Susanne Kitschun,
Leiterin des Projektes
Friedhof der Märzgefallenen
für den Paul Singer Verein

"Trotz alledem und alledem ..."
(in spite of everything)

For the history of the revolution in 1848, this cemetery hidden away at the edge of the the Volkspark (people's park) in Friedrichshain is as important as St. Paul's Church in Frankfurt am Main (seat of the first freely elected German legislative body in 1849) or Hambach Castle (site of the Hambacher Fest, an early rally for democracy in 1832). This is what the Paul Singer Association, the Foundation for Historic Churchyards and Cemeteries in Berlin and the District Authority of Berlin Friedrichshain-Kreuzberg hope to make clear through the historical restoration of the cemetery and the design of a new information concept. "The days of the March Revolution in 1848 in Berlin were part of a wider democratic process of emancipation throughout the states of the German Confederation that led to the appointment of liberal governments and of the National Assembly at St. Paul's Church in Frankfurt am Main which drew up the first constitution. The principles of parliamentary democracy outlined in the draft constitution as well as the catalogue of fundamental rights served as a model for our current constitution. These roots of democracy represent a positive symbol of German historical identity and must be preserved and communicated."[1]
The Cemetery of the March Revolution also plays an important role in the history of the labour movement. Today, the words "Trotz alledem und alledem ..." stand written for all to see at the cemetery. This socially critical song was adapted from the translation of an English original ("For a' that, and a' that", Robert Burns) by Ferdinand Freiligrath in June 1848.
It was to become an influential motto of the German labour movement. Rediscovered by Ernst Busch after the Second World War, the song was covered in the 1960s and 1970s by various singers in both East and West Germany, including Wolf Biermann and Hannes Wader.
Not only the motto of the labour movement but also the existing design of the cemetery shows that a clear view of the history of the revolution of 1848 is still lacking: its current state corresponds to the changes made in 1948/49 and 1957–60 which interpret the March Revolution from the viewpoint of the ideology of the German Democratic Republic (GDR). 1848 is also the year in which Karl Marx and Friedrich Engels wrote the communist manifesto. A citizens' uprising on the one hand and communist manifesto on the other illustrate the potential breadth of possible references that a new, contemporary redesign of the Cemetery of the March Revolution could offer.
sinai landscape architects began by identifying the questions they had about the March Revolution and the cemetery. These they then compared with the available knowledge in history books and developed a temporary installation on this basis.

„Trotz alledem und alledem ..."

In seiner Bedeutung für die Revolutionsgeschichte von 1848 ist dieser versteckte Friedhof am Rande des Volksparks Friedrichshain der Frankfurter Paulskirche oder dem Hambacher Schloss ebenbürtig. Das wollen der Paul Singer Verein und die Stiftung historische Kirchhöfe und Friedhöfe Berlin-Brandenburg sowie das Bezirksamt Friedrichshain-Kreuzberg, Berlin, mit der denkmalgerechten Restaurierung des Friedhofs und seiner informationellen Umgestaltung deutlich machen. „Die Tage der Märzrevolution in Berlin 1848 waren Teil eines umfassenden bürgerlich-demokratischen Emanzipationsprozesses in den Staaten des Deutschen Bundes, der zur Berufung liberaler Regierungen und zur verfassungsgebenden Nationalversammlung in der Frankfurter Paulskirche führte. Die dort aufgestellten Prinzipien parlamentarischer Demokratie des Verfassungsentwurfs, einschließlich eines Grundrechtekatalogs, bildeten das Vorbild für unser heutiges Grundgesetz. Diese Wurzeln der Demokratie gilt es als positives Identitätsangebot aus der deutschen Geschichte zu bewahren und zu vermitteln."[1]
Zugleich hat der Friedhof der Märzgefallenen eine wichtige Bedeutung für die Geschichte der Arbeiterbewegung. „Trotz alledem und alledem ..." wird heute sichtbar für alle über dem Friedhof zitiert. Dieses sozialkritische Lied hatte Ferdinand Freiligrath im Juni 1848 nach einer englischen Vorlage umgedichtet. Es wurde zum einflussreichen Motto der deutschen Arbeiterbewegung, nach dem Zweiten Weltkrieg von Ernst Busch wiederentdeckt und in den 1960er und 1970er Jahren von zahlreichen Liedermachern in Ost und West, darunter Wolf Biermann und Hannes Wader, interpretiert.
Nicht nur das Motto der Arbeiterbewegung, sondern auch die heute vorzufindende und vorerst erhaltene Gestaltung des Friedhofs, der 1948/49 und 1957–1960 im Sinne einer Interpretation der Märzrevolution durch die DDR-Geschichtsdeutung umgestaltet wurde, zeigt, dass ein klares Geschichtsbild zur Revolution von 1848 bis heute fehlt. Denn 1848 verfassten eben auch Karl Marx und Friedrich Engels das Kommunistische Manifest. Bürgerliche Revolution und Kommunistisches Manifest machen die Bandbreite der Bezugsmöglichkeiten deutlich, die sich einer heutigen erneuten Umgestaltung des Friedhofs der Märzgefallenen bietet. sinai Landschaftsarchitekten skizzierten ihre Fragen an die Märzrevolution und an diesen Ort. Ihre Fragen verglichen sie mit dem Wissen der Geschichtsbücher und Archive und entwickelten daraus eine temporäre Installation.

maerz_baustelle –
the March Revolution under construction

The winning competition entry by sinai and their partners leaves the hidden cemetery largely untouched, in keeping with its location at the edge of the Volkspark Friedrichshain, but announces its presence more demonstratively. In stark contrast to the atmosphere of the cemetery, and the character of the memorial from GDR times, the designers introduced a new element on the site: the maerz_baustelle.

The maerz_baustelle is signified by a row of three clearly-visible construction site containers that project out over the gentle slope of the terrain and over a newly-renovated fence that separates the site from the park and the neighbouring grounds of a clinic. Situated next to a protected old oak tree, the dark green containers have a translucent glass end wall on which a succession of images from the history of the March Revolution is displayed.

This bar, made of three shipping containers together with a circular rotunda of exhibition panels, was opened in 2012 as a place of remembrance and learning. The containers house an exhibition with information on the history and political significance of the revolution in March 1848 while the separate exhibition rotunda explains the history of the cemetery that it surrounds.

At the beginning of the project, the Cemetery of the March Revolution lay – in the words of the Paul Singer Association – in a state of "eternal slumber". This allusion to "Sleeping Beauty" in the fairy tale world of the Brothers Grimm underscores the influence of the educated middle classes on the interpretation of this place. But can such a place be re-awakened? Is there a story to the March Revolution that can be discovered?

While the March Revolution of 1848 is a part of the history of the civil-democratic process of emancipation, the cemetery itself is more an expression of the failure of this movement at a specific moment in time than a place that celebrates a stepping-stone on the path to democracy. The Cemetery of the March Revolution is therefore a place that communicates history from several perspectives. One cannot communicate the role of this place in the history of democracy in Germany independently of its role in the culture of remembrance and its historical interpretation in the German Democratic Republic, which despite its name was not a democracy. A linear interpretation of the historical development of democracy is not possible – and especially not here. This is the situation that the landscape architects have chosen to articulate: with a few carefully selected design elements they intervene in the perception of history, emphasising that there is still work to be done before one can answer the question of the meaning of this place for the history of democracy in Germany. The idea of the building site attracts attention to the cem-

maerz_baustelle

Der im Wettbewerb erfolgreiche Entwurf von sinai und Partnern belässt den Friedhof, entsprechend seiner Lage am Rande des Volksparks Friedrichshain, als versteckten, gleichwohl öffentlich präsentierten und zunehmend auch präsenten Ort. In deutlichem Bruch zur Atmosphäre eines Friedhofs und zum Charakter als Gedenkstätte aus DDR-Zeiten wird auf dem Gelände die maerz_baustelle platziert.

Die maerz_baustelle schafft eine eigene Aufmerksamkeit, und zwar allein schon durch die Container, die über die sanfte Kuppe des Geländes hinausragen und auch den kürzlich sanierten Zaun, der das Gelände vom Park und einem benachbarten Klinikareal trennt, überragen. Neben einer als Naturdenkmal ausgewiesenen alten Eiche zeigen die dunkelgrün lackierten Container an ihrer Stirnseite auf einer transluzenten Glaswand eine Folge wechselnder Bilder zur Geschichte der Märzrevolution.

Diese drei in Reihe aufgestellten Seecontainer und eine Ausstellungsrotunde wurden 2012 als Erinnerungs- und Lernort eingeweiht. Die Container beherbergen eine Informationsausstellung zur Geschichte und politischen Bedeutung der Revolution vom März 1848, während die räumlich abgesetzte Rotunde die Geschichte des Friedhofs erzählt, der sie umrahmt.

Zu Beginn des Projektes lag der Friedhof der Märzgefallenen „im Dornröschenschlaf", so fasst es der Paul Singer Verein in Worte. Dieser Bezug auf die Märchenwelt der Brüder Grimm unterstreicht die bildungsbürgerliche Interpretation des Ortes. Doch kann dieser Ort erweckt werden? Gibt es überhaupt diese eine Geschichte der Märzrevolution, die zu entdecken wäre?

Zwar ist die Märzrevolution von 1848 ein Aspekt des bürgerlich-demokratischen Emanzipationsprozesses, der Friedhof aber ist eher Ausdruck des vorübergehenden Scheiterns dieser Bewegung denn Erinnerungsort an einen geradlinigen Erfolg. Der Friedhof der Märzgefallenen wird damit zu einem Ort, der Geschichte aus mehreren Perspektiven vermittelt. Die Bedeutung dieses Ortes für die Geschichte der Demokratie in Deutschland kann nicht getrennt erzählt werden von der Bedeutung dieses Ortes für die Erinnerungskultur und Geschichtsschreibung zur Zeit der DDR, der Deutschen Demokratischen Republik, die keine Demokratie war. Eine lineare Geschichtsentwicklung ist – besonders für diesen Ort – nicht darstellbar.

Hier setzen die Landschaftsarchitekten an und greifen in die Wahrnehmung der Geschichte ein, indem sie mit den gewählten Gestaltungselementen betonen, dass die Beantwortung der Frage nach der Bedeutung dieses Ortes für die Geschichte der Demokratie in Deutschland einiger Arbeit bedarf. Das dafür gewählte Bild der Baustelle betont ohne Pathos den Ort und stellt seine Bedeutung zugleich in Frage – ein ebenso starkes

etery without pathos while at the same time calling it into question – an image that is as powerful as it is dissonant, and an approach that ultimately convinced the competition jury. To a certain degree, one might argue that the design concept declines to address the actual task: it offers no solution for the design of the cemetery as a place of remembrance and commemoration.

Instead, the landscape architecture treats the cemetery as an existing find and draws attention to it – all the while remaining sensitive to conservation objectives – by augmenting it with elements that are of a deliberately temporary nature, such as the construction site containers and information panels.

The decision to design a temporary installation is a response to a specific aspect of the original brief. The initiators of the competition wanted not only to provide information about the site and the happenings of 1848 and its consequences. A second key aim was to communicate how the cemetery would become a memorial. Part of this involves encouraging people to participate in this societal process.

wie sperriges Bild, das die Jury des Gestaltungswettbewerbs letztlich überzeugte. In gewisser Hinsicht verweigert sich der Entwurf gar der gestellten Aufgabe: Ein Gestaltungsentwurf für einen Friedhof als Erinnerungsort und Gedenkstätte wurde gerade nicht geliefert.

Stattdessen hat die Landschaftsarchitektur eingegriffen, indem sie den Friedhof nach Maßgaben denkmalpflegerischer Sensibilität anhand des Vorgefundenen in Szene setzt und diesem Bild bewusst temporäre Elemente, eben eine Baustelleneinrichtung aus Containern und Informationsplanen, entgegensetzt.

Der Entwurf einer temporären Installation beruft sich auf die Eigenart der Aufgabenstellung. Die Auslober des Gestaltungswettbewerbs wollten erreichen, dass nicht allein die Information über den Ort und die Geschehnisse von 1848 mitsamt ihrer Folgen im Mittelpunkt stehen. Ein zweites zentrales Ziel ist die Vermittlung der „Denkmal-Werdung" dieses Friedhofs. Damit verbunden ist die Aufforderung, sich an diesem gesellschaftlichen Prozess zu beteiligen.

**Site plan
1:750**

Lageplan
1:750

25 m

As a consequence, sinai conceived of the exhibition as a temporary event that appears to be preparing the ground for a later situation. For the landscape architects it was important that "the visual language of the exhibition architecture represents a state of transition and avoids the impression of looking finished."

Building sites create a sense of anticipation for what will arise in future. People want to see what is happening, what is being built. The presence of the construction site facilities on the cemetery is a kind of intrusion that stimulates people's curiosity about what there is to see, its history and ultimately its meaning. For a while, the exhibition will dominate the site. As the landscape architects put it, "this largely unknown place should be made to stand out clearly for a certain period of time. The monument itself is occupied in a manner that is quite provocative, yet without it being permanently altered."

Folgerichtig konzipierten sinai die Ausstellung als temporäres Ereignis, das einen späteren Zustand vorbereiten helfen soll. „Die Bildsprache der Ausstellungsarchitektur verkörpert den Zustand des Übergangs und meidet die Anmutung des Fertigen", das ist den Landschaftsarchitekten für diesen Ort wichtig.

Der Charakter einer Baustelle sorgt zugleich für große Aufmerksamkeit auf Zukünftiges. Was passiert dort, was entsteht? Die Neugierde auf diesen Ort, auf seine Geschichte und damit auf seine Bedeutung wird durch die Irritation der Baustelleneinrichtung auf dem Friedhof angeregt. Die Ausstellung dominiert für eine vorübergehende Zeit den Ort. Es ist die Absicht der Landschaftsarchitekten, „diesen weithin unbekannten Ort für eine gewisse Zeit offensiv nach außen treten zu lassen. Das Denkmal selbst wird auf durchaus provozierende Art und Weise besetzt, ohne es dauerhaft zu überformen."

Components
A maerz_container
B maerz_baustelle

Komponenten
A maerz_container
B maerz_baustelle

Pathway of the visitors
1 Chronology of events
2 Remembering/forgetting
3 Participation

Besucherführung
1 Ereignisgeschichte
2 Erinnern/Vergessen
3 Partizipation

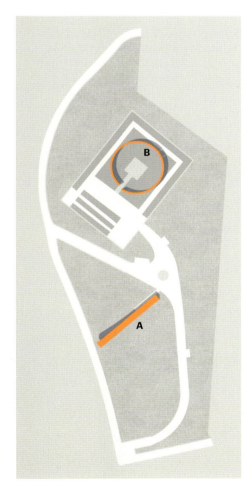

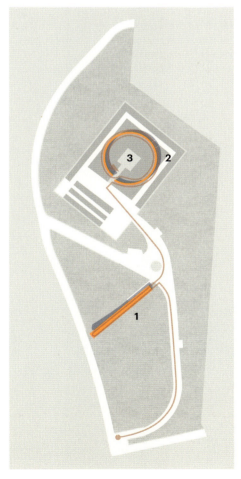

Can history occupy places? Events can certainly occupy places, and here, too the March Revolution set a precedent, having taken possession of public space in the interests of Germany by occupying it, as it were, with a message: the idea of democracy. At that time this occupation took the form of a battle with barricades and demonstrations. This is a motif that has recurred innumerable times over the years as an expression of civil demands, and also as a battle for public space. Recently we have seen water cannons turned against citizens in Stuttgart's Schlosspark, and demonstrations and counter-demonstrations on the streets of small towns or capital cities are images that we associate with expressions of public opinion in democratic societies.

The formal language of the maerz_baustelle is restrained in comparison to the dramatic events related in the pictures of the exhibition in the containers. While the containers are arranged perpendicular to the terrain, they are painted green to match the surrounding environment of the park and cemetery. The slogan "*Trotz alledem und alledem*" is the only textual information one can see from outside.

The presentation of the information is divided into three thematic sections, and it is apparent that each has been given an own form of communication in space. The linear arrangement of the containers follows the principle of a timeline and describes the political history of the March Revolution. It simultaneously traces the path of the revolutionaries, pointing out the historical locations in the city. History is expressed through the spatial arrangement and one's linear movement through it.

The timeline is a motif that sinai also use in their design for the Platz des 9. November 1989. In that case, however, the historical developments are explicitly inscribed in the floor in the form of steel strips marking the events and decisions of a single fateful day that was to have revolutionary consequences for Europe and the world, and led to the reunification of Berlin and Ger-

Kann Geschichte Orte besetzen? Die Ereignisse besetzen Orte, auch dafür steht die Märzrevolution, die den öffentlichen Raum für Deutschland quasi durch seine Besetzung neu entdeckte und ihn mit einer Botschaft, der Idee der Demokratie besetzte. Diese Besetzung passierte im Kampf, mittels Barrikaden und Demonstrationen. Das Motiv hat sich als Ausdruck bürgerschaftlicher Willensbekundungen seitdem vielfach wiederholt, auch als Kampf um den öffentlichen Raum. Wasserwerfer gegen Bürger im Stuttgarter Schlosspark, Demonstrationen und Gegendemonstrationen auf den Straßen von Klein- wie Hauptstädten gehören heute zum Wahrnehmungsbild demokratischer Meinungsbildung.

Die Gestaltsprache der maerz_baustelle ist im Vergleich zur Dramatik der in der Ausstellung in den Containern gezeigten Bilder sehr zurückhaltend. Die Container stehen zwar quer zum Raum, sind aber farblich an die grüne Umgebung des Parks und Friedhofs angepasst. Die Botschaft „Trotz alledem und alledem" ist die einzige von außen sichtbare Textinformation, der Slogan.

Das Informationsangebot ist in drei Themenfelder gegliedert, und es fällt auf, dass jedem von ihnen ein eigenständiger Vermittlungsprozess im Raum zugeordnet wird. Die lineare Anordnung der Container im Sinne eines Zeitstrahls erläutert die politische Geschichte der Märzrevolution und entspricht zugleich dem Weg der Revolutionäre und bezieht sich auf die historischen Schauplätze in der Stadt. Geschichte wird als Raumbild und lineares Bewegungsmuster lesbar. Das Motiv des Zeitstrahls hat sinai auch für den Entwurf für den Platz des 9. November 1989 verwendet. Allerdings ist dort die Geschichtsentwicklung ganz konkret in den Boden eingeschrieben, Stahlbänder markieren die Etappen und Entscheidungen eines einzigen Tages, die zu einer weltbewegenden Veränderung führten. Die Folge war die revolutionäre

maerz_baustelle: the historical impact of the Cemetery of the March Revolution displayed on building-site hoardings

maerz_baustelle: Wirkungsgeschichte des Friedhofs der Märzgefallenen auf der bespannten Baustellenwand

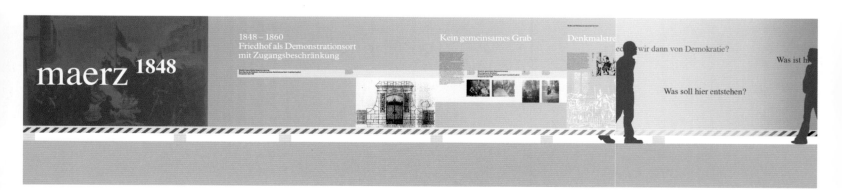

many. For the March Revolution, the historical consequences do not follow so directly. As such, the landscape architects did not see a justification for inscribing a timeline in the location. Instead, the tracing of the historical developments takes place in the containers, which are raised above the ground – the ground of a cemetery that commemorates the victims of a revolution and not the success of a revolution.

The rotunda in the centre of the cemetery, by contrast, has a spiral-shaped arrangement that imperceptibly leads the visitor along the path of the history of the cemetery to a peaceful space in the centre, a place of concentration and reflection befitting of a cemetery.

This history of the cemetery is related here as a concentric movement leading to a central point for commemoration and remembering.

The twin layers of the site fencing are clad on the inside and outside with a graphic skin. The outward-facing side presents the consequences and effects of the events and the history of the cemetery's reception along the chronology of the interventions and events. Visitors walk counter-clockwise from topic to topic along an imaginary timeline from 1848 to 2010. Important dates that represent turning points in the perception of the cemetery are articulated as gaps in the wall. The interior-facing surfaces are enclosed with white walls with the briefest of information on other comparable memorial sites. Questions have been written tentatively on the wall. These white walls serve as a kind of "guestbook" for the visitors, and groups can use the central space as a forum and place for holding discussions.

This peaceful, almost meditative space is intended as a space for concentration removed from its context. The actual building site for the future memorial is, after all, in one's minds.

Veränderung Europas und der Welt, die Vereinigung Berlins und Deutschlands. Für die Märzrevolution gilt diese geschichtliche Wirkung nicht in so unmittelbarer Weise. Daher sahen die Landschaftsarchitekten keine Veranlassung, einen Zeitstrahl in den Ort einzuschreiben. Vielmehr platzierten sie Geschichtsschreibung in Containern – über diesem Boden, der der Boden eines Friedhofs ist, der den Opfern und nicht dem Gelingen einer Revolution gehört.

Die Rotunde im Zentrum des Friedhofs dagegen, unauffällig spiralförmig aufgebaut, führt den Besucher entlang der Geschichte des Friedhofs auf einen inneren Ruheraum hin, einen Ort der Konzentration und Besinnung, wie er einem Friedhof zukommt. Die Geschichte des Ortes wird als konzentrische Bewegung erzählt, in deren Mittelpunkt das Gedenken und die Erinnerung stehen.

Der zweischalige Bauzaun ist innen und außen mit einer grafischen Haut versehen. Die Außenseite stellt dabei die Wirkungsgeschichte der Ereignisse und die Rezeptionsgeschichte des Friedhofs entlang der Chronologie der Eingriffe und Geschehnisse dar. Der Besucher erläuft sich so gegen den Uhrzeigersinn die Themenfelder entlang eines imaginären Zeitstrahls von 1848 bis 2010. Prägnante Daten, die Wendepunkte in der Wahrnehmung des Friedhofs darstellen, werden als Blickfugen in der Wand ausgebildet. Der Innenraum ist mit weißen Wänden gefasst, sehr sparsam gibt es Informationen zu vergleichbaren Gedächtnisorten, Fragen sind zurückhaltend auf die Wand aufgebracht. Ansonsten dient die weiße Wand den Besuchern als „Gästebuch". Gruppen können den Raum als Forum und Ort der Diskussion nutzen.

Dieser stille, fast meditative Raum dient der Entortung und Konzentration. Die Baustelle für das künftige Denkmal ist schließlich im Kopf zu suchen.

maerz_baustelle: the building-site wall leads in a spiral to the hidden central area of the cemetery
 maerz_baustelle: Die Baustellenwand führt spiralförmig zum verdeckten Zentralbereich des Friedhofs

maerz_container: documenting the events of March 1848. The end wall of the elevated container is a projection screen that is illuminated at night.

maerz_container: Dokumentiert werden die Geschehnisse im März 1848. An der Front der auskragenden Container bildet eine Projektionswand einen auffälligen Nachtaspekt.

Revolution in our minds

The image of the maerz_baustelle presents the work involved in developing the memorial as a communal task. The Cemetery of the March Revolution is marked by the design of the maerz_baustelle but not conclusively defined in terms of its historical importance. It is now down to the initiators to develop the disparate interpretation and strong imagery provided by the landscape architecture into a place of democratic learning.

The Cemetery of the March Revolution is an example for a way of dealing with "difficult places". The imagery of the containers symbolises transportability, relocation and the fact that democracy is not place-dependent, and is in turn a statement that the history which this place communicates is precisely not tied to this particular location, and that this is not the place of the revolution but a cemetery of the revolution of 1848.

This portrayal is typical for the unconventional approach that sinai take when working on memorial sites. Although their respective design solutions – like the underlying tasks themselves – are not comparable, and although the relative emphasis on exhibition or spatial structure varies with the respective spatial and communicative objectives of each project, the designs all follow a common principle: the conviction that history and space, and content and place can be revealed and experienced within a specific context. Space always has a serving function that can potentially reinforce, or also obscure, the content. In places of remembrance and learning, space must always make it possible to concentrate and at the same time create an atmosphere that can foster attentiveness. Space can stimulate this mood and this state of attentiveness. This communication-oriented, enlightening and didactic approach has been applied in many different ways in sinai's landscape architecture.

In sinai's work, history is never a one-dimensional message; it is always called into question. Communicating history through space simultaneously stimulates questions about history. Since 2011 the Cemetery of the March Revolution serves as an example for the ambivalence of history, which is always also a product of the ambivalence of the culture of remembrance.

Revolution im Kopf

Das Bild der maerz_baustelle thematisiert die Arbeit an der Gedenkstätte als bürgerschaftliche Aufgabe. Der Friedhof der Märzgefallenen wird mit der Gestaltung der maerz_baustelle markiert, aber nicht abschließend in seiner geschichtlichen Bedeutung definiert. Es ist nun an den Initiatoren, diesen von der Landschaftsarchitektur disparat interpretierten und zugleich bildstark markierten Ort zu einem Ort der demokratischen Bildung zu entwickeln.

Der Friedhof der Märzgefallenen wird damit zum Beispielort für den Umgang mit „schwierigen Orten". Die Containerlösung symbolisiert Transport, Standortwechsel, die Nicht-Ortsbindung der Demokratie und ist damit ein Statement, dass die an diesem Ort vermittelte Geschichte gerade nicht an diesem Ort gebunden ist, der ja nicht Ort der Revolution, sondern Friedhof der Revolution von 1848 ist.

Diese Inszenierung ist typisch für die unkonventionelle Arbeit des Büros sinai zum Thema Gedenkstätten. Auch wenn die jeweiligen Entwürfe – ebenso wie die Aufgabenstellungen – nicht vergleichbar sind, wenn die Schwerpunkte zwischen Ausstellung und Raumstruktur in einer jeweils eigenständigen räumlichen Geschichtsvermittlung unterschiedlich gesetzt werden, verbindet die Entwürfe dieses Prinzip: die Überzeugung, dass Geschichte und Raum, Inhalt und Ort in einem spezifischen Kontext erlebbar werden. Der Raum hat stets eine dienende Funktion, die einen Inhalt potenziell stärken oder aber auch verunklaren kann. Geht es um Gedenk- und Lernorte, muss der Raum Konzentration ermöglichen und zugleich eine Atmosphäre schaffen, die der Aufmerksamkeit zugutekommt. Raum kann diese Stimmung, die Aufmerksamkeitsbereitschaft, anregen. Diese kommunikationsgeprägte, aufklärerische und didaktische Haltung wird in der Landschaftsarchitektur von sinai in sehr vielfältiger Weise umgesetzt.

Geschichte wird in den Arbeiten von sinai nie zur eindimensionalen Botschaft, sondern immer in Frage gestellt. Durch die Vermittlung von Geschichte mittels Raum werden zugleich die Fragen nach Geschichte angeregt. So wird der Friedhof der Märzgefallenen seit 2011 als ein Beispiel für die Ambivalenz von Geschichte gestalterisch inszeniert, die immer auch eine Ambivalenz der Erinnerungskultur ist.

Berlin Wall Memorial,
Bernauer Strasse, Berlin-Mitte
2007–2009
2009–2011
Extended area ongoing

Gedenkstätte Berliner Mauer
Bernauer Straße, Berlin-Mitte
2007 – 2009
2009 – 2011
Erweiterter Bereich im Bau

**Berlin Wall Memorial
– Remembering Shapes
Our Expectation of the
Future**

Gedenkstätte Berliner
Mauer
– Erinnerung formt die
Erwartung an die Zukunft

The act of "crossing the border" has long become normality. Now integrated into the fabric of a working city, the Bernauer Strasse provides an opportunity to remember the construction, existence and fall of the Berlin Wall. What we now take for granted – the back and forth between two districts in the city, the way to work, the ability to visit friends and relatives in another neighbourhood or quarter – came to an abrupt end on 13 August 1961. The building of the Berlin Wall separated not only the Eastern Bloc from the West from 1961 to 1989; for the three million inhabitants of Berlin this dividing line in the city meant living in a socially divided city.

With the help of a few carefully chosen traces, the Berlin Wall Memorial on the Bernauer Strasse manages to evoke these memories. And not just among those who can remember what the Wall looked like, who can personally recall how it separated the district of Wedding in the West from Mitte in the East. Together with the curators of the memorial, the landscape architects have also managed to create opportunities for the large numbers of people who come to this place to retrace their own image of the Berlin Wall, many of whom only know the Wall from the accounts of others, and are often younger than the Wall itself and in some cases so young that they were not around in 1989 as the Wall fell and have no personal memory of it.

Längst ist der „Grenzübertritt" alltäglich geworden. In den Alltag eines Stadtraumes integriert, erleben wir entlang der Bernauer Straße die Erinnerung an den Bau, die Existenz und den Fall der Berliner Mauer. Was heute wieder selbstverständlich ist, das Hin und Her zwischen zwei Bezirken, Arbeitswege, Besuche bei Freunden und Familie in einem Kiez, einem Stadtquartier, war am 13. August 1961 jäh unterbrochen worden. Durch den Bau der Berliner Mauer trennten sich nicht nur Ostblock und Westen, sondern über drei Millionen Bürger Berlins erlebten diese bauliche Zäsur zwischen 1961 und 1989 als Alltag sozialer Trennungen.

Mit nur wenigen, gezielt eingesetzten Spuren vermag die Gedenkstätte Berliner Mauer an der Bernauer Straße diese Erinnerungen hervorzurufen. Und zwar nicht nur bei denjenigen, die das Bild der Mauer noch vor Augen haben, die sich persönlich erinnern, wie die Mauer den Wedding (West) von der Berliner Mitte (Ost) trennte. Sondern die Landschaftsarchitekten haben gemeinsam mit den Kuratoren der Gedenkstätte ein Angebot auch für jene geschaffen, die heute in großer Zahl diesen Ort besuchen, um ihrem Bild von der Berliner Mauer nachzuspüren, die diese Mauer nur noch vom Hörensagen kennen, die häufig jünger sind als diese Mauer und teils so jung, dass sie den Fall der Mauer 1989 nicht erlebt haben und erinnern.

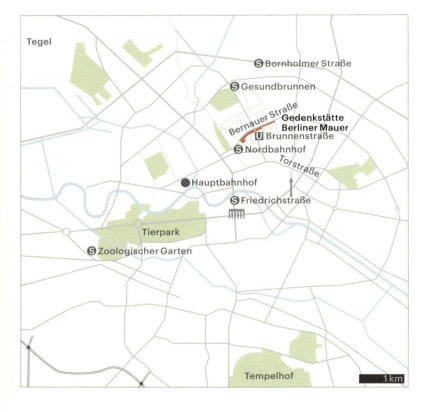

Why create a memorial along the Bernauer Strasse?

The design for the Berlin Wall Memorial was developed from sinai's winning competition submission in 2007 and extends over a length of 1.5 kilometres along the Bernauer Strasse from the Nordbahnhof S-Bahn Station and the Gartenstrasse in the West to the Brunnenstrasse and beyond to the Schwedter Strasse in the East. The neighbouring Park am Nordbahnhof and the Mauerpark, which both follow the path of the former Wall, adjoin the memorial site at the northwest and northeast ends respectively. In both parks, the memory of the Wall plays only a secondary role. Traces of the past can still be seen, but the Park am Nordbahnhof is primarily a ruderal landscape and the Mauerpark a space for recreation with the hippy-esque character of a cultural "free trade zone".

While the Park am Nordbahnhof and the Mauerpark are each in their own way special spaces in the city, adding an idyllic habitat and a sense of colour and flair to the urban realm, especially on Sundays, sinai's design for the actual memorial treats it as a 4.2-hectare-large space for everyday use.

The Berlin Wall Memorial is not a museum-like space but a specific place in the heart of Berlin. The former buildings from the turn of the past century that stood along the Brunnenstrasse were demolished in 1963, although some of the original side wings and former rearward buildings still jut into what is now the new memorial landscape, and a few new buildings have also been added. The buildings in Berlin-Mitte have now almost all been renovated and the residents are often new to the area. In the formerly West German district of Wedding, north of the Brunnenstrasse, large areas were completely renewed in the 1970s and the new buildings are now home to a heterogeneous mix of residents, as is

Warum der Gedenkort entlang der Bernauer Straße?

Die von sinai auf Grundlage eines Wettbewerbsgewinns von 2007 gestaltete Gedenkstätte Berliner Mauer reicht über 1,5 Kilometer entlang der Bernauer Straße vom Nordbahnhof und der Gartenstraße im Westen bis zur Brunnenstraße und darüber hinaus bis zur Schwedter Straße im Osten. Die benachbarten Parks auf dem Nordbahnhof und Mauerpark schließen nordwestlich und nordöstlich ebenfalls auf ehemaligen Mauerflächen an den Erinnerungsraum an. In beiden Parks spielt die Erinnerung an die Berliner Mauer nur eine untergeordnete Rolle. Spuren sind zwar präsent, aber es geht im Park auf dem Nordbahnhof um eine ruderale Stadtlandschaft und im Mauerpark um den Freiraum schlechthin, um eine hippieeske kulturelle Freihandelszone.

Während der Park auf dem Nordbahnhof und der Mauerpark auf ihre jeweils eigene Art aus der Stadtlandschaft herausfallen, ihr ein eher verträumtes und ein besonders lebendiges Sonntagsgesicht hinzufügen, inszenierte sinai die eigentliche Gedenkstätte als 4,2 Hektar großen Alltagsort.

Die Gedenkstätte Berliner Mauer ist kein musealer, aber ein spezifischer Ort inmitten Berlins. Die ehemalige gründerzeitliche Bebauung wurde nach 1963 entlang der Brunnenstraße abgerissen, einige Seitenflügel und Hinterhäuser ragen nun in die neue Gedenklandschaft hinein, an anderen Stellen sind Neubauten entstanden. Der Gebäudebestand in Berlin-Mitte ist heute umfassend saniert, die Bewohner sind häufig neu zugezogen. Im ehemaligen Westen dagegen, nördlich der Brunnenstraße im Bezirk Wedding, wurde in den 1970er Jahren eine Flächensanierung durchgeführt; der Neubaubestand ist heute Heimat einer heterogenen Bewohnerschaft, wie sie für den Wedding typisch ist. Dieser All-

Church of Reconciliation in the border strip, 1968

Die Versöhnungskirche im Grenzstreifen, 1968

typical for Wedding. The everyday activities of the city are reflected in the memorial – it is a pause within the heterogeneous texture of the city: the tram runs the length of the Bernauer Strasse, pedestrians cross the road, cyclists and cars descend at speed down the long incline that spans from the heights of Barnim in northeast Berlin to the glacial valley of the Spree River. It is a green band that accommodates the everyday goings-on in the city. And it is a special band with traces and signs that only exist here, that were specially developed for this memorial and that only have special meaning here. They give this place a both quotidian and dignified quality.

The memories of this place are many-layered: the building of the Wall, the escape attempts, both successful and fatal, the tunnels built in secret over many months. The decades of the Wall's existence are portrayed through these special recollections of an inner-city border zone.

The fall of the Wall and the overcoming of the division are also themes of the memorial site. In this phase of bound-(ary)less energy and enthusiasm, the segments of the Wall were rapidly dismantled. This led later to much debate. As the Parish of St. Sophia started removing the first segments of the wall that divided a cemetery, the question arose as to whether these could be added to the remaining existing segments of the Wall for the design of the Berlin Wall Memorial. The idea's supporters argued that this renewed gap closure would heighten the dramatic effect of the situation along the Wall, making it appear more intimidating. But would this add to its authenticity? Or is the positioning of the overgrown segments of the wall along the death strip, as it existed since 1989, more authentic? How drastically do the crimes of the GDR period need to be presented? This and other questions sparked a debate of the historical context of oppression – now overcome – the memory of the Berlin Wall should portray. The landscape architects and the directors of the memorial were united in the opinion that the impact of the authentic relics would only be convincing if these relics were not adjusted for effect. The design concept is, therefore, careful to differentiate between "actual traces" and "visual cues".

tag der Stadt spiegelt sich in der Gedenkstätte, einer Pause inmitten der heterogenen Stadt, wider: Die Straßenbahn fährt die Bernauer Straße hinauf, Fußgänger queren, Fahrräder und Autos gleiten mit hoher Geschwindigkeit den weiträumigen Hang hinab, der von der Hochfläche des Barnim im Nordosten Berlins ins Urstromtal der Spree führt. Es ist ein grünes Band, das den Alltag der Stadt begleitet. Und es ist ein besonderes Band, mit Spuren und mit Zeichen, die es nur hier gibt, die eigens für diese Gedenkstätte erdacht wurden und die ihre besondere Wirkung entfalten. Sie geben dem Ort Alltag und Würde zugleich.

Vielschichtig ist die Erinnerung an diesem Ort. Der Bau der Mauer; die Fluchten, gelungene und tödlich gescheiterte; die Tunnel, deren Bau einem monatelangen Krimi glich. Die jahrzehntelange Existenz der Mauer wird anhand der Besonderheiten eines innerstädtischen Grenzgebietes dargestellt.

Der Fall der Mauer, die Überwindung der Teilung ist ebenfalls Thema der Gedenkstätte. In diese Phase unbändiger Energie und Freude fiel der schnelle Abbau der Mauersegmente. Später führte dieser zu Diskussionen. Nachdem die Sophien-Kirchengemeinde direkt mit dem Fall der Mauer erste Mauersegmente, die einen Friedhof zerteilt hatten, entfernte, wurde anlässlich der Gestaltung der Gedenkstätte die Frage gestellt, ob diese nicht wieder in den Verlauf noch vorhandener Segmente einzufügen wären. Dieser erneute Lückenschluss hätte, so die Argumente, die Situation an der Mauer mit höherer Dramatik gezeigt, bedrohlicher. Authentischer? Oder ist die Positionierung der überwuchernden Mauersegmente auf dem Todesstreifen, wie sie seit 1989 bestand, der authentische Anblick? Wie drastisch müssen die Verbrechen der DDR-Zeit dargestellt werden? Anhand dieser und ähnlicher Fragen wurde debattiert, in welchem historischen Kontext des – überwundenen – Bedrohlichen die Erinnerung an die Berliner Mauer inszeniert werden sollte. Landschaftsarchitekten und Gedenkstättenleitung waren sich einig, dass die Kraft des authentischen Reliktes nur dann zur Wirkung kommt, wenn diese Relikte nicht nachgestellt würden. Daher wurde in der Gestaltung zwischen „echten Spuren" und „Sehhilfen" unterschieden.

Recharting: new traces and additional elements have been inserted alongside the built elements in the death strip

Rekartierung: Nachzeichnung und Ergänzung der baulichen Elemente im Todesstreifen

Sentry path

Postenweg

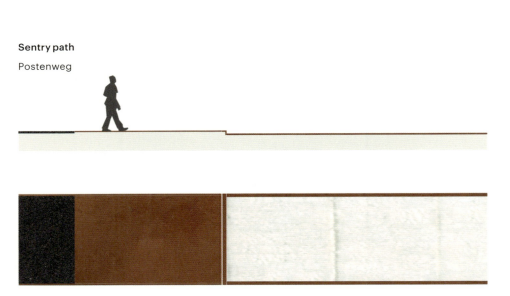

The events associated with the building and fall of the Berlin Wall cannot be conserved, and the memorial therefore makes no attempt to do this. Instead, the landscape architects have set about communicating the different topics and phases of memory using traces that reveal them in the present day. For example, traces of archaeological excavations, so-called "soundings", refer to the time before the building of the Wall and the clearing of the death strip. Visual cues, by contrast, include the wall of steles that traces the former course of the Wall, or the steel strips in the floor that mark the outlines of buildings that were demolished to build the Wall. Two site models made of CorTen steel are placed at the "entry points" to the memorial and show the historical course of the Wall in its urban context. The reproduction of the no longer existent watchtowers in an abstract form, or the marking of parts of the no longer visible inner security wall are further examples of such visual cues. This combination of both authentic traces as well as abstractions avoids the site becoming a cabinet of curiosities from the past. The remaining still intact section of the Berlin Wall, along with the sandy stretch of border strip, cannot be walked on, it can only be viewed from the tower of the neighbouring information centre. This conserved piece from the epoch of the Berlin Wall (a place of remembrance designed by Kohlhoff & Kohlhoff Architects from Stuttgart) was preserved before the design of the memorial began and opened in 1998. In the context of today's memorial landscape, however, it is a foreign object. But to the left and right of this fragment of "the real thing", the memorial achieves a remarkably sophisticated response within an everyday environment.

Zu konservieren sind die Ereignisse rund um den Bau und den Fall der Mauer allesamt nicht, die Gedenkstätte versucht dies auch gar nicht. Stattdessen setzen die Landschaftsarchitekten darauf, die verschiedenen Themen und Phasen der Erinnerung mittels gestalterischer Spuren in die Gegenwart zu vermitteln. So verweisen Spuren archäologischer Grabungen in sogenannten Sondagen auf die Zeit vor dem Mauerbau und auf die Zeit des Todesstreifens. Sehhilfen dagegen sind die Stelenwand, die den ehemaligen Mauerverlauf nachzeichnet, sowie Stahlbänder im Boden, die ehemalige Grundrisse durch den Mauerbau verschwundener Bauten markieren. Zwei in CorTen-Stahl ausgeführte Geländemodelle an den „Einstiegspunkten" zur Gedenkstätte zeigen den historischen Verlauf der Mauer im Stadtbild. Auch die Nachbildung nicht mehr vorhandener Wachtürme in abstrakter Form oder die Kennzeichnung von Teilen der kaum mehr zu identifizierenden Hinterlandmauer sind solche Sehhilfen. Es ist aufgrund dieser Verwendung sowohl authentischer Spuren als auch von Abstraktionen kein Panoptikum der Erinnerung entstanden – wenn man einmal von einem vollständig erhaltenen Abschnitt der Berliner Mauer samt sandigem Todesstreifen absieht, der nicht betreten, sondern vom Turm des benachbarten Informationszentrums aus besichtigt werden kann. Dieses Stück konservierte Epoche der Berliner Mauer (ein Erinnerungsort nach einem Entwurf von Kohlhoff & Kohlhoff Architekten, Stuttgart) war schon vor der Gestaltung der Gedenkstätte Berliner Mauer erhalten geblieben, wurde 1998 eingeweiht und bildet in der heutigen Gedenklandschaft einen Fremdkörper des vermeintlich Originären. Links und rechts davon aber ist die besondere Leistung des Gedenkraumes seine Differenziertheit im Alltäglichen.

Border wall

Grenzmauer

Inner security wall

Hinterlandmauer

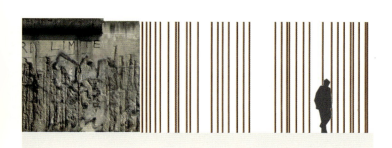

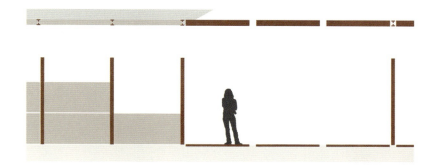

Making remembering possible

Can a place of remembrance correspond to one's personal experience, or to the expected image one has of the Wall? How can landscape architecture evoke memories or make remembering possible? In their design for the Berlin Wall Memorial, sinai have consistently put these questions to one side: rather than considering a single message, they focus on the multiplicity of impressions.

People respond to stimuli even when they are not aware of them, i.e. before they have processed them consciously. This phenomenon of priming, the subconscious perception of stimuli, is commonly exploited in advertising and entertainment, but it also applies to human perception and orientation in general and is therefore relevant in all spatial design disciplines. A particular strength of sinai's design for the memorial on the Bernauer Strasse lies in the fact that it is able to take this preconditioning into account. Wherever places of remembrance are created, it is likely that visitors have prior knowledge or expectations of the place and a degree of preconditioned curiosity is therefore to be expected. The actual design of the space was consequently able to respond to the visitors' interest in and preconceived opinion of "The Wall" without actually needing to visibly reproduce the Wall.

The design for this place of remembrance could draw on people's individual images of the Berlin Wall, including those that have become part of our collective memory through the media, as appropriate motifs. Large-format images – citations from our collective medial memory of the construction of the Wall, of the attempts to flee and the border regime – have been mounted on the firewalls of the neighbouring buildings in the former East sector that survived the building of the Wall.

Erinnerung ermöglichen

Kann ein Ort des Erinnerns der persönlichen Erfahrung oder der Erwartung an das Bild der Mauer entsprechen? Wie kann Landschaftsarchitektur Erinnerung auslösen, Erinnerung ermöglichen? Das Büro sinai hat im Entwurf für die Gedenkstätte Berliner Mauer diese Fragen konsequent hintangestellt, hat nicht die eine Botschaft, sondern die Vielzahl der Eindrücke zum Gegenstand des Entwurfs gemacht.

Menschen reagieren auf Reize, auch wenn sie diese nicht bewusst wahrnehmen, also nicht sofort im Bewusstsein verarbeiten. Dieses Phänomen des Priming, des unbewussten Wahrnehmens von Reizen, machen sich nicht nur Werbe- und Unterhaltungsindustrie zunutze, sondern es ist ganz generell auf die menschliche Wahrnehmung und Orientierung anwendbar und betrifft daher auch alle Disziplinen der Raumgestaltung. Die Stärke des Entwurfs von sinai Landschaftsarchitekten für die Mauergedenkstätte Bernauer Straße besteht gerade darin, eine solche Konditionierung einbezogen zu haben. Denn gerade dort, wo Räume der Erinnerung geschaffen werden, ist von einer Vorerwartung oder einem Vorwissen oder einer in gewisser Weise konditionierten Neugierde der Besucher auszugehen. So konnte sich die eigentliche Raumgestaltung auf das Informationsinteresse und die aus Vorerwartungen gespeiste Haltung der Besucher zum Thema „Mauer" beziehen, ohne diese Mauer allzu deutlich nachzubilden.

Signal fence

Signalzaun

Escape tunnel

Fluchttunnel

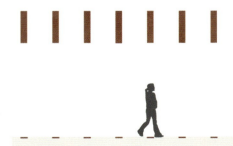

On the site of the former border strip itself, the view along the site reveals an impression that, today more than ever, is representative of the Berlin Wall: it is perceived as a brutal intervention in society, in the surrounding urban context and quarters, in the dense weave of neighbourhoods, family relations and friendships. To the present day, "The Wall" remains a symbol in our minds of the intrusion of politics in society – and also of its failure, in the fall of the Berlin Wall. The Wall severed and obstructed many friendships, new and longstanding, between people around the world, and especially in Berlin. In the townscape of the Bernauer Strasse this is made apparent through the buildings that are missing, through the last still interrupted road connection between East and West Berlin, and through the slice that has been cut out of the heterogeneous fabric of the city. It is a vacant space that demands attention and awakens memories. The memorial is characterised by this sense of emptiness, augmented with iconographic images and supplemented with carriers of information.

sinai's design makes this image visible by revealing divergent images, and makes it even more visible and tangible by designing an empty space as emptiness: a stretch of grass in which a few traces reveal the immense historical importance of this place; a green scar in the body of the city, a place that signals the eradication of everyday life. This negative form has not been filled in but made visible as a fracture in the city.

Die individuellen Bilder der Berliner Mauer, auch diejenigen im kollektiven Gedächtnis der Gesellschaft und ihrer Medien, konnten als Leitbilder für den Entwurf des Erinnerungsortes vorausgesetzt werden. Großformatige Bildzitate aus unserem kollektiven Mediengedächtnis zum Thema Mauerbau, Flucht und Grenzregime wurden an die Brandwände von benachbarten Gründerzeitbauten gebannt, die den Bau der Mauer im ehemaligen Ostteil der Stadt überstanden hatten.

Auf dem Areal des ehemaligen Mauerstreifens selbst wurde der Blick frei für eine Botschaft, die heute umso überzeugender die Berliner Mauer repräsentiert: Sie erscheint als ein brutaler Eingriff in die Gesellschaft, in ihre angestammten Quartiere und Orte, in das dichte Netz aus Nachbarschaften, Familienbeziehungen und Freundschaften. Bis heute steht „die Mauer" in unseren Köpfen als Symbol für diese Art des Eindringens von Politik in Gesellschaft. Doch auch dessen Scheitern wird symbolisiert: im Fall der Berliner Mauer.

Getilgt und verhindert wurden durch die Mauer langjährige alte und neue Beziehungen der Menschen, weltweit und ganz konkret vor Ort, in Berlin. Dies ist entlang der Bernauer Straße bis heute im Stadtbild ablesbar, und zwar durch das Fehlen von Gebäuden, durch eine letzte auch heute noch unterbrochene Straßenverbindung zwischen Ost- und Westberlin, durch die Schneise, die sich dort durch das heterogene Stadtbild fräste. Ein unbebauter Leerraum, der Aufmerksamkeit erzeugt und Erinnerung auslöst. Die Gedenkstätte ist eine durch diese Leere geprägte Stätte, aufgeladen mit ikonografischen Bildern und ergänzt mit Informationsträgern.

Der Entwurf von sinai hat dieses Bild in divergenten Bildern sichtbar gehalten, hat es sogar noch sichtbarer und spürbarer gemacht, indem ein leerer Raum als solcher gestaltet wurde: eine Rasenfläche, in der mit wenigen Spuren der immensen geschichtlichen Bedeutung des Ortes entsprochen wird: eine grüne Narbe im Stadtkörper, das Zeichen der Auslöschung des Alltags. Diese Negativform wurde nicht wieder gefüllt, sondern als Bruch in der Stadt sichtbar gehalten.

Watchtower

Wachturm

Edge of the adjoining buildings

Außenkanten der Grenzhäuser

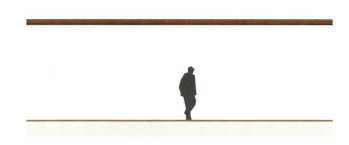

1
Cammann, Alexander:
„Stadtlandschaft mit
Todesstreifen", in: DIE ZEIT,
1 August 2011, No. 33

1
Cammann, Alexander:
„Stadtlandschaft mit
Todesstreifen", in: DIE ZEIT,
1.8.2011, Nr. 33

Remembering shapes our expectation of the future

"That a Central European metropolitan city with a few million inhabitants is cut in two with a concrete wall and that people who try to climb over it are shot at seems today like a sinister fantasy and not a contemporary reality," wrote Alexander Cammann in 2011. In the same article he declares that the Berlin Wall Memorial has succeeded in "impressively taking a stand against forgetting". "Without any of the noise of Cold War folklore," the memorial reflects "the historical and human tragedy of the division of Germany", "recounting the story for the 21st century in a considered and yet moving way. [...] Conceptually and aesthetically it is so convincing that it will surely soon count among the defining examples of museological memorial places in Europe."[1]
It is well known that the aesthetics of remembering is always rooted in the spirit of the time and therefore reflects the self-perception of society at the moment in which the design of the memorial place takes place. The design can, however, strive to avoid expressing this zeitgeist all too conspicuously, and this is what sinai landscape architects have tried to achieve.

Erinnerung formt die Erwartung an die Zukunft

„Dass man eine mitteleuropäische Millionenmetropole mit einer Betonwand durchtrennt und Menschen, die sie überklettern wollen, abschießt, erscheint heute eher als eine düstere Fantasy-Idee und nicht als zeithistorische Realität", schreibt Alexander Cammann 2011. Um zu konstatieren, dass es mittels der Gedenkstätte Berliner Mauer gelungen sei, „sich eindrucksvoll dem Vergessen entgegenzustemmen". „Ohne lärmige Kalte-Krieg-Folklore" werde „das historische und menschliche Drama der deutschen Teilung" hier „auf reflektierte, dennoch berührende Weise für das 21. Jahrhundert nacherzählt. [...] Konzeptionell und ästhetisch derart geglückt, dürfte die ganze Anlage bald zu den stilprägenden musealen Gedenkstätten Europas zählen."[1]
Selbstverständlich folgt die Ästhetik des Erinnerns immer auch einem Zeitgeist und verweist somit auf die Selbstwahrnehmung der Gesellschaft zum Zeitpunkt der Arbeit am Entwurf zu diesem Erinnerungsort. Der Entwurf aber kann sich darum bemühen, und das ist der Anspruch von sinai Landschaftsarchitekten, diesen Zeitgeist nicht vordergründig zum Ausdruck zu bringen. Erinnerung formt die Erwartung an die Zukunft – wenn wir hierin die eigentliche Herausforderung in der

Multi-media information system for the stations

Multimediales Infosystem der Themenstationen

Remembering shapes our expectation of the future – and if this is the actual challenge in the design of places of remembrance, it is especially important that the respective portrayal of memory is as universal as possible in its appeal. sinai's design even goes as far as to call the zeitgeist into question. Their intention is not to create a place of remembrance that emphasises or refocuses attention on one specific memory, but rather that opens up the city as a place for remembering. This is what differentiated their project from many of the other competition entries.

In the case of the Berlin Wall Memorial, the design should not focus primarily on the dramatic events of the building of the Wall in 1961, on the mistrust that characterised the following decades along the Wall, or even on the joy of the 1990s after the fall of the Wall – rather it should span the overall history of the place. The design of a place of remembrance means not to portray an individual memory but to create invitations to engage with history in both a conscious as well as subconscious field of perception. In other words, it means to support the process of remembering rather than to find an artistic interpretation of history.

Gestaltung von Erinnerungsräumen sehen, ist es von besonderer Bedeutung, dass die jeweilige Inszenierung der Erinnerung einem möglichst allgemeingültigen Anspruch folgt. Im Entwurf von sinai wurde sogar gezielt dem Zeitgeist misstraut. Ein Erinnerungsort, der nicht versucht, eine spezifische Erinnerung zu betonen, gar zu lenken, sondern der die Stadt öffnet für das Erinnern – diese Vorstellung leitete den Entwurf der Landschaftsarchitekten und machte ihn damit unterscheidbar von vielen anderen Arbeiten im Gestaltungswettbewerb.

Im Falle der Gedenkstätte Berliner Mauer sollte nicht zuvorderst die Dramatik des Mauerbaus 1961, der von Misstrauen geprägte Alltag der folgenden Jahrzehnte entlang der Mauer oder die Freude der 1990er Jahre über den Fall der Mauer zum Ausdruck gebracht werden, sondern eine zeitübergreifende Darstellung der Geschichte. Das Gestalten des Erinnerns ist nicht die Inszenierung einer individuellen Erinnerung, sondern das Schaffen von Angeboten zur Auseinandersetzung mit der Geschichte, und dies ebenso im bewussten wie im unbewussten Wahrnehmungsfeld. Das Gestalten des Erinnerns ist eher eine Unterstützung der Erinnerung denn eine künstlerische Interpretation von Geschichte.

"Death Markers" for those who died at the Bernauer Strasse (design: ON architektur)

"Todeszeichen" für die Opfer an der Bernauer Straße (Planung: ON architektur)

Incident markers in the floor that relate to the "Field Book" (design: ON architektur)

Ereignismarken im Boden mit Bezug zum "Feldbuch" (Planung: ON architektur)

"Window of Remembrance": the central site commemorating the victims of the Wall (design: ON architektur).

Zentraler Ort des Opfergedenkens: "Fenster des Gedenkens" (Planung: ON architektur)

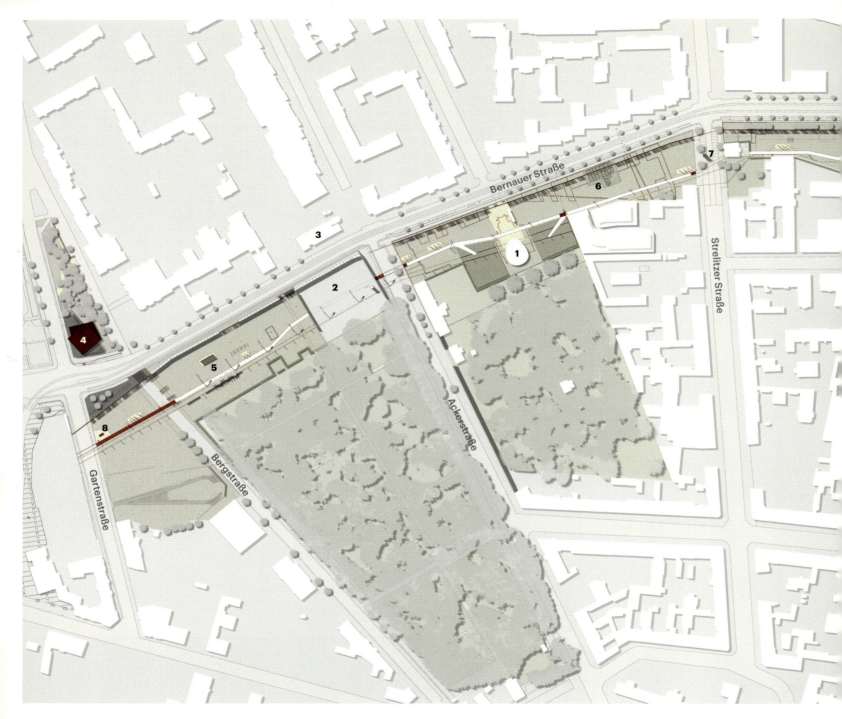

The Berlin Wall Memorial is a
1.4-kilometre strip between
Nordbahnhof and Mauerpark.

1 Chapel of Reconciliation
2 Monument
  (Kohlhoff & Kohlhoff)
3 Documentation centre
  with viewing tower
4 Visitor centre
5 "Window of
  Remembrance"
6 Remains of the Bernauer
  Strasse 10, a house on
  the border
7 Watchtower marker
8 Entry points with models

Die Gedenkstätte Berliner
Mauer auf einer Länge von
1,4 Kilometern zwischen
dem Nordbahnhof und
dem Mauerpark

1 Kapelle der Versöhnung
2 Mahnmal
  (Kohlhoff & Kohlhoff)
3 Dokumentationszentrum
  mit Aussichtsturm
4 Besucherzentrum
5 „Fenster des Gedenkens"
6 Relikt Grenzhaus
  Bernauer Straße 10
7 Nachzeichnung Wachturm
8 Einstiegsstationen
  mit Modellen

Bernauer Straße

Brunnenstraße

Ruppiner Straße

Swinemünder Straße

Wolliner Straße

Schwedter Straße

8

8

100 m

Many of the several thousand people who visit the Berlin Wall Memorial each day do not come from Berlin, or even from Germany. At the Bernauer Strasse, the memory people have of the Berlin Wall is therefore European or even international. How could it be that a state would go as far as to erect a wall in order to contain its people? "Our task is first of all to create an awareness of the issues and to communicate the value of freedom. Our role is also to raise questions," emphasises the director of the Berlin Wall Memorial, Dr. Axel Klausmeier. The memorial also conveys a further aspect that the Berlin Wall Foundation, as the body responsible for the memorial, accord special importance to, namely the memory of the role that civil society played in overcoming the Berlin Wall. The architect, urban designer and project manager for the foundation, Dr. Günter Schlusche, calls this a "civil impulse", the memory of which needs to be upheld, not by conserving it as in a museum, but by supporting it as an active, political means of giving meaning: "Memory will only be anchored in the fabric of the city when there is an interest in upholding this memory, as motivated by such a civil impulse. This applies for all memorial sites and places of remembrance."

Viele der mehreren tausend täglichen Besucher der Gedenkstätte Berliner Mauer kommen nicht aus Berlin, auch nicht aus Deutschland. Die Erinnerung an die Berliner Mauer ist an der Bernauer Straße eine europäische und eine internationale. Wie konnte es möglich sein, dass ein Staat so weit gehen konnte, eine Mauer zu errichten, um sich seines Volkes zu versichern? „Unsere Aufgabe es ist es, grundsätzlich erst einmal Bewusstsein für das Thema zu wecken und den Wert von Freiheit zu vermitteln. Wir sind auch da, um Fragen aufzuwerfen", betont der Direktor der Gedenkstätte Berliner Mauer, Dr. Axel Klausmeier. Der Gedenkstätte ist zugleich eine Botschaft anzumerken, auf die der Träger dieser Gedenkstätte, die Stiftung Berliner Mauer, besonders hinweist, nämlich die Erinnerung an die zivilgesellschaftliche Leistung der Überwindung der Berliner Mauer. Dr. Günter Schlusche, Architekt, Stadtplaner und Projektbeauftragter der Stiftung, nennt dies einen „zivilgesellschaftlichen Impuls", den es mittels dieser Gedenkstätte nicht in musealer Bewahrung, sondern im Sinne einer aktiven politischen Be-Deutung im Gedächtnis zu halten gelte: „Das Erinnern kann nur dann im Stadtbild verankert werden, wenn das Interesse an dieser Erinnerung einem solchen zivilgesellschaftlichen Impuls folgt. Dies gilt für alle Gedenkstätten und Orte der Erinnerung."

View from the watchtower over the memorial site and monument (design: Kohlhoff & Kohlhoff)

Blick vom Aussichtsturm auf Gedenkstättengelände und Mahnmal (Entwurf: Kohlhoff & Kohlhoff)

In the case of remembering along the Berlin Wall, this impulse came first and foremost from the Protestant Parish of Reconciliation whose Chapel of Reconciliation on the Bernauer Strasse was consecrated in the year 2000. A simple rammed-earth structure surrounded by a translucent skin of vertical wooden strips, it has a powerful atmosphere of concentration and serves as place for contemplation and reflection for many visitors to the memorial. Church services as well as exhibitions are held in the chapel which stands on part of the foundations of the former Church of Reconciliation that directly adjoined the border strip and was therefore demolished in 1985.

The building of the chapel in the border strip was a remarkable step given that the then prevailing urban development policy envisaged the building over of the majority of the stretch of the Berlin Wall. But once built, it represented a first impulse towards the creation of a place of remembrance. Later it became clear that the memory of the Berlin Wall could not be reduced to a selection of individual points. Schlusche explains the shift in political direction as follows: "The Wall was not a selective intervention; it was a totally other dimension of urban experience, namely the experience of the division of a city. In 2006, the State of Berlin recognised this with a resolution for a decentralised concept for remembering the Berlin Wall, in which the Memorial along the Bernauer Strasse was to play a special role. From then on it was clear that places of remembrance should reflect this dimension of urban experience, and that they should have a certain urban presence."

Im Falle des Erinnerns an die Berliner Mauer ging dieser Impuls wesentlich von der Evangelischen Versöhnungsgemeinde aus, die an der Bernauer Straße schon im Jahr 2000 die Kapelle der Versöhnung einweihte. Der schlichte, mit einer transluzenten Hülle aus Holz verkleidete Stampflehmbau mit einer außergewöhnlichen Atmosphäre der Konzentration dient vielen Besuchern der Mauergedenkstätte als Ort der Einkehr und des Nachdenkens. Gottesdienste und auch Ausstellungen finden in dieser Kapelle statt, die teils auf den Grundmauern der 1985 im Mauerstreifen gesprengten Versöhnungskirche errichtet wurde.

Die Errichtung der Kapelle war ein außergewöhnlicher Schritt, ging doch die Stadtentwicklungspolitik damals noch von einer weitgehenden Überformung des Bandes der Berliner Mauer aus. Doch der Impuls war damit gesetzt, einen Erinnerungsort zu schaffen. Später wurde dann deutlich, dass das Erinnern an die Berliner Mauer nicht auf wenige einzelne Orte reduzierbar ist. Schlusche begründet diesen Wandel in der Politik: „Die Mauer war kein punktueller Eingriff, sondern eine völlig andere Dimension der Stadterfahrung, eben die Erfahrung der Teilung einer Stadt. Dem hat das Land Berlin 2006 mit dem Beschluss für ein dezentrales Konzept des Erinnerns an die Berliner Mauer entsprochen, in dem die Gedenkstätte Bernauer Straße eine besondere Rolle einnimmt. Nun war klar, dass Orte des Erinnerns die Dimension der Stadterfahrung, also eine gewisse stadträumliche Prägnanz, aufweisen sollten."

Detail of the border wall

Detail Grenzmauer

Monument:
CorTen steel walls

Mahnmal:
Cortenstahlwände

A museum for the Berlin Wall is less suitable for this kind of experience as museums document primarily the events and their traces in the context of their historical development, which presumes a linear causality to the progression of time and events. It is through this that the past becomes history. The Wall Memorial, as a part of the present-day city, subscribes instead to a different idea in which the central role is played by a normal space in the city which is, so to speak, invested with its history.

Ein Mauermuseum ist für diese Art der Erfahrung weniger geeignet, zeigt ein solches doch vor allem das Geschehen und seine Spuren im Sinne einer Geschichtsentwicklung, der eine lineare Kausalität der Abfolge von Zeit und Ereignissen eingegeben ist – erst dadurch wird Vergangenheit ja zu Geschichte. Die Mauergedenkstätte als Teil der Gegenwart folgt dagegen einer anderen Idee, in deren Mittelpunkt ein Alltagsort steht, der quasi aufgeladen ist durch seine Geschichte.

Monument: between the two CorTen steel walls, a section of the border strip has been preserved, including the border wall and inner security wall.

Mahnmal: Zwischen den Stahlwänden sind die Grenzsicherungen des Todesstreifens erhalten geblieben: Grenzmauer und Hinterlandmauer.

Markings and information

For the design and communication of this spatial axis, the landscape architects worked together with curators, architects and exhibition designers. Islands of information have been placed on the site, each with a thematic focus. As visitors walk around the site, they acquire different perspectives on the Berlin Wall and can trace, often in detail, the political history and especially the daily reality of the Wall. A few metres further on, the factual information gives way to the need for appropriate symbols of remembering. Special attention is given to remembering those who died along the Wall in the form of both individual places of remembrance and a joint object. The names of the dead are read out and their portraits are gathered in a sculptural wall. This object leaves an impression that is very personal while also serving as a factual record.

For a spatially structured narrative of this kind, the landscape architects needed to create an adequate spatial framework. To tell such a narrative, historical traces and contemporary evidence are indispensable. The newly built items are, however, always careful not to assume greater importance than what is experienced, what is imagined and what happened. In this context, the commitment to respecting the authenticity of the site helped ensure that interventions never lean towards the fake.

Markierung und Information

Kuratoren, Architekten und Ausstellungsgestalter haben diese Raumachse gemeinsam mit den Landschaftsarchitekten ins Bild gesetzt. Inseln der Information wurden nach Themen gegliedert im Raum platziert. Der Besucher erläuft sich diese verschiedenen Betrachtungsmöglichkeiten der Berliner Mauer, die teils sehr detailliert die politische und vor allem die Alltagsgeschichte nachzeichnen. Wenige Meter entfernt tritt die sachliche Information zurück hinter das Bedürfnis nach angemessenen Symbolen des Erinnerns. Besonders den Toten an der Mauer wird in Form individueller Erinnerungen und eines gemeinsamen Objektes gedacht. Die Namen der Toten werden verlesen, ihre Bilder sind in einer skulpturalen Wand versammelt. Ein Eindruck, der ganz persönlich, aber auch als sachliche Bestandsaufnahme wirkt.

Für diese Art einer raumgegliederten Erzählung mussten die Landschaftsarchitekten eine adäquate räumliche Grundlage schaffen. Auf historische Spuren und Zeitzeugnisse kann diese Raumerzählung selbstverständlich nicht verzichten. Aber das Gebaute nimmt an keiner Stelle mehr Bedeutung für sich in Anspruch als das Erleben, das Vermutete und das Geschehene selbst. Insbesondere die Verpflichtung gegenüber dem Authentischen half, die Grenze der Inszenierung nicht hin zum Fake zu überschreiten.

Reinforcement rods were partially laid bare by the "wall peckers" in 1989/90.

Mauerspechte legten 1989/90 die Armierung der Grenzmauer teilweise frei.

An irregular arrangement of steel rods indicates the former course of the Wall.

Nachzeichnung der Grenzmauer mit lockerer Reihung von Stahlstäben

The marking of the "gap in the Wall": parts of the Wall that were thought to stand on the site of a mass grave were removed in 1990.

Nachzeichnung in der „Mauerlücke": Mauerelemente über einem vermuteten Massengrab wurden 1990 entfernt.

The traces made are left clearly visible, an approach that also conforms to conservation concerns in dealing with the history of the Berlin Wall. The Office for the Protection of Historic Monuments elaborated a strategy in detailed discussions with the landscape architects. The director of the Berlin Wall Foundation, Dr. Axel Klausmeier, had himself undertaken detailed research into the remaining legacy of the Berlin Wall and the possibilities for its conservation, also voicing his concerns over how these traces could be successfully incorporated into a new landscape of remembrance – the question being how to preserve their authenticity. Instead of specifying a predetermined pattern of remembering, the strategy makes it possible to remember individual traces and fates – it communicates the impacts of history. These are demarcated by circular metal markings set into the ground along the Bernauer Strasse. Inscribed on each of these is a name together with the date of the attempted escape, or of their death.

Dabei bleiben die Spuren durchaus sichtbar, auch im Sinne eines denkmalpflegerischen Umgangs mit der Geschichte der Berliner Mauer. Die Denkmalpflege hat diese Aufgabe hier in intensiver Diskussion mit den Landschaftsarchitekten gelöst. Der Leiter der Stiftung Berliner Mauer, Dr. Axel Klausmeier, hat selbst umfassend zu den Zeitzeugnissen der Berliner Mauer und den Möglichkeiten ihrer Konservierung geforscht und auch durchaus skeptisch die Frage eingebracht, wie eine Integration dieser Spuren in eine neu gestaltete Gedenklandschaft gelingen könne – die Frage der Authentizität.

Statt der Vorgabe bestimmter Erinnerungen erfolgt hier das Ermöglichen des Erinnerns an individuelle Spuren und Schicksale – die Vermittlung der Wirkungsmacht der Geschichte. Dies wird entlang der Bernauer Straße durch in den Boden eingelassene, kreisrunde metallene Markierungen möglich. Auf diesen ist jeweils ein Name und das Datum der Flucht oder auch des Todes markiert.

Archaeological windows showing excavations in Bergstrasse

Freigelegte Bergstraße mit archäologischen Fenstern

The widest part of the death
strip between Gartenstrasse
and Bergstrasse. The inner
security wall can be seen in
the background

Todesstreifen mit seiner
größten Ausdehnung
zwischen Gartenstraße und
Bergstraße. Im Hintergrund
die Hinterlandmauer

For Klausmeier, the strength of the landscape architecture concept is that "the existing elements of the memorial are now linked together much more strongly". Of elementary importance is the design principle of "maintaining the numerous remaining relics of the border installations as they are, i.e. without any form of reconstruction" and of tracing the presence of lost structures using supplementary CorTen steel elements. Instead of a reconstruction, the landscape architects designed a programme of built interventions and supplementary elements. To ensure the authenticity and credibility of the memorial, all pre-existing structures and traces were secured wherever possible. These original relics make it possible to conduct future research on the Berlin Wall, and to examine and evaluate possible new hypotheses and research questions.

Die Stärke des landschaftsarchitektonischen Entwurfs sieht Klausmeier darin, dass dieser „bereits bestehende Elemente der Gedenkstätte nun sehr viel stärker zusammenbindet". Von struktureller Bedeutung ist dabei die Entwurfsidee, die „zahlreichen erhaltenen baulichen Reste der Grenzanlagen bei jeglichem Verzicht auf Rekonstruktionen" mit Nachzeichnungen der verloren gegangenen Strukturen mit Hilfe von CorTen-Stahlelementen zu ergänzen. Die Landschaftsarchitekten entwickelten also statt einer Rekonstruktion ein Programm der baulichen Interventionen und Ergänzungen. Im Sinne der Authentizität und Glaubwürdigkeit der Gedenkstätte wurden vorgefundene Strukturen und Spuren wo immer möglich gesichert. So kann anhand dieser Zeugnisse die spätere Forschung zur Berliner Mauer noch neue Thesen und Forschungsfragen überprüfen.

Parallel succession of border security facilities: lighting masts, sentry path, signal fence, inner security wall

Parallele Abfolge der Grenzsicherungsanlagen: Lichttrasse, Postenweg, Signalzaun, Hinterlandmauer

Parallel to this, the foundation have worked together with contemporary witnesses to gain a better impression for later generations of the different perspectives in the East and West and their everyday experiences of the Wall. Today, Klausmeier describes the "former crime scene of the Berlin Wall" as a "non-formal place for learning and educating": "It is a place of learning for understanding the meaning of freedom, of the principles of a constitutional state and of democratic values, as well as for realising that these are both important and by no means self-evident. It also reminds us that no wall is built to last for ever."

Zugleich wurde die Arbeit mit Zeitzeugen gestärkt, um anhand der unterschiedlichen Perspektiven in Ost und West die Alltagserfahrungen mit der Mauer für die folgenden Generationen zu bewahren. Klausmeier beschreibt den „einstigen Tatort Berliner Mauer" heute als „außerschulischen Lern- und Bildungsort". „Ein Lernort für das Verständnis und die Bedeutung von Freiheit, für die Prinzipien des Rechtsstaates und von demokratischen Grundwerten sowie für die Gewissheit, dass diese wichtigen Güter nicht selbstverständlich sind. Aber auch dafür, dass keine Mauer für die Ewigkeit errichtet ist."

Border patrol path and remains of the inner security wall

Kolonnenweg und Relikt der Hinterlandmauer

Tracing the course of the Wall

The design of the memorial space needed to combine the documentary aspect of this urban space, and of some of its elements, with its everyday function in the city and with the needs of visitors interested in understanding its history. To provide orientation, a series of different elements have been introduced: the course of the Wall is delineated by CorTen steel posts while steel strips in the floor mark the outlines of former buildings. So-called "event markers" set into the surface denote the scene of special events where they happened and serve as traces for visitors to follow and as invitations for reflection. These traces are incorporated as "irritations" into the everyday urban setting.

Especially interesting for visitors is the marking of the escape tunnels that were built beneath the site in the 1960s. As described earlier, the Bernauer Strasse rises slightly from west to east. At this point it was possible to dig tunnels of relatively short length above the water table but beneath the Bernauer Strasse. There are a number of such tunnels along the Bernauer Strasse that were built in concerted efforts by escape helpers to assist relatives, friends as well as paying clients to escape from East Berlin. These tunnel escapes remain legendary to the present day and the curiosity generated by the steel plates in the floor marking the tunnels is correspondingly great. The steel plates are laid across the grass much like long zebra crossings and are relatively inconspicuous, functioning as "visual cues" that are often only seen on second glance. Visitors passing by happen upon them as they cross the space and on closer inspection find an inscription showing the year in which the tunnel was built. At a nearby information point, they can find out more about the huge effort of building them and the difficulties involved in assisting people to escape.

Nachzeichnung des Verlaufs

Die dokumentierende Funktion dieses Stadtraumes, einzelner seiner Elemente, galt es in der Gestaltung des Gedenkortes mit dem Alltag der Stadt und dem Interesse der Besucher an einem Nachvollziehen der Geschichte zu verbinden. Verschiedene Elemente geben Orientierungshilfe: die Nachzeichnung des Mauerverlaufs mittels der CorTen-Stahlstreben, die Bodenmarkierungen in Stahlbändern, welche ehemalige Grundrisse zeigen, und die sogenannten „Ereignismarken", die in den Boden eingelassen besondere Ereignisse direkt am Ort eines Geschehens markieren und eine Spur legen zum Nachlesen und Nachdenken. In den Alltagsraum sind diese Nachzeichnungen als Irritationen integriert.

Besonders interessant ist für die Besucher die Markierung der Fluchttunnel, die in den 1960er Jahren unter dem Gelände hindurch gegraben wurden. Die Bernauer Straße steigt wie beschrieben von West nach Ost leicht an. An dieser Stelle war es möglich, Tunnel oberhalb des Grundwasserspiegels auf relativ kurzer Strecke, eben unter der Bernauer Straße hindurch, zu graben. Entlang der Bernauer Straße findet sich eine Vielzahl von Tunneln, die als konzertierte Aktionen von Fluchthelfern gegraben wurden, um Verwandten, Freunden oder auch zahlenden Kunden zur Flucht aus Ostberlin zu verhelfen. Die Tunnelfluchten sind bis heute legendär. Die Neugierde, die die Stahlplatten im Boden zur Markierung dieser Tunnel auslösen, ist entsprechend groß. Dabei sind diese Stahlplatten, die beinahe wie Zebrastreifen den Rasen der Gedenkstätten queren, eine äußerst schlichte und auch erst auf den zweiten Blick wahrnehmbare funktionale „Sehhilfe". Die Besucher laufen darüber hinweg, sind irritiert, finden auf einer der Markierungsplatten eine Inschrift mit der Jahreszahl des Tunnelbaus und informieren sich dann an einem der Informationspunkte über diese Leistungen und Umstände der Fluchthilfe.

Remains of the inner security wall
—
Cluster of Ailanthus trees (tree of heaven) between removed segments of the Wall

Reste der Hinterlandmauer
—
Hain mit Götterbäumen zwischen abgestellten Mauersegmenten

One tunnel marker is particularly intriguing as it does not take the shortest route from east to west but runs almost parallel to the Bernauer Strasse. Was it a mistake, a wrong bearing? Inquisitive visitors will discover the reason: it was a Stasi tunnel. The GDR State Security actually built a tunnel to discover the presence of other tunnels by running it perpendicular to the imagined shortest escape routes. One could hardly find a more compelling way of expressing and revealing the paranoia of the border regime. The history of the Berlin Wall that is told along the path of the memorial is full of surprises and by no means one-dimensional. For a stretch of time, the Berlin Wall was part of everyday life in Berlin where now the memorial is a part of the city. This everyday life had its own complexities and also its own logic. And for this reason, there is no single truth about the Wall – this too is communicated in this place. Nevertheless, the memorial still adopts a standpoint with respect to the Wall's history and communicates it through its materiality and its reductive design.

Border patrol path and remains of the inner security wall

Kolonnenweg und Relikt der Hinterlandmauer

Große Neugierde löst vielmals eine Tunnelmarkierung aus, die nicht den kürzesten Weg von Ost nach West bezeichnet, sondern fast parallel zur Bernauer Straße verläuft. Ein Richtungsirrtum, eine falsche Peilung? Der suchende Besucher findet den Hinweis: Stasi-Tunnel. Die Staatssicherheitsorgane der DDR hatten hier einen Tunnel-Suchtunnel gegraben, der quer zu den kürzestmöglichen Fluchtwegverbindungen verlaufen musste. Konsequenter ist das paranoide Erkenntnisinteresse des Grenzregimes kaum nachzuerzählen und aufzuklären. Die Geschichte der Berliner Mauer wird im Verlauf dieses Gedenkweges durchaus überraschend und keineswegs eindimensional erzählt. Die Mauer war für einige Zeit Alltag, wo heute der Gedenkort ein Bereich der Stadt ist. Dieser Alltag hatte seine eigene Komplexität, auch seine eigene Logik. Und deshalb gibt es nicht die eine Wahrheit über die Mauer – auch das sagt dieser Ort. Der aber dennoch eine Haltung zu dieser Geschichte einnimmt und diese auch vermittelt in seiner Materialität und schlichten Gestaltung.

Individual remembrance:
the "Window of Remem-
brance" alongside the
St. Sophia Parish Cemetery

Individuelle Erinnerung:
„Fenster des Gedenkens"
am Friedhof der
Sophiengemeinde

Large-format images on the firewalls of buildings along Bernauer Strasse

Großformatige Drucke auf Brandwänden entlang der Bernauer Straße

Chapel of Reconciliation,
erected on the former death
strip on the site of the former
Church of Reconciliation that
was demolished

Kapelle der Versöhnung, errichtet auf dem Todesstreifen
anstelle der gesprengten
Versöhnungskirche

The design of the traces

"The traces need to function in the ordinary context of the city and this means that they must be durable. That eliminates many potential materials for very pragmatic reasons," explains A. W. Faust. The same applies for the use of plants as materials: the Wall did not grow organically but was made by man – it was a hard element in the city. That left stone or steel as possible options. Stone as an "eternal" building material conveys an impression that would have been just as inappropriate as an organic structure, given that the memorial also remembers the fall of the Wall. CorTen steel was therefore a natural choice, being both durable while symbolising transience through its materiality. In addition, this material was also used elsewhere in the context of remembering the Wall.

But the key to finding an appropriate way of remembrance lies in the very design idea of tracing the course of the Wall without giving it presence as a built object. What the landscape architects have achieved is to trace the new condition of permeability of this once impenetrable wall by placing thousands of vertical rods made of CorTen steel along the former line of the Wall, not in single file but in a three-dimensional constellation. The result is an impression of the memory of the Wall as an object in the urban surroundings, but one that is visually permeable, that can be stepped through and crossed. At the same time it creates an impression of solidity when seen from certain viewpoints – an

Spuren gestalten

„Die Spuren müssen im Alltag der Stadt funktionieren, das setzt ihre Belastbarkeit voraus. Und schließt viele Gestaltungsmaterialien aus, aus ganz pragmatischen Gründen", erläutert A.W. Faust. Das betrifft auch pflanzliche Materialien: Die Mauer war keine organisch gewachsene, sondern eine von Menschen gemachte, harte Stadtspur. Es blieben Stein oder Stahl. Die Botschaft des „ewigen" Materials Stein wäre allerdings ebenso unangemessen wie eine organische Struktur, erinnert die Gedenkstätte doch zugleich an den Fall der Mauer. CorTen-Stahl lag daher als Material nahe: Vergänglichkeit symbolisierend und zugleich belastbar. Zudem war dieses Material im Kontext des Mauergedenkens schon an anderer Stelle verwendet worden. Der Schlüssel zur angemessenen Erinnerung liegt aber in der Entwurfsidee, die Mauer nachzuzeichnen, ohne sie als Bauwerk zu betonen. Eigentlich ist es eher eine Nachzeichnung der neuen Durchlässigkeit dieser einst undurchdringlichen Mauer, die den Landschaftsarchitekten gelang, indem sie tausende Rundstäbe aus CorTen-Stahl entlang des ehemaligen Mauerverlaufs aufreihten, nicht linear, sondern dreidimensional aufgestellt, so dass eine Erinnerung an die Mauer als Körper im Stadtraum entstand, der heute durchschritten, gequert und durchblickt werden kann, während

Harvesting the field of rye belonging to the Parish of Reconciliation

Ernte am Roggenfeld der Versöhnungsgemeinde

optical trick achieved with the means of design. In its materiality it is reminiscent of the reinforcement bars of the reinforced concrete wall, once a symbol for the Wall's impenetrability and then later – after the fall of the Wall – for the destructibility of the Wall and of the system behind it: after the 9 November 1989, so-called "wall peckers" began to break out pieces of the Wall, leaving the reinforcement bars exposed, rusting and hanging strangely loose out of the damaged structure.

Today the row of rods, or steles, serves as an echo of this image while at the same time creating an entirely new one: that of permeability. The ease with which this structure is able to accommodate multiple associations can be attributed to the confident design of the intervention and the choice of material. The designers are careful not to over-dramatise, instead choosing a gesture that first acquires presence through its repetition, in turn evoking a range of associations. The deconstructed quality of this object in space allows it to convey at times an impression of the Wall and at times an image of its destruction: its qualities are not apparent simply by standing in front of it and looking at it as the physical embodiment of a message; to appreciate it one needs to move around it and walk along on it – on both sides of the former border.

die Stäbe aufgrund ihrer dichten Anordnung je nach Blickwinkel zugleich den Eindruck einer geschlossenen Wand vermitteln. Es ist ein Vexierspiel mit den Mitteln der Raumgestaltung, und in der Materialität zugleich eine Reminiszenz an die Armiereisen der stahlbewehrten Mauer, die erst die Undurchdringlichkeit und dann – nach dem Fall – die Zerstörbarkeit des Bauwerks und des Systems symbolisierten: Die „Mauerspechte" brachen nach dem 9. November 1989 Stück für Stück den Beton aus der Mauer, die Armiereisen blieben und hingen seltsam rostig und schlaff in dem zerstörten Baukörper.

Die Stelenreihe erinnert heute an dieses Bild und schafft zugleich ein ganz neues, das der Durchlässigkeit. Dass diese vielfache Assoziation ganz unaufdringlich gelingt, ist der großen Sicherheit in der Gestaltung und in der Materialwahl zu verdanken. Hier wurde bewusst nichts dramatisiert, sondern eine Geste gewählt, die erst in der Wiederholung einen Raumeindruck, und mit diesem eine Vielfalt der Assoziationen, freisetzt. Diese Aufgelöstheit des Raumkörpers, der sich mal zum Bild der Mauer, mal zum Bild des Mauerfalls verändert, funktioniert nicht als materiell gewordene Botschaft, vor der die Betrachter stehen bleiben, sondern sie funktioniert, indem sich die Besucher im Raum bewegen – auf beiden Seiten entlang der ehemaligen Grenze.

Markings: the outline of the former Church of Reconciliation

Nachzeichnung: Grundriss der Versöhnungskirche

**Markings: the Stasi-built
search tunnel**

Nachzeichnung: „Gegen-
tunnel" der Stasi

Stasi-Tunnel

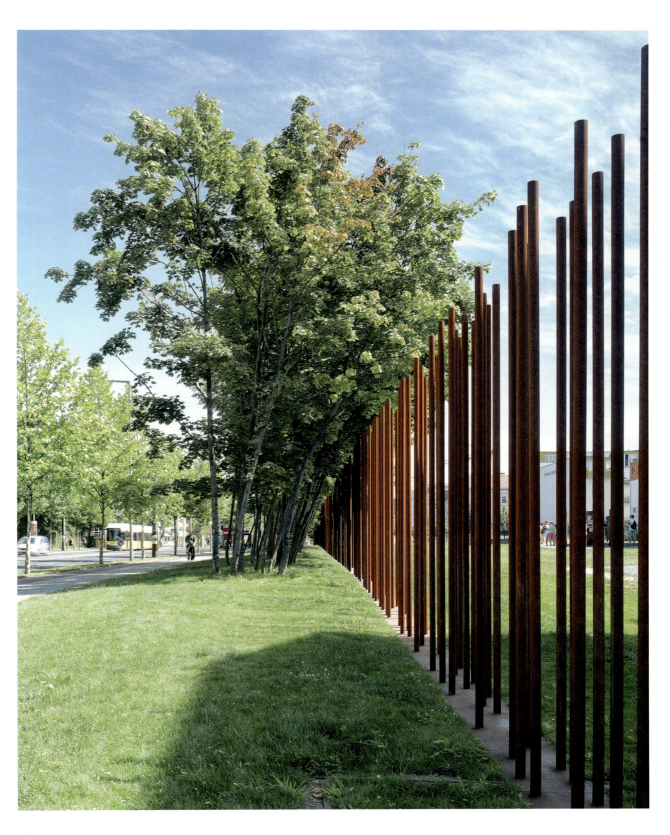

Maples growing on the
wastelands of the Wall
between Strelitzer Strasse
and Brunnenstrasse

Ahornaufwuchs der Mauer-
brache zwischen Strelitzer
Straße und Brunnenstraße

No continuity

With their design for the Berlin Wall Memorial and the maintaining of this open strip in the city, the landscape architects have formulated a counterpoint to the idea of resurrecting the "European city" as proposed by Berlin's planning policies in the 1990s, which envisaged re-establishing, or simulating, a sense of continuity in the city's development. The decision to express this site as a break in the townscape of the city also acknowledges that the history of Berlin is fractured. For Schlusche, this approach to "cultivating remembrance" marks a new departure in the recent history of Berlin's urban development. In the context of the critical discourse surrounding the "Planwerk Innenstadt", the new planning concept for the city centre drawn up by the Berlin Senate Administration for Urban Development in 1999, the selection of sinai's design for this site represents a shift in the official standpoint: urban planning should not attempt to paper over the developments of a city, or attempt to simulate the normality of the European city; it is possible to respond to the fractures within a city, as seen in this socially disparate urban area between Berlin-Mitte and Berlin-Wedding, with the means of design – which in turn creates the potential to reconnect.

Rather than perpetuating an image, an epoch, or a timespan in history, the layers of the city's development are made visible as heterogeneous points of reference. History is not accorded a specific value, declared as being good or right or wrong, but is communicated by cultivating remembrance – the urban realm itself offering the answers.

To this end, we need spaces like this one that truly bring to life a place of the dead, of remembrance, of images – spaces that makes history present.

Keine Kontinuität

Die Landschaftsarchitekten haben mit der Gedenkstätte Berliner Mauer durch das Freihalten des Schneisenraumes eine Kontraposition formuliert zur Wiederaufnahme der Idee der europäischen Stadt in der Berliner Planungspolitik der 1990er Jahre, die eine Kontinuität der städtischen Entwicklung simulieren sollte. Diese Betonung des Bruches im Stadtbild ist zugleich ein Bekenntnis zu den Brüchen in der Geschichte Berlins. Schlusche sieht in dieser Art der „Kultivierung des Erinnerns" zugleich einen neuen Abschnitt der jüngeren Städtebaugeschichte Berlins markiert. Aufgrund des kritischen Diskurses zum „Planwerk Innenstadt" der Berliner Senatsverwaltung für Stadtentwicklung wurde in der Entscheidung für diese Gestaltung eine neue Position bezogen: Die Entwicklungen einer Stadt sollen nicht baulich kaschiert werden, es soll nicht eine Normalität der europäischen Stadt simuliert werden, sondern es kann eine „Stadt der Brüche" in diesem Stadtraum höchster sozialer Diskrepanz zwischen Berlin-Mitte und Berlin-Wedding zum gestalterischen Ausdruck kommen – die nun wiederum verbindend wirken kann.

Nicht ein Bild, eine Epoche, ein Ausschnitt der Geschichte wird fortgeschrieben. Sondern die Schichten der Stadtentwicklung bleiben als heterogene Referenzpunkte im Blick. Geschichte wird nicht per se als Wert, als gut, richtig oder falsch deklariert, sondern sie wird in einer Kultivierung des Erinnerns vermittelt, die einer stadträumlichen Aufklärung gleichkommt.

Dazu bedarf es eines solchen wahrhaft lebendigen Ortes der Toten, der Erinnerung, der Bilder – eines Raumes mit gegenwärtiger Geschichte.

The former death strip passed over part of the St. Sophia Parish Cemetery between Ackerstrasse and Bergstrasse.

Der vormalige Todesstreifen auf Friedhofsflächen der Sophiengemeinde zwischen Ackerstraße und Bergstraße.

Atmospheric contrast: restored grave monuments alongside the former death strip

Atmosphärischer Kontrast: wiederhergestellte Grabanlagen auf dem vormaligen Todesstreifen

Platz des 9. November 1989,
Berlin-Prenzlauer Berg, 2010

Platz des 9. November 1989,
Berlin-Prenzlauer Berg, 2010

**Platz des
9. November 1989
– A Moment
in Time and Space**

Platz des
9. November 1989
– Ein Augenblick
in Zeit und Raum

"A space that commemorates a single day" is how sinai landscape architects have interpreted the task of designing this small square. Set back slightly from the road, history brushed past the small public space on the evening of the fall of the Berlin Wall, elevating it to a place of special significance. Its design traces the events of an evening in November in the context of time and space.

In north Berlin, the Bösebrücke, also known as the Bornholmer Brücke, passes over the former inner German border and connects the districts of Prenzlauer Berg and Wedding. Until 1989, this bridge was the site of the checkpoint at Bornholmer Strasse, the first border crossing to be opened on the evening of the 9 November 1989, heralding the end of the division of Berlin. At one end of the bridge, parallel to the Bornholmer Strasse, a 155-metre-long section of the former "inner security wall" still stands, and today forms the rear wall of the new Platz des 9. November 1989.

The Platz itself is a place that commemorates and informs. The term *Platz* – which in German means both place and square – corresponds here to a landmark that denotes a place and time rather than to an urban square and focal point within the urban structure of the city. The Platz des 9. November 1989 is a transit space, part of a crossing point between two districts in Berlin separated by a deep railway cutting. The fact that this crossing point, which had been impassable for so many years, was unexpectedly opened for everyone on the 9 November 1989, turned this space into a place.

„Ein Erinnerungsraum für einen Tag." So interpretieren sinai Landschaftsarchitekten die Aufgabe, einen kleinen Platz zu gestalten. Dieser Platz wurde an seinem eher abseits liegenden Standort von der Geschichte quasi gestreift. Mit der Öffnung der Mauer wurde dieser Ort zu einem besonderen Ort. Seine Gestaltung stellt einen Abend im November in einen zeitlichen und räumlichen Kontext.

Im Norden Berlins, über die ehemalige innerstädtische Grenze hinweg, verbindet die Bösebrücke, häufig auch Bornholmer Brücke genannt, die Stadtteile Prenzlauer Berg und Wedding. An dieser Brücke lag bis 1989 der Grenzübergang Bornholmer Straße – der Übergang, an dem die Teilung Berlins am Abend des 9. November 1989 erstmals überwunden wurde. Entlang der Bornholmer Straße sind noch 155 Meter der ehemaligen Hinterlandmauer erhalten. Diese fassen heute den Platz des 9. November 1989.

Der Platz selbst ist ein Ort der Information und der Erinnerung. Dabei ist „Platz" eher zu verstehen als eine Markierung von Ort und Zeit denn als ein städtischer Platz, wie er die Stadtstruktur bestimmen oder gar einen Höhepunkt des Stadtbildes darstellen kann. Der Platz des 9. November 1989 ist ein Transitraum, Teil eines Übergangs zwischen zwei Stadtteilen über eine breite, eingetiefte Eisenbahntrasse hinweg. Dass dieser Übergang so lange versperrt und dann am Abend des 9. November 1989 für alle so überraschend wieder geöffnet wurde, macht diesen Ort zum Platz.

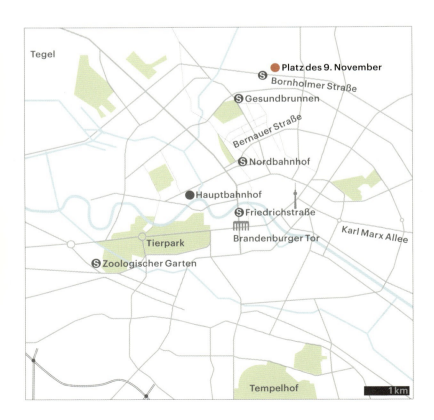

In their design for the space, the landscape architects have deliberately avoided creating a grand gesture, opting instead to design the process of crossing the space as a process of remembering the occurrences of the 9 November as they unfolded over the day. Strips of steel embedded in the ground structure the space – and the day – into timespans. A loose arrangement of autumn-flowering cherry trees planted on the site grows gradually denser to form a grove-like cluster echoing the growing crowds of East Berliners who gathered at this spot. Information panels on the square trace the developments of the day, showing large-format photos of the euphoric scenes seen here and all over the world after the opening of the barrier on the Bornholmer Brücke. East and West Berlin were once again re-united, and with it the Federal Republic of Germany and the GDR, and the Eastern Bloc and the West. The Bornholmer Brücke is synonymous with the "opening of a valve", which by 23:30 had become a "flood", an event that would change the course of history.

Die Landschaftsarchitekten haben auf große Gesten einer Platzgestaltung konsequent verzichtet und das Durchqueren dieses Raumes als Erinnerung an die Zeit, an diesen Tag des 9. November gestaltet. Stahlbänder im Boden gliedern den Platz, den Tag in Zeitabschnitte. Eine sich zum Hain verdichtende Pflanzung von im Herbst blühenden Winterkirschen bringt den wachsenden und sich aufstauenden Anstrom der Bürger Ostberlins zum Ausdruck. Informationstafeln auf dem Platz zeichnen diese Entwicklung des Tages nach und zeigen in großformatigen Fotos die euphorischen Reaktionen vor Ort und in aller Welt auf die Öffnung des Schlagbaumes an der Bornholmer Brücke. Ost- und Westberlin und damit die Bundesrepublik Deutschland und die DDR, Ostblock und Westen, waren für alle wieder miteinander verbunden – auf der Bornholmer Brücke wurde ein „Ventil geöffnet", ab 23.30 Uhr dann sogar „geflutet", und die Geschichte nahm weltweit eine neue Entwicklung.

Bornholmer Brücke,
9 November 1989

Bornholmer Brücke,
9. November 1989

Moment by moment: the key events of the 9 November 1989 are marked in the floor as a timeline. A grove of cherry trees clusters around the "moment" of the first border crossing.

9:00 h	The ministries of the GDR draw up a draft for a new travel regulation.
12:30 h	Draft of the new travel regulation passed to the Council of Ministers and the SED Politbüro.
16:00 h	SED Secretary General Egon Krenz reads out the new travel resolution in the SED Central Committee.
18:00 h	SED Central Committee International Press Conference begins. The transmission is live.
18:53 h	The SED spokesman Günter Schabowski announces that the new travel regulations is "effective immediately, without delay!"
19:05 h	"GDR opens border" – newsflash, AP news agency
19:30 h	"Private trips can be applied for" – Aktuelle Kamera, DDR 1
20:00 h	"GDR opens border" – Tagesschau current affairs TV programme, ARD
20:15 h	Approx. 50 GDR citizens have gathered at Bornholmer Straße – East Berlin Volkspolizei report
20:40 h	"It is not possible to let you depart here and now." – East Berlin Volkspolizei, Bornholmer Straße
21:20 h	Approx. 500 GDR citizens now at the Bornholmer Straße: "Those who are most rebellious. Let them go." – Instruction from Stasi Colonel
22:42 h	"The gates in the Wall are wide open", Hanns Joachim Friedrichs, Tagesthemen current affairs TV programme, ARD
23:20 h	Tens of thousands at the Bornholmer Straße: "Open the gates! Open the Gates! We'll be back, we'll be back!"
23:30 h	"We're flooding now! We're opening the gates!" – Stasi Officer, Bornholmer Straße
00:15 h	"Unbelievable", "Crazy", "Amazing" – 20,000 people cross the Bornholmer Brücke.

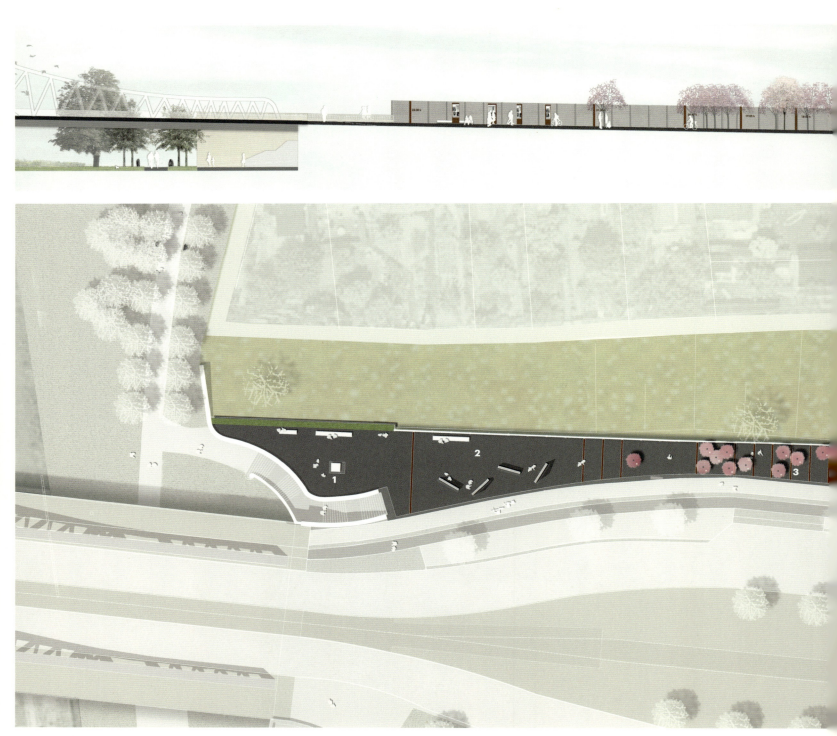

Moment für Moment: Die prägenden Ereignisse des 9. November 1989 sind als Chronografie in den Boden eingelassen. Ein Hain von Zierkirschen verdichtet sich um den „Moment" der ersten Grenzübertritte.

9:00 h	DDR-Ministerien arbeiten an neuer Reiseregelung.
12:30 h	Entwurf der Reiseregelung geht an DDR-Ministerrat und SED-Politbüro.
16:00 h	SED-Generalsekretär Egon Krenz verliest Reiseregelung im ZK der SED.
18:00 h	Beginn der internationalen Pressekonferenz des ZK der SED – Liveübertragung
18:53 h	Reiseregelung gilt „ab sofort, unverzüglich!", Günter Schabowski, SED-Pressesprecher
19:05 h	„DDR öffnet Grenze", Eilmeldung, AP
19:30 h	„Privatreisen nach dem Ausland können beantragt werden", Aktuelle Kamera, DDR 1
20:00 h	„DDR öffnet Grenze", Tagesschau, ARD
20:15 h	Ca. 50 Reisewillige an der Bornholmer Straße, Bericht der Ost-Berliner Volkspolizei
20:40 h	„Es ist nicht möglich, Ihnen hier und jetzt die Ausreise zu gewähren", Ost-Berliner Volkspolizist, Bornholmer Straße
21:20 h	Ca. 500 Reisewillige an der Bornholmer Straße: „Die am aufsässigsten sind, die lass raus", Stasi-Oberst
22:42 h	„Die Tore in der Mauer stehen weit offen", Hanns Joachim Friedrichs, Tagesthemen, ARD
23:20 h	Zehntausende an der Bornholmer Straße: „Tor auf! Tor auf! Wir kommen wieder, wir kommen wieder!"
23:30 h	„Wir fluten jetzt! Wir machen alles auf!", Stasi-Offizier, Bornholmer Straße
00:15 h	„Wahnsinn" – „Irre" – „Nicht zu fassen", 20.000 Menschen haben die Bösebrücke passiert.

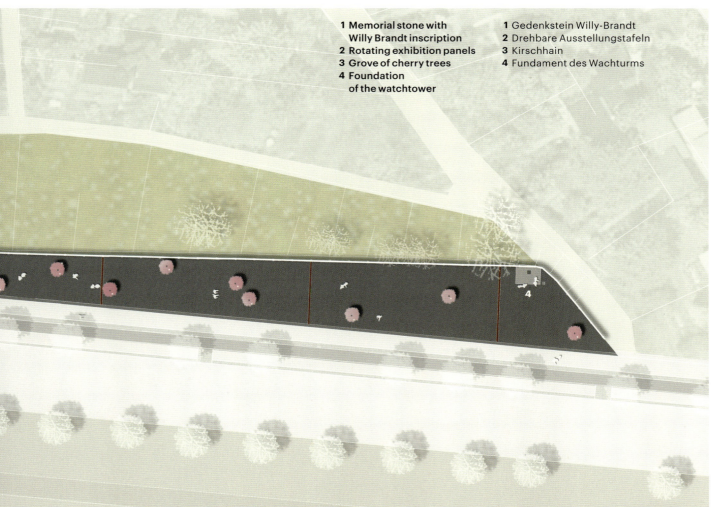

1	**Memorial stone with Willy Brandt inscription**	1	Gedenkstein Willy-Brandt
2	**Rotating exhibition panels**	2	Drehbare Ausstellungstafeln
3	**Grove of cherry trees**	3	Kirschhain
4	**Foundation of the watchtower**	4	Fundament des Wachturms

5 m

Measuring the course of a day

The design for the Platz des 9. November 1989 condenses the events of this "historic day", as the national newsreader Hanns Joachim Friedrichs spontaneously dubbed it at 22:42 on 09/11/1989, into a place of remembering. Developments earlier in the day had caused many Berliners to gather at the Bornholmer Brücke in the hope of being able to cross the border, until at 21:20 this then actually happened.

"Our design approaches this 'moment' as a historic point in time and as a motif to remember. The 9 November had already been proclaimed a historic day before the day was over. But what makes this day any different to those before it? When we look back, we don't remember this day as an abstract unit of time. Instead we remember it (like many other days before it) as a series of individual moments, as the successive build-up of previously unforeseen new developments. Many of the moments of this day have become iconic, a product of their recurring presence in the media: the majority of people in Germany can recall Günter Schabowski announcing 'As far as I know … effective immediately, without delay' or the cries of 'Wahnsinn' [Unbelievable] from later that night. So far these remembered moments have lost none of their emotional impact, and it is these powerful moments of the day that this place should commemorate. For us, the most decisive moment of the night is one that we can only imagine as (as far as we know) it was never documented: namely the moment in which the first person broke free from the growing masses and walked over the bridge." (sinai landscape architects)

The path to the bridge leads along the length of the Platz which has been given a simple, anthracite-coloured water-bound gravel surface. At intervals, steel strips delineate this surface, each of which has a time-stamp in hours and minutes and a short quote welded onto it. The succession of these steel strips marks the progression of the day, their frequency increasing as one walks from east to west, echoing the heightening intensity of the events of the 9 November as they began to unfold towards the evening. "We have structured the Platz chronologically, because this is the clearest way of remembering the not always logical progression of decisions made by those responsible that evening," explain sinai landscape architects.

The idea of representing time as a succession of snapshots inscribed in space that signify or stimulate the perception of a historic moment, rather than attempting to portray history, is a design principle that sinai have used repeatedly. There are few examples of this approach in contemporary landscape architecture; instead inspiration is more likely to be found in the visual arts. Modern landscape architecture often takes the approach of programming or deprogramming a space, in order to create an "environment" in which people as the recipient subjects and objects of the design can feel at

Taktung eines Tages

Ein „historischer Tag", wie es der Fernsehmoderator Hanns Joachim Friedrichs am 9.11.1989 um 22.42 Uhr in den „Tagesthemen" spontan formulierte, wird durch diese Gestaltung des Platzes zu einem Erinnerungsraum verdichtet. Aufgrund der Ereignisse dieses Tages erhofften die Berliner einen Grenzübertritt und warteten nun an der Bornholmer Brücke, bis hier um 21.20 Uhr die Grenze tatsächlich geöffnet wurde. „Unsere Platzgestaltung nähert sich dem ‚Moment' als historische Zeiteinheit und als Erinnerungsmotiv. Noch am selben Tag wurde der 9. November als historischer Tag benannt. Doch was machte diesen Tag anders als die Tage davor? Beim erinnernden Blick zurück bleibt der Tag als Erinnerungseinheit abstrakt. Er stellt sich (wie viele andere Tage zuvor) als Fluss von Einzelmomenten dar, als sich aufbauender Strom von ungeahnten Neuigkeiten. Viele der Momente dieses Tages gehören zum häufig wiederholten Kanon unserer medial vermittelten Erinnerung, sie sind bei einem Großteil der Menschen in Deutschland abrufbar, von Schabowskis ‚nach meiner Kenntnis … ist das sofort, unverzüglich umzusetzen' bis zum ‚Wahnsinn' der späteren Nacht. Bisher haben diese Erinnerungsmomente ihre emotionale Wirkung nicht verloren. Die starken Momente dieses Tages sollen daher den Ort prägen. Und wir wollen uns als den entscheidenden Moment in dieser Nacht den (unseres Wissens) nicht dokumentierten Augenblick vorstellen, als sich der erste Mensch aus dieser dichten und anschwellenden Menschenmenge löst und sich auf den Weg über die Brücke macht." (sinai Landschaftsarchitekten)

Der Weg hin zur Brücke über den länglichen Platz führt heute über eine schlichte anthrazitfarbene wassergebundene Wegedecke. Der Belag wird unterbrochen durch die Stahlbänder, auf die Uhrzeiten in Stunden und Minuten sowie kurze Zitate aufgeschweißt sind. In einer sich verdichtenden Folge bilden diese Stahlbänder die Taktung eines Tages ab, dessen Ereignisfolge in ihrer Intensität zum Abend hin zunahm – so wie heute die immer dichter werdende Folge der zu querenden Stahlbänder auf dem Weg von Ost nach West. „Chronologisch haben wir diesen Platz gegliedert, denn chronologisch behalten wir die ja durchaus nicht eindeutige Entscheidungsfolge der Verantwortlichen an diesem Tag am klarsten in Erinnerung", erläutern sinai Landschaftsarchitekten ihre Planung.

Die Idee, Zeit als Folge von Momentaufnahmen in Raum einzuschreiben, die Geschichte gerade nicht nachzugestalten, aber ihrer Wahrnehmung Anregung und Zeichen im Raum zu geben, ist ein von sinai wiederholt angewendetes Entwurfsprinzip. Es gibt dafür in der gegenwärtigen Landschaftsarchitektur wenige Vorbilder; diese sind eher in der bildenden Kunst zu suchen. Denn während Landschaftsarchitektur heute oftmals an Programmierungen oder Deprogrammie-

1

Grothaus, Christian J.: "Das Eliasson-Alphabet oder: Eine Spielanleitung für Raum und Zeit", in: Tabula Rasa, Zeitung für Gesellschaft und Kultur, Jena 2012, c.f. www.tabularasa-jena.de/artikel/artikel_4297/

1

Grothaus, Christian J.: Das Eliasson-Alphabet oder: Eine Spielanleitung für Raum und Zeit, in: Tabula Rasa, Zeitung für Gesellschaft und Kultur, Jena, 2012, zit. n. www.tabularasa-jena.de/artikel/artikel_4297/

home, or feel stimulated, can relax, recharge their batteries, and so on. Visual artists, by contrast, ask more fundamental questions such as how "people relate to their immediate environment and to one another, how they assure themselves of their own physical presence in the environment and how they define their identity as subjective, aware individuals" (Philip Ursprung). The atmosphere, the general way of perceiving a place, space, object or image has no single, categorical "meaning" for the artist or author of a design, in this case the landscape architect. Instead the meaning is "coupled with the act of the viewer experiencing the presence of art, who is, in the best performative manner, involved in a situational construct that shapes the here and now."[1] sinai landscape architects' designs are not about transforming time into space as a kind of simplified sundial principle. Instead, here time is represented in space using symbolic references to the unfolding headlines of a day to create such a "situational construct" in which the visitor (and not the spatial surroundings) connects with the different personal memories they have of this day. The space does not portray history, but supplies invitations to tell one's own story of this day in one's head.

In its composition, the space is not structured around a dominant message, choosing instead to leave itself open to casual appropriation, and to personal interpretation of the dividing and connecting role of its elements (the Berlin Wall, once a division, is today the Bornholmer Strasse that connects). As such, it remains a normal space for the different activities of everyday city life. The Platz is not a prominent space in the city, even after its redesign. It is an almost incidental space that acquires historical meaning through the visitors' connection with the space in their minds as a product of its design. "History as a means of transforming space" is communicated in the form of an invitation to read the historical context of a space.

rungen von Raum arbeitet, um mittels eines Werks ein „Umfeld" zu schaffen, in dem die Menschen als empfangende Subjekt-Objekte sich wohlfühlen, angeregt sind, sich entspannen, sich regenerieren und vieles andere mehr, fragt die bildende Kunst grundlegender danach, „wie Menschen mit ihrer unmittelbaren Umgebung und untereinander in Beziehung stehen, wie sie sich der Anwesenheit ihrer Körper in der Umgebung versichern und ihre Identität als subjektiv wahrnehmende Individuen artikulieren" (Olafur Eliasson). Die Atmosphäre, generell die Art der Wahrnehmung eines Ortes, eines Raumes, eines Objektes oder Bildes ist also keine eindeutige, einseitige „Bedeutung" durch den Künstler, den Entwurfsverfasser, hier den Landschaftsarchitekten, sondern die Bedeutung ist „gekoppelt an das Engagement der Betrachter, die die Präsenz der Kunst erfahren, denn in bester performativer Manier werden sie in ein situatives Gefüge involviert, das das Hier und Jetzt gestaltet".[1]

Es geht den Entwürfen von sinai Landschaftsarchitekten gerade nicht um die Transformation von Zeit in Raum, um ein simplifizierendes Sonnenuhr-Prinzip, sondern die Abbildung von Zeit im Raum wird mittels symbolischer Bezüge auf die Nachrichtenlage eines Tages zu eben jenem „situativen Gefüge", in dem der Besucher sich selbst (nicht den umgebenden Raum) in verschiedene, individuelle Erinnerungen an diesen Tag versetzen kann. Der Raum ist nicht Abbild einer Geschichte, sondern Anregung für die eigenen Erzählungen dieser Geschichte im Kopf.

In seiner Komposition wurde der Raum nicht auf eine Botschaft hin hierarchisiert, sondern er gibt dem Zufall der Inbesitznahmen, der Grenzziehungen für trennende und verbindende Elemente (einst die Berliner Mauer, heute die verbindende Bornholmer Straße) beiläufigen Ausdruck und belässt damit den verschiedenen Phasen städtischen Alltags ein alltägliches Raumgefüge. Der Platz ist kein betonter Ort im Stadtgefüge, auch nach seiner Umgestaltung nicht. Er ist ein zufälliger Raum, der durch die gestalterisch angeregte Begegnung in den Köpfen der Besucher zum geschichtlichen Ort wird. „Geschichte als Raumtransformation" wird als Anregung, als Leseangebot eines geschichtlichen Kontextes im Raum vermittelt.

Steel strip on the ground with inscription: the moments are what one remembers

Beschriftetes Bodenband: Moment als Erinnerungs-einheit

2
Schröder, Thies: "Identity via Transformation", in: Zeitgeist Berlin Invalidenpark, Zurich 2006, p. 51

3
Ursprung, Philip: "Irony's Edge: Christophe Girot's Invaliden Park and the Spatiality of History", in: Zeitgeist Berlin Invalidenpark, Zurich 2006, p. 129

4
Ibid., p. 133

2
Schröder, Thies: Identität durch Transformation, in: Zeitgeist Berlin Invalidenpark, Zürich 2006, S. 51

3
Ursprung, Philip: „Irony's Edge: Christophe Girots Invalidenpark und die Räumlichkeit der Geschichte", in: Zeitgeist Berlin Invalidenpark, Zürich 2006

4
Ebda., S. 133

An approach comparable to that of sinai's – and consequently one that contrasts markedly with many memorial site designs that focus predominantly on the creation of moods and atmospheres – is Christophe Girot's design for the Invalidenpark in Berlin from 1992. "Christophe Girot's notion of a timescape is [...] about an awareness of time – and the passage of time. His parks draw their identity from time, from the past and the future alike. Remembrance and renewal are not mutually exclusive in Girot's thinking – on the contrary, they impinge on each other." [2] The outcome of a personal process of tracing the site, Girot's design for the park is for Philip Ursprung one of those projects "that best articulate the horizon that is unique to Berlin, this incomparable openness shot through with historical contradictions and rough caesuras," [3] and an example that challenges how we deal with historical sites. This approach to dealing with history has "nothing to do with repression, nor nostalgia. History is neither evoked as something tragic, disparate, unrepresentable – as in Peter Eisenman's Memorial to the Murdered Jews of Europe – nor is it simulated and made palatable as in Kollhoff's facades and interiors." [4] sinai's work also reflects this approach: the Platz des 9. November 1989 is a "drawing" in the urban realm, a design concept in which the focus lies on the design and reception of a place that has become connected with history. As such, this design concept transcends a whole range of design interpretations of history and yet still manages to address a number of the concrete expectations we have of "history".

Vergleichbar mit diesem Ansatz von sinai Landschaftsarchitekten – und damit in deutlichem Kontrast zu vielen Entwürfen für Gedenkstätten, welche sich vordringlich um die Formulierung von Stimmungen und Atmosphären bemühen – ist wohl Christophe Girots Entwurf für den Invalidenpark in Berlin von 1992 zu lesen. „Es geht Girot mit seiner Idee einer ‚Landschaft der Zeit' [...] um ein Bewusstsein für Zeit – und für Zeitläufte. Seine Parks sind Räume, die ihre Identität aus der Zeit, der Vergangenheit wie der Zukunft, speisen. Erinnern und Erneuern schließen sich für Girot nicht aus, sie bedingen einander." [2] Philip Ursprung, der Girots auf einer individuellen Spurensuche des Entwerfers fußenden Park zu denjenigen Projekten zählt, „welche diesen spezifisch berlinischen Horizont, diese einzigartige Offenheit und zugleich die historischen Widersprüchlichkeiten und rohen Brüche Berlins am treffendsten artikulieren", fragt an dessen Beispiel nach dem Umgang mit historischem Raum. Ein solcher Umgang mit Geschichte habe „weder mit Verdrängung zu tun, noch mit Nostalgie. Geschichte wird weder als etwas Tragisches, Disparates, Undarstellbares evoziert, wie beispielsweise in Peter Eisenmans Denkmal für die ermordeten Juden Europas, noch wird sie simuliert und damit konsumierbar gemacht wie in den Fassaden und Innenräumen von Kollhoff." [3] Auch sinai kann diese Haltung für sich beanspruchen: Der Platz des 9. November 1989 ist eine „Zeichnung" im Stadtraum, die Gestaltung und Empfindung dieses mit Geschichte identifizierten Ortes in den Mittelpunkt des Entwurfs stellt. Damit weist dieser Entwurf über vielerlei gestalterische Interpretationen von Geschichte hinaus und wird mancherlei Erwartung an „Geschichte" im Konkreten dennoch gerecht.

A narrow strip of land with remains of the inner security wall was turned into the Platz des 9. November 1989.

Ein schmales Geländeband mit einem Relikt der Hinterlandmauer wurde zum Platz des 9. November 1989.

Time signals

Visitors to the site today can trace the progression of a day as they cross the new Platz. Time signals inscribed in the ground mark out the headlines of the 9 November 1989, starting with the morning briefing of the GDR border guards at 09:00 and progressing on to the legendary announcement by Günter Schabowski, member of the Socialist Unity Party of Germany (SED) Politburo and officiating speaker of the Central Committee, at 18:57 during a press conference; the subsequent gathering of crowds at the checkpoint and the opening of the Bornholmer Strasse border crossing at 21:20 as well as the reactions of the people and media to this event. Freestanding panels augment these markings on the ground with photos and written information in several languages.

The motif of inscribed steel strips in the floor is borrowed from sinai's work on the design of the Berlin Wall Memorial along the Bernauer Strasse, where inlaid steel strips mark the outlines of buildings and structures that existed before the Wall was built. However, the chronospatial delineation of an urban space as implemented here in such a direct form, is an approach only really imaginable for a site of such towering importance for the communication of history. The Platz itself has no formal climax, centre or focal point, echoing the fact that historical developments did not lead up to this particular day. In both its historical as well as its temporal dimensions, the fall of the Berlin Wall was a succession of decisions and developments that did not follow a greater plan. As a place of moments, it is not in need of a monumental memorial. The fact that the Platz des 9. November 1989 seems almost incidental is part of the idea.

Zeitzeichen

Heute erlebt der Besucher des Platzes die Abfolge eines Tages nach, wenn er sich über diesen Platz bewegt. Die Zeitzeichen sind hier die Nachrichten des 9. November 1989, von der Lagebesprechung der Grenztruppen der DDR um 9.00 Uhr morgens bis zum berühmten Satz in der Pressekonferenz des SED-Politbüromitgliedes und Sprechers des Zentralkomitees Günter Schabowski um 18.57 Uhr, dem darauffolgenden Andrang an den Grenzübergängen und der Öffnung des Übergangs an der Bornholmer Straße um 21.20 Uhr und den Reaktionen der Menschen und Medien auf diese Nachricht. Stelltafeln illustrieren diese Zeitmarkierungen im Boden durch Fotos und informierende mehrsprachige Texte.

Das Motiv der markierenden Stahlbänder im Boden konnte aus der Arbeit von sinai zur Gestaltung der Mauergedenkstätte entlang der Bernauer Straße entlehnt werden; dort zeichnen Stahlbänder die vor dem Mauerbau vorhandene Bebauungsstruktur in ihren Grundrissen nach. Dass aber ein Platz quasi chronoräumlich gegliedert wird, ist in dieser sehr unmittelbaren Umsetzung wohl nur für einen solch gewichtigen Informations- und Vermittlungsort der Geschichte vorstellbar. Einen gestalterischen Höhepunkt, ein Zentrum oder einen Mittelpunkt hat der Platz nicht, denn auch die geschichtliche Entwicklung baute sich ja nicht um diesen Tag herum auf. Der Fall der Berliner Mauer war in seiner historischen wie in seiner unmittelbaren zeitlichen Abfolge eine Folge von Entscheidungen und Entwicklungen, die keinem größeren Plan folgten. Ein Platz der Momente bedarf keiner monumentalen Gestaltung der Erinnerung. Dass der Platz des 9. November 1989 heute eher beiläufig wirkt, ist Teil der gestalterischen Idee.

Cherry trees cluster around the strip at 21:20 hours.

Kirschbäume verdichten sich am Band 21.20 h.

That the design of this site chooses to focus on the significance of the moment rather than to monumentalise history is characteristic of our present approach to remembering the fall of the Wall. It corresponds to the prevailing spirit of objectivity in our historical interpretation of the Berlin Wall. Berlin and Germany, only just reunified, capture the emotionality of the moment as reflected in images from the media coverage. sinai, too, make use of these emotions frozen in photography. A more powerful symbol would be inappropriate, at least at the present time. While the 9 November 1989 was an achievement, it resists the obviously representative symbolism so typical of monuments for battles, liberation or for places of mourning or defeat. Rather than representing, the Platz symbolises that it is appropriate, at relevant places, to highlight the transformation of the city by focussing attention on these specific changes. And landscape architecture is one possible way of generating that attention.

Whether such an approach, whether this design will do justice to the emotionality of this occasion, of this moment in history in the long term can only be supposed. To a large degree, this will depend on how the information provided and the overall semiotic character of the Platz is received in future, and in turn on how viewers' expectations will change with regard to how the 9 November 1989 is perceived and valued. The design of the Platz in its current form lays down certain aspects but also leaves room for a variety of ways of approaching the place, ranging from the chance encounter in passing to the ritualistic tracing of a historic moment.

Es ist bezeichnend für unsere gegenwärtige Erinnerung an den Mauerfall, dass für die Gestaltung dieses Platzes die Bedeutung des Moments einer Monumentalisierung der Geschichte vorgezogen wird. Dies entspricht der vorherrschenden Versachlichung der Geschichtsschreibung zur Berliner Mauer. Das gerade erst vereinigte Berlin, das vereinigte Deutschland fixiert die Emotionalität dieses Moments in den Bildern der reflektierenden Medienberichterstattung. sinai bedient sich dieser in Fotografie gefrorenen Emotionen. Ein stärkeres Symbol dagegen wäre – derzeit – fehl am Platze. Denn der 9. November 1989 wurde zwar errungen, er entzieht sich aber der eindeutigen repräsentativen Symbolik, wie sie beispielsweise für Denkmale eines Sieges, einer Befreiung oder für Orte der Trauer, der Niederlage so typisch sind. Dieser Platz repräsentiert nicht, er symbolisiert vielmehr, dass es angemessen ist, der Stadt in ihrer Veränderung an entscheidenden Orten eine Aufmerksamkeit zu widmen, indem auf eben diese Veränderungen hingewiesen wird. Die Landschaftsarchitektur ist eine Möglichkeit, diese Aufmerksamkeit zu erreichen.

Ob eine solche, ob genau diese Gestaltung der Emotionalität dieses Anlasses, dieses Moments der Geschichte auf Dauer gerecht wird, ist nur zu vermuten. In hohem Maße hängt dies auch davon ab, wie das Informationsangebot und insgesamt der Zeichencharakter dieses Platzes zukünftig angenommen werden, wie also die Erwartung der Betrachter an die Wahrnehmung und Bewertung des 9. November 1989 sich verändert.

**Foundation
of the watchtower**

Fundament
des Wachturms

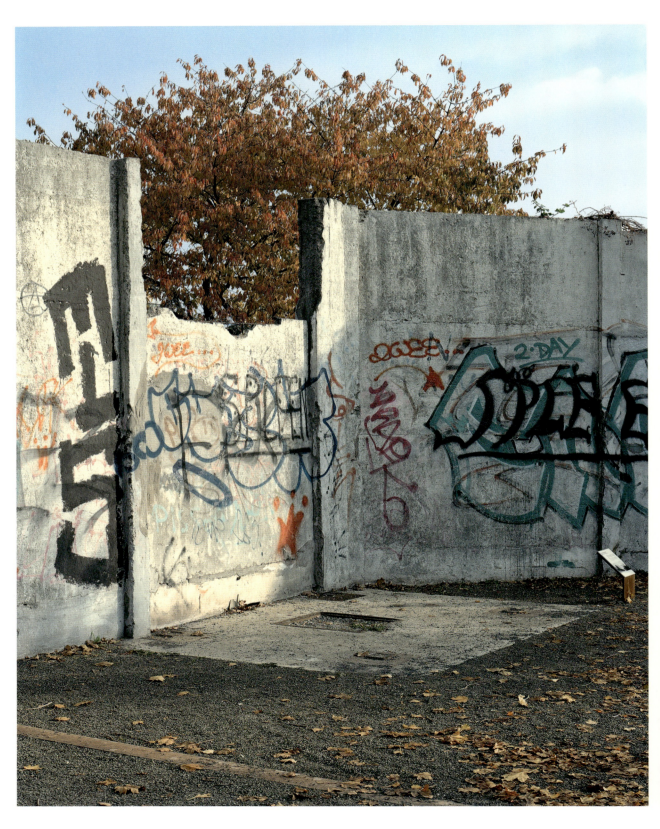

Detail of 18:00 hours
on the inner security wall

Detail 18.00 h an der
Hinterlandmauer

Today, one can already see the different ways in which people respond to the Platz, whether they are casual passers-by or visitors who have deliberately made their way here. Using the means of landscape architecture, sinai have laid down a structure that records that day as an increasingly dramatic succession of decisions and events. In all other respects, however, and therefore very much in the spirit of the times, the landscape architecture refrains from passing judgement or pre-determining the historical significance of this moment at the Platz der 9. November 1989. Remembrance at this place takes the form of a communicative invitation with uplifting intention. Beyond this place, however, the memory of these events no longer has the power to shape the city, or has not yet regained sufficient emotional power.

Der Platz in seiner jetzigen Gestaltung gibt einiges vor, lässt aber zugleich Raum für ein weites Spektrum zwischen einer beiläufigen Wahrnehmung und der ritualisierten Begegnung mit dem Geschichtsmoment. Schon heute ist der Unterschied sichtbar, mit dem beiläufige Passanten oder den Ort aktiv aufsuchende Gäste auf das Angebot dieses Platzes reagieren. sinai hat hier mittels der Landschaftsarchitektur eine Struktur vorgegeben, die den Tag als spannungsreiche Abfolge von Entscheidungen und Nachrichten in Erinnerung hält. Darüber hinaus allerdings hält sich die Landschaftsarchitektur, damit durchaus zeitgeistig, in der Wertung und Gewichtung dieses Moments am Platz des 9. November 1989 eher zurück. Das Erinnern ist an diesem Ort vor allem eine nachrichtliche Aufforderung mit intendierter positiver Stimmung. Die Stadt über diesen Ort hinaus zu prägen vermag diese Erinnerung nicht mehr oder noch nicht wieder.

Rotating exhibition panels with large-format photos showing key moments of the 9 November

Drehbare Ausstellungsträger mit großformatigen Momentaufnahmen des 9. November

Night views of the urban
space next to the busy
Bornholmer Strasse

Nachtaspekte des stark
frequentierten Alltagsraums
Bornholmer Straße

**About sinai
landscape architects**

Das Büro sinai
Landschaftsarchitekten

1
Piltz, Eric: Trägheit des
Raums, in: Döring, Thielmann
(Ed.): Spatial Turn, Bielefeld
2008, p. 94

1
Piltz, Eric: Trägheit des
Raums, in: Döring, Thielmann
(Hg.): Spatial Turn, Bielefeld
2008, S. 94

Few other landscape architects in Germany and beyond have undertaken such a large variety of challenging design projects for places that, due to their specific historical significance, can be regarded as "difficult", as complex and many-layered. In their work, sinai landscape architects have concerned themselves with the March Revolution of 1848, with the beginnings of the socialist movement and with the idea of freedom. They have developed designs for sites from the National Socialist past, for places dedicated to the victims, as well as places used by the perpetrators. They have done work on the consequences of the Second World War, on flight, expulsion and reconciliation. And they have created designs for places that remember the division of Germany, the Berlin Wall and also the fall of the Wall in Berlin. There are many different ways and means of relating history in space. sinai have found an approach of their own that rather than making history itself the central aspect, provides ways of reading history as the key elements of the design of spaces. Nothing is portrayed; instead visitors are offered help in forming their own impression. This happens not only through the provision of background information such as archive material but also in concrete form, by making these reading aids a characteristic element of the design of the spaces. The markings of traces are given a new material identity that is a product of both the history of the place as well as the aesthetics of the system of these reading aids.

The decisive aspect is therefore how history is told with the means of landscape architecture. This narrative approach to designing requires contextual and sensitive design that attempts to reveal the nature or atmosphere of a place rather than to declare it.

For sinai, space is not conceived of as a defined container such as a city, region, park or courtyard but as an "instrument of analysis" with which they "place emphasis on its relationality". "Relational means not to assume that an area of investigation is existent purely in its spatial structure and that what is to be investigated is to be found there and within its limits. Rather, the interaction between physical conditions and (human) actions is investigated, whereby space is the product of these interactions and is itself an expression of the ideas of spatiality, boundaries and the representation thereof."[1]

The landscape architects themselves view this comprehension of space, which reflects parallel developments in the fields of social science and history, as the key to their designs. In these designs they develop "form through content". The open space, the landscape is for sinai landscape architects the connective fluid. Designing open spaces therefore means to be constantly working in contexts. Based on their ongoing consideration of urban objectives at a larger scale, the landscape architects are able to precisely identify and to reveal the specific quality of an open space.

The realisation that cultural and atmospheric quality can only arise in the context of a holistic consideration of the larger urban sphere has led sinai to consciously seek intersections with other disciplines. Their dealings with engineers and scholars of humanities, with architects,

Wohl keine anderen Landschaftsarchitekten in Deutschland und auch darüber hinaus haben in den letzten Jahren eine so große Vielzahl an anspruchsvollen Entwürfen für Orte erarbeitet, die aufgrund ihrer geschichtlichen Bedeutung als „schwierig" eingeschätzt werden, als komplex und vielschichtig. sinai Landschaftsarchitekten haben sich in ihrer Landschaftsarchitektur mit der Märzrevolution 1848 in Deutschland, mit den Anfängen der sozialistischen Bewegung wie mit der Idee der Freiheit auseinandergesetzt. Sie haben Entwürfe erdacht zu den Orten des Nationalsozialismus, zu Orten, die den Opfern gewidmet sind, wie zu Orten der Täter. Sie haben gearbeitet zu den Folgen des Zweiten Weltkrieges, zu Flucht, Vertreibung und Versöhnung. Und sie haben Entwürfe geschaffen zu den Orten der deutschen Teilung, der Berliner Mauer, wie auch zum Fall dieser Mauer in Berlin.

Nun kann man Geschichte auf sehr unterschiedliche Art und Weise im Raum erzählen. sinai haben ihren besonderen Weg gefunden, der nicht die Geschichte selbst in den Mittelpunkt stellt, sondern die Lesehilfen zur Geschichte zu den Schlüsselelementen der Gestaltung von Räumen macht. Nichts wird abgebildet, sondern dem Betrachter werden Hilfen angeboten, sich ein Bild zu machen. Und dies nicht nur auf der Ebene der Hintergrundrecherche, also der Bereitstellung von Archivmaterial, sondern ganz konkret, indem diese Lesehilfen zu den prägenden Elementen der Gestaltung der Räume werden. Nachzeichnungen von Spuren erhalten eine neue materielle Identität, die sich aus der Historie ebenso wie aus der Ästhetik dieser Lesehilfen begründet.

Entscheidend ist also das Wie des Geschichte-Erzählens mit den Mitteln der Landschaftsarchitektur. Dieses narrative Entwerfen ist ein kontextbezogenes, behutsames Gestalten mit der Absicht, eine Gestimmtheit des Ortes zu erwirken, gerade keine Bestimmtheit. sinai begreifen Raum nicht als Abgrenzung fassbarer Einheiten wie Stadt, Region, Park oder Hof. Vielmehr ist Raum ihr „Analyseinstrument", womit sie die „Relationalität in den Vordergrund stellen". „Relational meint dabei, nicht davon auszugehen, dass ein Untersuchungsgebiet in seiner räumlichen Struktur vorhanden ist und das zu Untersuchende darin und in dessen Grenzen stattfindet. Vielmehr wird die Wechselbeziehung von physischen Bedingungen und (menschlichen) Handlungen untersucht, wobei Raum das Ergebnis dieser Wechselbeziehungen ist und sich in den Vorstellungen von Räumlichkeit, Grenzen und der Darstellungen derselben äußert."[1]

artists, scenographers and many others has given rise to an extended notion of open space that aims to encapsulate the quality of our living environment as a whole. Without this collaboration with architects, artists and exhibition designers, and their respective openness to creating something together, many important projects would not be as unified as they are.

The landscape architects view what they find at the site "as a kind of translocated panel painting, comprised of allusions, of references to history, landscape and politics". These references they regard "not as physical deposits at the respective place, but as purely mental associations". To reveal these in the visitors' intellectual consideration of the place, a "neutral covering layer" is helpful. Relics are placed within this neutral context as are newer markings of traces, so that with the help of landscape architecture, people are stimulated to think about the place.

All of sinai landscape architects' realised projects are the product of prize-winning competition entries. The members of the competition juries as well as of the institutions and foundations that develop and operate memorial sites, comprise historians, museum education specialists, sociologists and political scientists. In most cases sinai are able to convince them. Is that because the landscape architects are specialists in the communication of history? Or because "landscape" can also always be read as a form of political or historical development?

The places that sinai design are historical places, places that communicate history. In their design, however, every one of them is reinvented and interpreted. sinai do not align their work with any supposed historical truth, and they do not bring out the spirit of a place from a particular historical epoch; their designs interpret the respective task from the viewpoint of the present. Not "the history" but the stories of history, their references and structures are what interest the landscape architects. History and space are the means of concentration. sinai landscape architects undertake a far wider spectrum of tasks than are shown in this book. sinai also steer and develop the building of parks, work on theories and concepts for the park of the future, develop urban and architectural projects in collaboration with others and even spin legends around a place where this lends it a distinctive profile. Whether designing "green" parks or "stony" urban spaces such as squares and promenades, the design approach is no different. Of central importance is always how the user perceives the space. In many cases, these designs lend spaces renewed legibility and reactivate spaces in the landscape of the city that were previously considered "non-spaces or ancillary spaces".

Die Landschaftsarchitekten selbst nennen dieses Verständnis von Raum, das mit Entwicklungen in den Sozial- und Geschichtswissenschaften übereinstimmt, den Schlüssel zu ihren Entwürfen. In diesen Entwürfen entwickeln sie „Form durch Inhalt". Der Freiraum, die Landschaft ist für sinai Landschaftsarchitekten das verbindende Fluidum. Die Gestaltung von Freiraum bedeutet die ständige Arbeit in Kontexten. Basierend auf der andauernden Auseinandersetzung des Büros mit übergeordneten städtebaulichen Aufgaben können die spezifischen Qualitäten eines Freiraums in seinem Umfeld präzise identifiziert und entfaltet werden. Aus der Erkenntnis, dass kulturelle und atmosphärische Qualität nur in einer ganzheitlichen Betrachtung der städtischen Sphäre entstehen kann, sucht sinai bewusst die Schnittstellen zu anderen Disziplinen. Aus der Auseinandersetzung mit Ingenieuren und Geisteswissenschaftlern, mit Architekten, Künstlern, Szenographen und vielen anderen entsteht ein erweiterter Freiraumbegriff, der auf die Qualität unserer Lebenswelt als Ganzes zielt. Ohne diese Zusammenarbeit mit den Architekten, Künstlern und Ausstellungsgestaltern und deren Offenheit, etwas Gemeinsames zu schaffen, wäre die Geschlossenheit von wichtigen Entwürfen nicht möglich.

Das Vorfindbare betrachten die Landschaftsarchitekten „als transloziertes Tafelbild, gespeist durch Verweise, geschichtliche, landschaftliche und politische Bezüge". Diese Verweise verstehen sie aber „nicht als physische Anhaftungen am jeweiligen Ort, sondern als rein geistige". Um diese in der gedanklichen Auseinandersetzung des Betrachters mit dem Ort erkennbar werden zu lassen, hilft eine „neutrale Deckschicht". Relikte ebenso wie Nachzeichnungen werden in diesen neutralen Kontext gestellt, so dass mittels Landschaftsarchitektur ein Nachdenken über den Ort möglich wird. Alle realisierten Entwürfe von sinai Landschaftsarchitekten wurden in Wettbewerben ausgezeichnet. In den Wettbewerbsjurys ebenso wie in den Einrichtungen und Stiftungen, die Gedenkstätten entwickeln und betreiben, trafen die Landschaftsarchitekten auf Historiker, Museumspädagogen, Soziologen und Politikwissenschaftler. Meist konnten sinai diese überzeugen. Weil die Landschaftsarchitekten besondere Spezialisten sind in der Vermittlung von Geschichte? Weil die „Landschaft" immer auch als politische, als geschichtliche Entwicklung gelesen werden kann? Die Orte, die sinai entwerfen, sind Geschichtsorte, vermitteln Geschichte. Doch sie sind in ihrer Gestaltung allesamt neu erfunden und interpretiert. sinai orientieren sich gerade nicht entlang einer vermeintlichen historischen Wahrheit, erarbeiten nicht den Geist des Ortes aus einer bestimmten historischen Epoche heraus, sondern die Entwürfe interpretieren die jeweilige Aufgabe aus dem Jetzt. Nicht „die Geschichte", sondern Geschichten, Bezüge und Strukturen interessieren die Landschaftsarchitekten. Geschichte wie Raum sind Mittel der Konzentration.

In their work on places of historical remembrance, however, the landscape architects apply different standards. These designs require particular sensitivity and a comprehensive understanding of the social and political conditions often over several recent centuries. A. W. Faust compares this aspect of the landscape architects' work with that of a detective or an investigator. The search for traces is only successful when these traces can be made visible, when there are expectations, hypotheses and viewpoints associated with a situation, space or history. One needs to know what one is looking for in the design process: history is not something that is there for you to simply excavate. History arises through a consideration of the present and past, of places, of spaces and of constellations.

A special quality of the work produced by sinai landscape architects is that it is not the work of historians employing the means of design, or designers employing the means of historical studies but the work of landscape architects relying solely on their creativity in dealing with history. Designing is a way of telling stories – and that applies not only for those places that society has high expectations of due to their historical significance. This is in each and every case the purpose of the design project, which is discussed in teams both inside and outside the office. sinai have no departments for specific tasks or kinds of work; instead each project is developed by a team of designers assembled specifically for that project who have a mix of different disciplinary backgrounds. The designers need a range of skills: they must have a good command of structures and details, be able to sensitively select materials and plants, understand construction schedules, costs and landscaping construction technologies as well as be able to read and interpret the respective design brief. From the very outset, the initial design concept is influenced by design considerations for its possible implementation and vice versa.

In sinai's office, each design project is discussed at length, as is the process of design in general. This process of verbal elaboration and discussion serves to uncover each place layer by layer. sinai call this the "verbal entry in the place". This is accompanied by sketching in order to "make a place graphically accessible". The process of drawing supports the discourse on the design, the verbal process of uncovering: in the same way as time has laid down layers over a place, these are then discussed, sketched and uncovered. What exists on site, and what period does it relate to? What is important? What should be there? What will be added? The discussions aim to produce as many approaches to the design as possible, most of which will be discarded. Working on a task involves working on sorting the traces that the respective place presents.

sinai Landschaftsarchitekten bearbeiten ein weitaus größeres Spektrum an Aufgaben, als dieses Buch zeigt. sinai steuern und entwickeln den Bau von Parkanlagen, arbeiten an Theorien und Konzepten für den Park der Zukunft, entwickeln mit anderen städtebauliche und Architekturentwürfe und erfinden auch schon mal Legenden zum Ort, wenn diese der Profilierung dienen. Zwischen „grünen" Parks und „steinernen" Stadträumen wie Plätzen und Promenaden wird in der Methode des Entwerfens nicht unterschieden. Im Mittelpunkt steht immer die Raumwahrnehmung der Nutzer. Häufig gelingt es in diesen Entwürfen, den Raum neu lesbar zu machen und dabei auch scheinbar abseitige „Nicht- und Nebenräume" im Stadtbild zu reaktivieren.

An ihre Arbeiten zu den Gedenkorten der Geschichte allerdings legen die Landschaftsarchitekten andere Maßstäbe an. Denn diese Entwürfe erfordern eine besondere Sensibilität und ein umfassendes Verständnis der sozialen und politischen Verhältnisse durch die letzten Jahrhunderte hindurch. A.W. Faust vergleicht diese Arbeit der Landschaftsarchitekten mit der von Ermittlern. Spuren suchen ist nur dann erfolgreich, wenn diese Spuren sichtbar werden können, wenn es Erwartungen, Hypothesen und Haltungen zu einer Situation, zum Raum, zur Geschichte gibt. Man muss wissen, wonach man sucht in einem Entwurfsprozess. Denn Geschichte ist nicht etwas Vorhandenes, das man ausgraben kann. Sondern Geschichte entsteht in der Auseinandersetzung mit Gegenwart und Vergangenheit, mit Orten, mit Räumen, mit Konstellationen.

Es ist die besondere Qualität der Arbeiten von sinai Landschaftsarchitekten, dass sich hier nicht Historiker der Mittel der Gestaltung bedienen oder Gestalter der Mittel der Geschichtswissenschaft, sondern dass die Landschaftsarchitekten allein auf ihre Kreativität im Umgang mit Geschichte vertrauen. Gestalten ist Geschichten erzählen – das gilt nicht nur an den Orten, für die besondere gesellschaftliche Erwartungen an das Geschichtsbewusstsein gelten.

Dazu dient der Entwurf, der in Teams innerhalb und auch außerhalb des Büros diskutiert wird. Es gibt im Büro sinai keine Abteilungen mit spezifischen Aufgabenschwerpunkten, sondern für jede der Aufgaben ein eigens zusammengestelltes, multidisziplinär durchwobenes Team aus Entwerfern. Ein solcher Entwerfer muss vieles können: Strukturen und Details beherrschen, Material und Pflanzen gezielt auswählen, Bauabläufe, Kosten und Landschaftsbautechniken ebenso kennen wie die jeweilige Aufgabenstellung lesen und interpretieren können. Die Entwurfsplanung und die mögliche Ausführungsplanung beeinflussen sich vom ersten Schritt an gegenseitig.

Es wird im Büro sinai viel diskutiert über den jeweiligen Entwurf, über das Entwerfen generell. Dieses Sprechen und Diskutieren dient dazu, Schicht für Schicht eines Ortes aufzudecken. sinai nennt dies den „verbalen Einstieg in den Ort". Dazu kommt die Skizze, um „sich einen Ort grafisch gefügig zu machen". Die Zeichnung unterstützt den Diskurs zum Entwurf, den verbal getragenen Prozess des Aufdeckens: Ebenso wie die Zeit Schichten über einen Ort gelegt hat, werden diese nun diskutiert, skizziert und aufgedeckt. Was ist vor Ort vorhanden, was ist von wann? Was ist von Bedeutung? Was sollte vorhanden sein? Was wird hinzugefügt?

Every member of a design team is obliged to make suggestions, is encouraged to formulate their own impressions and ideas, to sketch them and to defend them. This discourse does more to consolidate the position of the office with respect to a specific task than reading the competition brief or specialist literature. Elements do not recur from project to project; instead a joint position is defined in response to the respective actual task by generating ideas and positions among the members of the team and then subjecting these to cross-examination. Through this workshop-like process, the office usually arrives at three or more well-reasoned potential design variants.

The search for a suitable expression begins with the production of variants of aspects of the overall design and the parallel production of structure plans and sketches that capture an expression. These are then examined to reveal coherences and correspondences. This evolutionary process of plan generation is a process of selection and determination that ultimately leads to a chosen design concept.

A.W. Faust describes this procedure – sinai do not regard this as a method – as "investigation", suggesting that designs are developed in a dialectic process: traces are found, antithetically interpreted and assembled to form an overall picture. The team formulates a series of hypotheses: what do we think we know about the place? Which impressions are unfounded, which are corroborated by research? "Sometimes this is an agonising process of groping in the dark" until an inner logic to the design starts to emerge that would seem to be plausible. Finally, "in moments of absolute concentration," the reward presents itself: the knowledge and certainty that the configuration sketched on paper represents a design that has the potential to hold together a space. Chance is likewise a valid part of this process; sometimes it is a word, an object or an idea that when turned back and forth grows stronger rather than weaker and eventually strong enough to transport the design concept.

Through this way of designing, landscape architecture is capable of cultivating plausible images and stories into a *spatial story* that relates to the specific place. The space itself comprises elements that clarify. A prerequisite for this kind of design is a specific social interest in the respective space and place. History as fact without the reading of such spatial stories is for sinai not relevant.

An obligation to history as a space of resonance for the impressions created by the landscape architecture requires an understanding of ideas such as freedom, respect or responsibility. In view of Germany's history, this approach is especially challenging, but one that has produced special places in difficult places. Timeless places for reflecting on time.

Möglichst viele Zugänge zum Entwurf werden in diesen Diskussionen angeregt, die meisten wieder verworfen. Die Arbeit an der Aufgabe ist die Arbeit an der Sortierung der Spuren, die der jeweilige Ort anbietet. Alle Beteiligten in einem Entwurfsteam haben eine Art Vorschlagspflicht, sind aufgefordert, ihre Eindrücke und Ideen zu formulieren, zu skizzieren, zu verteidigen. In diesem Diskurs – und weniger in der Lektüre von Auslobungstexten oder Fachliteratur – verfestigen sich die Positionen des Büros in Hinblick auf die jeweilige Aufgabe. Wiederkehrende Elemente gibt es nicht, die gemeinsame Haltung wird jeweils anhand der konkreten Aufgabe definiert, indem Haltungen der Teammitglieder abgefragt und diese dann gegenseitig hinterfragt werden. In einem solchen Werkstatt-Prozess entstehen meist mindestens drei gut begründbare mögliche Entwürfe.

Diese Suche nach dem Ausdruck erfolgt in Varianten zu Aspekten der Basisentwürfe, bevor dann in parallel entstehenden Strukturplänen und Ausdrucksskizzen sich überlagernde Stimmigkeiten sichtbar werden. Diese Plangenese führt zu Festlegungen und letztlich zu einem Entwurf.

A.W. Fausts Bild von dieser Vorgehensweise – eine Methode will sinai darin nicht sehen – als „Ermittlung" deutet darauf hin, dass Entwürfe von sinai Landschaftsarchitekten in einem dialektischen Prozess entstehen: Spuren sichern, antithetisch deuten und zu einem Gesamtbild fügen. Im Team werden Thesen formuliert: Was glauben wir über den Ort zu wissen? Welche Eindrücke sind haltlose Indizien, welche lassen sich in der Recherche verfestigen? „Teils sind dies quälende Runden, ein Tasten und Suchen." Bis sich dann eine innere Logik des Entwurfs aufgrund von Plausibilitäten herausschält. Und „in Momenten der absoluten Konzentration" zu einer Belohnung führt, zu dem Wissen und der Gewissheit, dass auf dem Papier ein Wirkungsgefüge skizziert wird, das durch genau diese Art der Gestaltung einen Raum zusammenhalten kann. Auch der Zufall ist bei diesen Analysen zugelassen, manchmal ist es ein Begriff, ein Objekt, eine Idee, die durch das Drehen und Wenden nicht schwächer, sondern stärker wird und dann einen Entwurf tragen kann.

Die Landschaftsarchitektur leistet es mittels dieser Art des Entwerfens, plausible Bilder und Geschichten in einer *spatial story* mit Bezug auf den jeweiligen Ort zu kultivieren. Der Raum selbst enthält Elemente der Aufklärung. Voraussetzung dieser Art von Gestaltung ist ein spezifisches gesellschaftliches Interesse an dem jeweiligen Raum und Ort. Geschichte als Faktum ohne das Lesen dieser Raum-Geschichten ist für sinai dagegen nicht relevant.

Die Verpflichtung gegenüber der Geschichte als Resonanzraum für die Inszenierungen der Landschaftsarchitektur erfordert ein Verständnis für Ideen wie Freiheit, Respekt oder Verantwortung. Angesichts der deutschen Geschichte eine besondere Herausforderung, aus der besondere Räume an schwierigen Orten entstehen. Zeitlose Räume der Reflektion der Zeit.

Appendix   Anhang

Essay

Peter Reichel was professor for historical principles of politics at the University of Hamburg until 2007. He now lives and works in Berlin and Usedom and writes articles for journals and radio. His most recent publication is "Glanz und Elend deutscher Selbstdarstellung. Nationalsymbole in Reich und Republik" (2012). Of his many publications, the most well-known include: "Der schöne Schein des Dritten Reiches. Gewalt und Faszination des deutschen Faschismus" (new edition in 2006), "Politik mit der Erinnerung. Gedächtnisorte im Streit um die nationalsozialistische Vergangenheit" (1995) and "Erfundene Erinnerung. Weltkrieg und Judenmord in Film und Theater" (2004).

Photography

Klemens Ortmeyer studied architecture in Braunschweig and now works as an international architectural photographer. He focuses on developing portraits of cities and the documentation of architecture projects. Ortmeyer sees photography as a form of communicating information. He has worked regularly with sinai Landschaftsarchitekten since 2008.

Book design

Weidner Händle Atelier is a graphic design office specialising in exhibition graphics, wayfinding systems, visual identities and book design. They have undertaken projects with Norman Foster in London, Valencia and Bilbao, and with sinai for the Bergen-Belsen Memorial, the Berlin Wall Memorial and the Cemetery of the March Revolution. Berthold Weidner taught at the Merz Akademie in Stuttgart, the Academy of Design in Bolzano and the Darmstadt University of Applied Sciences.

Author and editor

Thies Schröder studied landscape planning in Berlin and is an author and editor. He has produced monographs and books on the subject of landscape architecture and urban and regional development and has held teaching appointments at the Technische Universität Berlin, the ETH Zurich and the Leibniz Universität Hanover. Schröder heads the communications agency ts|pk thies schröder planung & kommunikation as well as the Perspektivmedien UG (with his partners), the Ferropolis GmbH and L&H Verlag publishers.

Essay

Peter Reichel lehrte bis 2007 an der Universität Hamburg Historische Grundlagen der Politik, lebt und arbeitet seitdem in Berlin und auf Usedom, schreibt für Zeitungen und Rundfunk und veröffentlichte zuletzt „Glanz und Elend deutscher Selbstdarstellung. Nationalsymbole in Reich und Republik" (2012). Zu seinen bekanntesten Büchern gehören: „Der schöne Schein des Dritten Reiches. Gewalt und Faszination des deutschen Faschismus" (Neuausgabe 2006), „Politik mit der Erinnerung. Gedächtnisorte im Streit um die nationalsozialistische Vergangenheit" (1995), „Erfundene Erinnerung. Weltkrieg und Judenmord in Film und Theater" (2004).

Fotograf

Klemens Ortmeyer studierte Architektur in Braunschweig. Als Architekturfotograf ist er heute international tätig. Städteporträts und Projektdokumentationen gehören zu den Arbeitsschwerpunkten. Fotografie versteht Ortmeyer als Informationsvermittlung. Seit 2008 kommt es immer wieder zu Zusammenarbeiten mit sinai Landschaftsarchitekten.

Buchgestaltung

Weidner Händle Atelier, Gestaltungsbüro mit den Schwerpunkten Ausstellungsgrafik, Orientierungssysteme, visuelle Erscheinungsbilder und Buchgestaltung. Projekte mit Norman Foster in London, Valencia, Bilbao, mit sinai bei der Gedenkstätte Bergen-Belsen, der Gedenkstätte Berliner Mauer und dem Friedhof der Märzgefallenen. Berthold Weidner lehrte an der Merz Akademie Stuttgart, der Akademie für Design Bozen und der Hochschule Darmstadt.

Autor und Redakteur

Thies Schröder, Studium der Landschaftsplanung in Berlin, Autor und Redakteur. Monographien und Themenbände u. a. zu Landschaftsarchitektur, Regional- und Stadtentwicklung. Lehraufgaben führten Schröder an die TU Berlin, die ETH Zürich und die Leibniz Universität Hannover. Schröder leitet die Kommunikationsagentur ts|pk thies schröder planung & kommunikation sowie die Perspektivmedien UG gemeinsam mit Partnern, die Ferropolis GmbH und den L&H Verlag.

The office of sinai is a melting pot of different talents. In 2006, the three partners A. W. Faust, Bernhard Schwarz and Klaus Schroll pooled their skills and today run their office as a team that act and interact in the interest of a project as a whole: there is no division between design, detail planning, project controlling and strategic development, only different constellations of team members and collaborators that bring together their respective strengths in all the different fields.

This understanding of the living environment of the city and space as an interdisciplinary and holistic task becomes apparent in their collaborations with urban planners, architects, engineers and scenographers. sinai's work covers a range of activities from project design to project development and controlling. In their work they strive to derive a form out of the content of the respective individual task, i.e. to find an appropriate expression that corresponds to the nature of the place. For sinai, the completion of a project marks the beginning of a process of observation. What they learn about how these places are used feeds back into the design of new projects that range from urban parks, squares, garden shows and living, working and research environments to the "difficult places" that feature in this book. All of these projects have resulted from competition entries won by sinai, which are conceived and designed in teams led by A. W. Faust.

A. W. Faust studied philosophy in Munich after completing his training as a gardener at a tree nursery. In Berlin, he studied landscape management and worked freelance for various landscape architecture offices. In 2001, A. W. Faust founded sinai.exteriors as a home for the nomadic in planning and as a project for landscapes of thought in motion. In 2006, this became sinai Gesellschaft von Landschaftsarchitekten mbH together with Bernhard Schwarz and Klaus Schroll.

Klaus Schroll studied landscape management and landscape planning in Munich-Weihenstephan and Berlin. Prior to founding sinai in 2006 together with his partners, he worked in planning offices such as Atelier Dreiseitl in Überlingen and for project developers and agencies in Potsdam and Wolfsburg focusing on project management.

Bernhard Schwarz joined the office of Landschaft planen + bauen in Berlin after completing his studies in landscape planning, heading it together with his partners from 1989 to 2001. Thereafter he worked as a project developer and controller. As a founding member of sinai in 2006, he combines his experience as a landscape architect and project controller, developing new strategies for navigating projects.

Es ist die Bündelung der Talente, die das Büro sinai auszeichnet. Die drei Partner A.W. Faust, Bernhard Schwarz und Klaus Schroll haben 2006 ihre Fähigkeiten zusammengeführt und leiten heute ein Büroteam, das im Sinne eines Gesamtprojekts agiert und interagiert: keine Trennung zwischen Entwurf, Ausführungsplanung, Projektsteuerung und Strategieentwicklung, sondern wechselnde Gruppen und Kooperationen, die jeweils Stärken in allen Bereichen zusammenführen. Das Verständnis der Lebenswelt Stadt und Raum als interdisziplinäre, ganzheitliche Aufgabe zeigt sich in der Zusammenarbeit mit Stadtplanern, Architekten, Ingenieuren, Szenographen. sinai bearbeiten ein weites Spektrum in der Objektplanung, Projektentwicklung und Projektsteuerung. Im Mittelpunkt steht der Anspruch, eine Form aus dem Inhalt der jeweiligen Aufgabe abzuleiten, also in der Gestalt dem Gehalt des Ortes zu entsprechen. Mit der Fertigstellung des Werks beginnt für sinai der Beobachtungsmoment. Erkenntnisse aus der Nutzung fließen stetig in neue Projekte ein, von Stadtparks, Plätzen, Gartenschauen, Wohn-, Wirtschafts- und Wissenschaftsbauten bis hin zu den „schwierigen Orten", die im Mittelpunkt dieses Buches stehen. Diese Arbeiten gingen allesamt aus Wettbewerbserfolgen hervor, die durch A.W. Faust konzeptionell und entwurflich geprägt sind.

A.W. Faust studierte nach seiner Ausbildung zum Baumschulgärtner in München Philosophie. Danach Studium der Landespflege in Berlin und freie Mitarbeit für mehrere Landschaftsarchitekturbüros. A.W. Faust gründete 2001 sinai.exteriors – eine Heimat für das Nomadische in der Planung, ein Projekt für Landschaften des bewegten Denkens. 2006 wurde daraus gemeinsam mit Bernhard Schwarz und Klaus Schroll die sinai Gesellschaft von Landschaftsarchitekten mbH.

Klaus Schroll entschied sich für ein Studium der Landespflege und Landschaftsplanung in München-Weihenstephan und Berlin. Seine Tätigkeiten in Planungsbüros wie Atelier Dreiseitl in Überlingen sowie für Entwicklungsträger und Projektgesellschaften in Potsdam und Wolfsburg mit dem Schwerpunkt der Projektabwicklung führten ihn 2006 mit der Neugründung des Büros sinai in diese Partnerschaft.

Bernhard Schwarz leitete nach seinem Studium der Landschaftsplanung das Büro Landschaft planen + bauen von 1989 bis 2001 gemeinsam mit Partnern in Berlin. Danach tätig als Projektentwickler und -steuerer. Als Gründungspartner bei sinai verbindet er seit 2006 die beiden Erfahrungen als Landschaftsarchitekt und Projektsteuerer zu neuen Strategien in der Projektnavigation.

Sumika Aisawa
Susanne Aoki
Sandra Ballerstedt
Jana Bernhardt
Marlene Biehl
Stephanie Braconnier
Jörg Bresser
Pia Custodis
Anja Dassel
Elena Emmerich
Sebastian Exner
Theresa Fehrmann
Timo Fritz
Gero Goldmann
Jan Gordon
Jedidiah Gordon-Moran
Matthias Grobe
Lisa Hankow
Josephine Hansen
Peter Hausdorf
Agnes Hofmeister
Sophie Holz
Britta Horn
Frederica Jambor
Hanna Jonsson
Ingmar Jorgowski
Christoph Jung
Jérome Kost
Malin Krause
Franziska Krija
Johanna Kühnelt
Denny Mlotzek
Frederike Müller
Maja Neumann
Burkhard Paetow
Henning Pagels
Theresa Quade
Beate Quaschning
Sebastian Radke
Bernd Rengers
Heiko Ruddigkeit
Ole Saß
Elke Schmidtke
Merle Schwabe
Martin Tietz
Jakob Trzebitzky
Holger Vahrenhorst
Maja van der Laan
Verena Wilke
Lotte Wülfing
Lene Zingenberg

Project Data

Translated names of institutions are not meant to represent official versions of these names.

Grounds of the Bergen-Belsen Memorial, Lohheide

Competition procedure
Ideas and design competition, 2003, 1st prize
Sponsor of the competition and client
Foundation for Memorials in Lower Saxony, represented by Lüneburg Heath State Building Department
Master plan **2005**
Construction **2006–2012**
Project partners:
Design and construction of documentation centre
KSP Engel & Zimmermann Architekten, Braunschweig
Exhibition design **Hans Dieter Schaal, Attenweiler**
Graphic design of exhibition and outdoor areas
Weidner Händle Atelier, Stuttgart
Artistic concept for master plan
stoebo – Oliver Störmer & Cisca Bogman, Berlin

Forum Vogelsang, Euskirchen

Competition procedure
International invited two-phase design competition, 2008, 1st prize
Sponsor of the competition
City of Euskirchen
Vogelsang framework concept **2011**
Client for framework concept
Standortentwicklungsgesellschaft Vogelsang GmbH (SEV), Schleiden
Construction of Forum **2012–2014**
Client for Forum
Vogelsang ip gGmbH, Schleiden
Project partners:
Design and Construction of Forum Vogelsang
Mola + Winkelmüller Architekten, Berlin

Mühldorfer Hart Concentration Camp Memorial, Waldkraiburg near Mühldorf am Inn

Competition procedure
Limited invited design competition, 2012, 2nd prize
Sponsor of the competition and client
Foundation of Bavarian Memorial Sites, Munich
Project partner **chezweitz & partner, Berlin**

Flossenbürg Concentration Camp Memorial

Competition procedure
Multiple commissioning procedure, 2009, winner
Sponsor of the competition and client
Foundation of Bavarian Memorial Sites, represented by the Bavarian State Building Authority
Construction **2013–2015**

Outdoor areas of the Centre of the Federal Foundation Flight, Expulsion, Reconciliation, Berlin-Kreuzberg

Competition procedure
Limited invited competition, 2013, 2nd prize
Sponsor of the competition
Federal Institute of Real Estate, Berlin Office, in conjunction with the Ministry for Transport, Building and Urban Development (BMVBS) and the Federal Government Commissioner for Culture and the Media (BKM), Federal Office for Building and Regional Planning (BBR)
Project partners:
Artistic concept
stoebo – Oliver Störmer & Cisca Bogman, Berlin

Cemetery of the March Revolution Memorial, Berlin-Friedrichshain

Competition procedure
Competitive design process, 2010, winner
Sponsor of the competition, organiser and client
Paul Singer e.V., project office for the Cemetery of the March Revolution
Construction **2011–2012**
Project partners and implementation:
Architecture
Mola + Winkelmüller Architekten, Berlin
Exhibition design
ON architektur, Berlin
Graphic design
Weidner Händle Atelier, Stuttgart

Berlin Wall Memorial, Berlin-Mitte

Competition procedure
Open competition, 2007, 1st prize
Sponsor of the competition
Federal State of Berlin, represented by the Senate Office for Urban Development, the Governing Mayor, the Senate Chancellery, Federal Republic of Germany, represented by the Federal Government Commissioner for Culture and the Media, Berlin Wall Association
Client
Federal State of Berlin, represented by the Senate Office for Urban Development, Berlin Wall Foundation, represented by Grün Berlin Park und Garten GmbH
Construction **2009–2011**
Extended area **ongoing**
Project partners:
Visitor centre, border house canopy
Mola + Winkelmüller Architekten, Berlin
Exhibition design, Window of Remembrance
ON architektur, Berlin
Graphic design of exhibition and building firewalls
Weidner Händle Atelier, Stuttgart

Platz des 9. November 1989, Berlin-Prenzlauer Berg

Competition procedure
Multiple commissioning procedure, 2009, winner
Sponsor of the competition
The Governing Mayor of Berlin, Senate Chancellery – Office for Cultural Affairs, Federal State of Berlin
Client
Federal State of Berlin, Senate Office for Urban Development, Department of Urban Planning and Open Space, IC 3 Landscape Gardening, Berlin
Construction **2010**
Project partners:
Exhibition concept
Berlin Forum for History and the Present
Exhibition architecture **ON architektur, Berlin**
Graphic design of exhibition **Gewerk, Berlin**

Außengelände der
Gedenkstätte Bergen-Belsen, Lohheide

Verfahren
Ideen- und Realisierungswettbewerb 2003,
1. Preis
Auslober und Auftraggeber
Stiftung Niedersächsische Gedenkstätten,
vertreten durch Staatliches Baumanagement
Lüneburger Heide
Masterplan 2005
Realisierung 2006 – 2012
Projektpartner:
Hochbau Dokumentationszentrum
KSP Engel & Zimmermann Architekten,
Braunschweig
Ausstellung Hans Dieter Schaal, Attenweiler
Grafik Ausstellung und Freiraum
Weidner Händle Atelier, Stuttgart
Künstlerische Konzeption Masterplan
stoebo – Oliver Störmer & Cisca Bogman,
Berlin

Forum Vogelsang,
Euskirchen

Verfahren
Internationaler, begrenzt zweiphasiger
Realisierungswettbewerb 2008, 1. Preis
Auslober Stadt Euskirchen
Rahmenkonzept Vogelsang 2011
Auftraggeber Rahmenkonzept
Standortentwicklungsgesellschaft Vogelsang
GmbH (SEV), Schleiden
Realisierung Forum 2012 – 2014
Auftraggeber Forum
Vogelsang ip gGmbH, Schleiden
Projektpartner:
Hochbau Forum Vogelsang
Mola + Winkelmüller Architekten, Berlin

KZ-Gedenkstätte Mühldorfer Hart,
Waldkraiburg bei Mühldorf am Inn

Verfahren
Beschränkter Realisierungswettbewerb 2012,
2. Preis
Auslober und Auftraggeber
Stiftung Bayerische Gedenkstätten, München
Projektpartner chezweitz & partner, Berlin

Gedenkstätte
KZ Flossenbürg

Verfahren
Mehrfachbeauftragung 2009, Gewinner
Auslober und Auftraggeber
Stiftung Bayerische Gedenkstätten, vertreten
durch die Bayerische Staatsbauverwaltung
Realisierung 2013 – 2015

Außenanlagen Bundesstiftung Flucht,
Vertreibung, Versöhnung, Berlin-Kreuzberg

Verfahren
Beschränkter Wettbewerb 2013, 2. Preis
Auslober
Bundesanstalt für Immobilienaufgaben,
Direktion Berlin, in Zusammenarbeit mit dem
Bundesministerium für Verkehr, Bau und
Stadtentwicklung (BMVBS) und dem Beauf-
tragten der Bundesregierung für Kultur
und Medien (BKM),
Bundesamt für Bauwesen und Raumordnung
(BBR)
Projektpartner:
Künstlerische Konzeption
stoebo – Oliver Störmer & Cisca Bogman,
Berlin

Gedenkstätte Friedhof der Märzgefallenen,
Berlin-Friedrichshain

Verfahren
Gutachterverfahren 2010, Gewinner
Auslober und Auftraggeber
Paul Singer e.V., Projektbüro Friedhof
der Märzgefallenen
Realisierung 2011 – 2012
Projektpartner und Realisierung:
Hochbau
Mola + Winkelmüller Architekten, Berlin
Ausstellungsgestaltung ON architektur, Berlin
Grafik Weidner Händle Atelier, Stuttgart

Gedenkstätte Berliner Mauer,
Berlin-Mitte

Verfahren
Offener Realisierungswettbewerb 2007,
1. Preis
Auslober
Land Berlin, vertreten durch die Senats-
verwaltung für Stadtentwicklung, den Regie-
renden Bürgermeister, die Senatskanzlei,
Bundesrepublik Deutschland, vertreten durch
den Beauftragten der Bundesregierung für
Kultur und Medien,
Verein Berliner Mauer
Auftraggeber
Land Berlin, Senatsverwaltung für Stadt-
entwicklung, sowie Stiftung Berliner Mauer,
vertreten durch Grün Berlin Park
und Garten GmbH
Realisierung 2009 – 2011
Erweiterter Bereich im Bau
Projektpartner:
Besucherzentrum, Überdachung Grenzhaus
Mola + Winkelmüller Architekten, Berlin
Ausstellungsgestaltung, Fenster des Gedenkens
ON architektur, Berlin
Grafik Ausstellung und Brandwände
Weidner Händle Atelier, Stuttgart

Platz des 9. November 1989,
Berlin-Prenzlauer Berg

Verfahren
Mehrfachbeauftragung 2009, Gewinner
Auslober
Der Regierende Bürgermeister von Berlin,
Senatskanzlei Kulturelle Angelegenheiten,
Land Berlin
Auftraggeber
Land Berlin, Senatsverwaltung für
Stadtentwicklung, Abteilung Stadt-und
Freiraumplanung,
IC 3 Landschaftsbau, Berlin
Realisierung 2010
Projektpartner:
Ausstellungskonzeption
Berliner Forum für Geschichte und Gegenwart
Ausstellungsarchitektur ON architektur, Berlin
Grafik Ausstellung Gewerk, Berlin

Colophon
Impressum

**Graphic design,
layout and typography**
Gestaltung, Layout und
Typografie
Berthold Weidner
Weidner Händle Atelier,
Stuttgart

Translation into English
Julian Reisenberger, Weimar
Copyediting of Translation
Michael Wachholz, Berlin

Editor at sinai
Redaktion bei sinai
Ole Saß

Editor for the Publisher
Lektorat
Andreas Müller, Berlin

A CIP catalogue record for
this book is available from the
Library of Congress,
Washington D.C., USA.

Bibliographic information
published by the German
National Library
The German National Library
lists this publication in the
Deutsche Nationalbibliogra-
fie; detailed bibliographic
data are available on the
Internet at
http://dnb.d-nb.de.

© 2013 Birkhäuser Verlag
GmbH, Basel
P.O. Box 44, 4009 Basel,
Switzerland
Part of De Gruyter

Printed on acid-free paper
produced from chlorine-free
pulp. TCF ∞

Printed in Germany

ISBN 978-3-03821-566-0

9 8 7 6 5 4 3 2 1

www.birkhauser.com

Illustration Credits
Bildnachweis

Unless otherwise stated,
all photos in this book
have been taken by Klemens
Ortmeyer and all drawings
have been provided by sinai
Landschaftsarchitekten.
Soweit nicht anders erwähnt,
stammen alle Fotos in diesem
Buch von Klemens Ortmeyer.
Alle Zeichnungen wurden,
wenn nicht anders erwähnt,
von sinai Landschafts-
architekten zur Verfügung
gestellt.

35
© Imperial War Museum
(BU 4043)

43 top/oben
NCAP / aerial.rcahms.gov.uk,
The Royal Commission on the
Ancient and Historical
Monuments of Scotland

43 middle/Mitte
Landesamt für
Geoinformation und
Landentwicklung
Niedersachsen

73
Archiv vogelsang ip,
Schleiden

95
Historical aerial photograph/
historisches Luftbild:
Bayerische Vermessungs-
verwaltung

109
KZ-Gedenkstätte
Flossenbürg

110
Historical aerial photograph/
historisches Luftbild:
Bayerische Vermessungs-
verwaltung

121
Stiftung Flucht, Vertreibung,
Versöhnung

133
akg-images

145
photonet.de/Lehnartz

150, 151
Berthold Weidner

167 right/rechts
Berthold Weidner

181
Andreas Schoelzel Fotografie

186
Burkhard Paetow, sinai
Landschaftsarchitekten